Palgrave Executive Essentials

Today's complex and changing business environment brings with it a number of pressing challenges. To be successful, business professionals are increasingly required to leverage and spot future trends, be masters of strategy, all while leading responsibly, inspiring others, mastering financial techniques and driving innovation.

Palgrave Executive Essentials empowers you to take your skills to the next level. Offering a suite of resources to support you on your executive journey and written by renowned experts from top business schools, the series is designed to support professionals as they embark on executive education courses, but it is equally applicable to practicing leaders and managers. Each book brings you in-depth case studies, accompanying video resources, reflective questions, practical tools and core concepts that can be easily applied to your organization, all written in an engaging, easy to read style.

Debbie Sanders · Joseph Perry · Richard Saundry

Collective Employment Relations

A Strategic Guide

Debbie Sanders
Make Work Better Ltd.
Lancing, UK

Joseph Perry
Atelier HR Ltd.
London, UK

Richard Saundry
Westminster Business School
University of Westminster
London, UK

ISSN 2731-5614 ISSN 2731-5622 (electronic)
Palgrave Executive Essentials
ISBN 978-3-031-65470-1 ISBN 978-3-031-65471-8 (eBook)
https://doi.org/10.1007/978-3-031-65471-8

© The Editor(s) (if applicable) and The Author(s), under exclusive license to Springer Nature Switzerland AG 2024, corrected publication 2025

This work is subject to copyright. All rights are solely and exclusively licensed by the Publisher, whether the whole or part of the material is concerned, specifically the rights of translation, reprinting, reuse of illustrations, recitation, broadcasting, reproduction on microfilms or in any other physical way, and transmission or information storage and retrieval, electronic adaptation, computer software, or by similar or dissimilar methodology now known or hereafter developed.
The use of general descriptive names, registered names, trademarks, service marks, etc. in this publication does not imply, even in the absence of a specific statement, that such names are exempt from the relevant protective laws and regulations and therefore free for general use.
The publisher, the authors and the editors are safe to assume that the advice and information in this book are believed to be true and accurate at the date of publication. Neither the publisher nor the authors or the editors give a warranty, expressed or implied, with respect to the material contained herein or for any errors or omissions that may have been made. The publisher remains neutral with regard to jurisdictional claims in published maps and institutional affiliations.

This Palgrave Macmillan imprint is published by the registered company Springer Nature Switzerland AG
The registered company address is: Gewerbestrasse 11, 6330 Cham, Switzerland

If disposing of this product, please recycle the paper.

This book is dedicated to Gerry, Nic, Jonathan, Michelle and our parents.

Acknowledgements

The authors would like to thank all those who we interviewed as part of the development of this book. We would also like to thank Lydia Cassidy and Michelle Nicholson for their help with proofreading and editing and Leonie Sittner and Alec Selwyn from Palgrave Macmillan for their advice and guidance.

Praise for *Collective Employment Relations*

"This is a timely contribution to the debate about the future of employee and Union relations. If there is one thing practitioners agree on, it is that we must rediscover the skills of negotiation and compromise to address the good work agenda, productivity challenges and technological change. The narrative asks searching questions of the prevailing HR orthodoxy of the last few decades and is essential reading for those studying and working in the field of employee relations."

—Mike Clancy, *General Secretary, Prospect, UK*

"A brilliant book which is essential reading for anyone studying industrial relations or who works with trade unions and must create an industrial relations strategy. The authors capture the essential skills needed by every industrial relations practitioner."

—Emily Cox, *Director of Colleague Relations, Lloyds Banking Group, UK*

"This is a very welcome and timely book, which explains how collective employment relations and collective voice, despite being marginalised within many HR departments, have become increasingly relevant in recent years. It makes a compelling case for a more strategic approach to the development of high-trust employment relations and for engaging constructively with trade unions. Drawing on a wealth of case study examples, it offers clear guidance to practitioners in developing and evaluating organisational policies around consultation, negotiation and conflict management. Written in an engaging and accessible style, it will be a superb resource for under-graduate students, those taking CIPD-accredited courses, as well as for managers and trade union representatives."

—Chris Rees, *Professor of Employment Relations, Royal Holloway, University of London, UK*

Contents

Part I Introduction and Context

1 Introduction — 3
1.1 Introduction — 4
1.2 A Changing Context — 5
1.3 Trade Unions—Challenge and Revitalisation — 5
1.4 The Case for Collective Voice — 7
1.5 Where Are the Leaders with Experience of Collective Voice? — 9
1.6 Collective Voice—A Strategic Advantage — 10
1.7 A Strategic Approach to Collective Employment Relations — 11
1.8 A New Agenda for Employment Relations Practice — 13
1.9 Rationale and Structure — 14
References — 16

2 Context and Concepts in Contemporary Collective Employment Relations — 19
2.1 Introduction — 19
2.2 Collective Employment Relations—Trust, Voice and Engagement — 20
2.3 Trust and Voice—A Question of Perspective? — 22
2.4 The Rise and Fall of Collective Voice — 23
2.5 The Implications of Employee Silence — 27

	2.6	The Challenge of Contemporary Employment Relations	34
	2.7	Conclusion	38
	References		39

Part II Strategy and Implementation

3 Creating an Effective Employment Relations Strategy — 45
  3.1 Introduction — 45
  3.2 Why Have an Employment Relations Strategy? — 46
  3.3 What Determines the Strategic Approach Taken by an Organisation? — 47
  3.4 Attitudes and Relationships — 49
  3.5 Employment Relations Strategy in Practice — 55
  3.6 What Factors Influence a Change in Approach to Employment Relations? — 57
  3.7 Building an Implementation Plan — 59
  3.8 Conclusion — 65
  References — 65

4 Building Employment Relations Teams — 67
  4.1 Introduction — 68
  4.2 Organisation Design and Employment Relations Strategy — 69
  4.3 Different Models for Delivering Collective Employment Relations — 70
  4.4 Employment Relations Accountabilities and Skills — 75
  4.5 Developing Specific Employment Relations Accountabilities — 78
  4.6 Overcoming Problems — 82
  4.7 Conclusion — 83
  References — 84

5 Constructive Behaviours for Effective Employment Relations — 85
  5.1 Introduction — 85
  5.2 Trust, Mistrust and Employment Relations — 86
  5.3 Behaviours for Building Trust — 89
  5.4 (Re)structuring Attitudes — 94
  5.5 The Power of Interests — 99
  5.6 Changing Behaviours in Practice — 101
  5.7 Conclusion — 103
  References — 104

Part III Working with Unions and Collective Voice

6   Informing and Consulting—Practical Processes and Structures for Employee Voice — 107
  6.1 Introduction — 107
  6.2 Employee Voice in Practice — 109
  6.3 Information and Communication — 110
  6.4 Consultation — 114
  6.5 Co-determination — 118
  6.6 Managing Structures — 120
  6.7 The Management of Meetings — 123
  6.8 Training, Facilities and Time to Participate — 127
  6.9 Conclusion — 128
  References — 129

7   Negotiation in Collective Employment Relations — 131
  7.1 Introduction — 131
  7.2 The Third Core Process—Negotiation — 132
  7.3 Pay Negotiation—A Worked Example — 136
  7.4 What is 'Good' Negotiation? — 147
  7.5 Collaboration and Integration—A Different Approach? — 148
  7.6 Conclusion — 150
  References — 151

8   Problem-Solving with Trade Unions — 153
  8.1 Introduction — 154
  8.2 Benefits of Problem-Solving — 154
  8.3 What is Problem-Solving? — 155
  8.4 Problem-Solving and Employment Relations — 156
  8.5 Conditions for Effective Problem-Solving — 159
  8.6 Problem-Solving Needs Structure — 162
  8.7 Practical Considerations When Setting up Problem-Solving Groups — 164
  8.8 Key Steps in the Problem-Solving Process — 166
  8.9 Conclusion — 172
  References — 174

Part IV Managing Conflict

9   Managing Industrial Action — 177
- 9.1   Introduction — 177
- 9.2   The Cost of Strike Action — 178
- 9.3   Strike Action—Roles and Responsibilities — 179
- 9.4   How Do You End Up with a Strike? — 183
- 9.5   The Employer's Perspective — 185
- 9.6   Conflict in Action — 187
- 9.7   Mediating Collective Conflict — 191
- 9.8   Planning and Communication — 193
- 9.9   Conclusion — 196
- References — 197

10   Rebuilding Employment Relationships — 199
- 10.1   Introduction — 199
- 10.2   The Long-Term Impact of Collective Conflict on Relationships — 200
- 10.3   Rebuilding Relationships—Key Principles — 201
- 10.4   Mediation and Positive Relationships — 204
- 10.5   Key Steps in a Facilitated Joint Session — 205
- 10.6   Addressing the Root Causes of Conflict — 209
- 10.7   Sustaining Change — 211
- 10.8   Challenges and Barriers to Successful Rebuilding — 213
- 10.9   Conclusion — 215
- References — 216

11   Measurement, Evaluation and Reporting — 217
- 11.1   Introduction — 217
- 11.2   Why Evaluate Your Collective Employment Relations Strategy? — 218
- 11.3   Establishing if Your Strategy is Working — 219
- 11.4   Increased Scrutiny from Investors and Shareholders — 220
- 11.5   The Cost of Collective Conflict — 222
- 11.6   The Management of Workforce Risk — 223
- 11.7   Methods of Evaluating and Auditing Collective Employment Relations — 225
- 11.8   Collecting Qualitative and Quantitative Data on Collective Employment Relations — 231
- 11.9   Employment Relations Measures — 232

	11.10	Problems With Measurement, Evaluation and Reporting	233
	11.11	Conclusion	234
	References		235

12 Concluding Remarks—Building a Strategic Approach to Employment Relations 237

	12.1	The Aims of the Book	237
	12.2	Influencing Organisational Leaders	238
	12.3	The Importance of Collective Voice	238
	12.4	Building Employment Relations Capacity	240
	12.5	Ten Steps to Build a Strategic Approach to Employment Relations	241
	Reference		242

Correction to: Informing and Consulting—Practical Processes and Structures for Employee Voice C1

Index 243

About the Authors

Debbie Sanders is an employment relations specialist with over 30 years' experience as a consultant, researcher, writer, and lecturer in this field. She has also led ER teams in unionised companies and been a union official. Today she runs Make Work Better, an employment relations consultancy, where she designed and delivers an executive education programme for some of the UK's largest unionised organisations, helping to build capability in collective employment relations.

Joseph Perry has extensive employment relations experience in unionised public, private and third-sector organisations including transport, law enforcement, utilities and politics. He has led HR and ER functions and worked internationally supporting organisations to achieve their goals through the effective management of collective employment relations and high performing teams. Joseph co-delivers the UKs only executive education programme for employment relations with Debbie Sanders. He studied Industrial Relations at the University of Keele.

Professor Richard Saundry is a leading academic authority on the management of discipline, grievance and workplace conflict. Having previously held posts at the Universities of Leeds, Sheffield, Central Lancashire and Plymouth, he is currently working on the development of the groundbreaking Skilled Managers research project at the University of Westminster. He is an author of 'Managing Employment Relations', the core CIPD text for Employee Relations, and edited 'Reframing Resolution' (Palgrave Macmillan, 2016). His research has been published in a wide range of leading international academic journals.

List of Figures

Fig. 1.1	A strategic approach to employment relations	12
Fig. 2.1	Union Density (OECD), 2000–2019 (*Data Source* OECD)	25
Fig. 2.2	Global Union Density, 2000–2016 (*Data Source* International Labour Organisation)	26
Fig. 2.3	Employee Engagement—% actively engaged, 2012–2022 (*Data Source* Gallup)	28
Fig. 2.4	Approval of Trade Unions, USA (*Data Source* Gallup)	30
Fig. 2.5	What three words best describe trade unions?	32
Fig. 3.1	Strategy—context and choice	48
Fig. 3.2	Employment relations strategy	56
Fig. 3.3	Step change plan for implementation of employment relations strategy	64
Fig. 4.1	Centralised employment relations operating model	72
Fig. 4.2	Specialist employment relations function within HR	73
Figure 1	Case Study 4.1 Line manager lifecycle	81
Fig. 5.1	Trust and resolution—a virtuous circle	87
Fig. 5.2	Attitudinal structuring Based on: Walton and McKersie (1991)	97
Fig. 5.3	Positions, interests and needs	99
Figure 1	Case Study 6.1 A structure for communication and information sharing	112
Fig. 6.1	Pros and cons of works councils (Based on: Hubler [2015])	119
Figure 1	Case Study 6.3 Consultation and negotiation structure	122
Fig. 6.2	What words would you use to describe management-union meetings?	123
Fig. 6.3	Skills needed by employee representatives	128

Fig. 7.1	What words do you associate with negotiation?	133
Fig. 7.2	What words do you associate with negotiation from a perspective of collaboration?	149
Fig. 9.1	Collective disputes procedure	186

List of Tables

Table 2.1	Frames of reference	22
Table 2.2	The political economy of employment relations	24
Table 4.1	Organisational design for collective employment relations	71
Table 4.2	Roles, accountabilities and skills	76
Table 4.3	Defining employment relations capabilities	80
Table 5.1	Attitudes and relationships	88
Table 7.1	Example: negotiating planning template	138
Table 1	Case Study 7.3 The Writers' Strike—issues and outcomes	146
Table 8.1	Suitable topics for using problem-solving	157
Table 8.2	Effective structures for problem-solving	163
Table 8.3	Example of five whys	165
Table 9.1	Communications and industrial action	196
Table 10.1	Structured joint process	207
Table 1	Case Study 11.1 Annual Survey	228
Table 11.1	Measures—employment relations strategy	231
Table 11.2	Measures—line manager capability	231
Table 11.3	Measures—effectiveness of collective forums	232

Part I

Introduction and Context

1

Introduction

Abstract Trade unions have been in decline in most countries across the world leaving many organisations bereft of Human Resource (HR) teams, managers and leaders with experience of working with unions. Collective employment relations has become increasingly marginalised within HR functions and organisational practice as opposed to being a key element of either organisational or people strategy. However, the Covid-19 pandemic had a profound effect on the workplace with workers expressing dissatisfaction with pay gaps, inequality and the precariousness of their jobs. Consequently, collective employment relations and collective voice have become increasingly relevant, requiring organisations to relearn skills and build capacity to be able to meet this challenge. We argue that developing a strategic approach to collective employee voice has huge benefits, which enables change to be managed effectively, problems to be solved with worker input, inclusive cultures to be developed and agreements to be made based on trust. This chapter sets the scene for the rest of the book. It explains the rationale and the aims and objectives of the book. It outlines the structure and gives readers a clear route map to follow as they think about employment relations in their organisations or during their studies.

Keywords Context · Strategy · Collective voice · Organisational benefits

1.1 Introduction

Studying and working in the field of collective employment relations is always challenging and interesting. Occasionally, strikes, labour disputes and campaigns dominate the media, but these high-profile events are just the tip of the iceberg. What is going on under the waterline is even more important. The world of work is changing rapidly with the growth of platform working and the rise of Artificial Intelligence (AI). However, this new environment is increasingly characterised by feelings of mistrust, unfairness and lower levels of employee engagement (Brinkley, 2023). This has negative consequences for organisations and the people that work in them.

The scale of change will require real engagement with employees and their representatives if employers wish to retain and motivate their workers. It will need the development of creative solutions based on trust, new agreements and problem solving on a grand scale to reduce anxiety, manage uncertainty and build healthy workplace cultures. Therefore, it is increasingly important that those of us working in (or hoping to work in) HR and leadership have the knowledge and skills to navigate these challenges. However, while there is a rich tradition of academic research and literature which critically examines the dynamic nature of collective employment relations, there are relatively few sources to which practitioners can turn to explore how this theory can be put into practice.

This book aims to fill this gap and provide a practical guide for those studying and working in the field of collective employment relations. It not only provides a critical analysis of the background and context, but also uses case studies, examples, exercises and original interviews to give the reader a contemporary and detailed understanding of this specialist field. There are also opportunities to reflect and discuss areas such as employment relations strategy, the role of leaders, the practice of negotiation and conflict management. Employers have several choices when it comes to listening to employee voice. They can work with a union; they can combine a union strategy with a direct listening strategy; or they can focus solely on direct employee voice. However, the starting point for this book is our belief that if employers are to create productive and efficient workplaces, and recruit and retain motivated people, they need to embrace the potential offered by effective collective voice and high-trust relationships with trade unions. This chapter develops this case and explains the rationale and structure of the book.

1.2 A Changing Context

The Covid-19 pandemic had a profound effect on many people's attitudes to work and at work. Issues of mental health, family and work-life balance became more important. As we argue later in the book, there is growing evidence that many workers will no longer do a job which doesn't match their priorities and values. A new generation of demotivated workers see work as transactional and ingrained with a lack of equity and inclusivity (Guggenberger et al., 2023; Newman, 2022). Leaders are seen as being out of touch with their employees as the gap between the highest and lowest paid seems to get inexorably wider. For example, in the UK, workers are increasingly aware of the negative impacts of work on mental health and work has become progressively less important for people across advanced economies (The Policy Institute, 2023). Increasingly, they no longer believe that hard work brings a better life. Motivation has been affected by feelings of inequality and unfairness in the workplace (Brinkley, 2023). In addition, burnout is increasingly being talked about across many countries, with organisational psychologists suggesting this is a larger commentary on the state of the work economy and current corporate culture (Stark et al., 2023).

The pandemic highlighted this widening income inequality, in-work poverty and the precariousness of work for many workers. Frontline workers want better pay, more flexibility, and greater control and stability over their work schedule. Perhaps most importantly, they appear to be more prepared to challenge the status quo and fight for their interests (McRae et al., 2023). This is being supported by traditional trade unions which have seen their influence and bargaining power increase. A new generation of workers is also turning to, and creating, new forms of collective representation with the ability to develop international worker networks across global organisations (such as Make Amazon Pay and Apple Together). This has significant implications for managers and organisational leaders who had become increasingly used to having untrammelled authority.

1.3 Trade Unions—Challenge and Revitalisation

In this context, it's not surprising that perceptions of trade unions are at the most favourable they've been since the 1960s. In the US, young workers are more enthusiastic about unions than they have been for decades. This seeming rise in popularity can be linked to anger over wage stagnation, wage rates and benefits for workers versus rising corporate profits in large companies. It has also been exacerbated by the experiences of the pandemic and the negative experiences of workers in health and social care, hospitality, warehousing and retail. These workers are increasingly turning towards collective ways of expressing their discontent and furthering their interests. Moreover, increasing costs of living and tight labour markets mean that for the first time for many years, worker bargaining power is on the rise. At the same time, the positive role of organised labour and trade unions is increasingly front and centre of policy and political debate.

Despite this positive perception, as we explain in Chapter 2, trade unions have been declining in most regions of the world, except in certain African and Latin American countries (Visser, 2019). The move from manufacturing to services, outsourcing of traditionally unionised job roles, increased non-standard and precarious roles, plus automation, have all created a more challenging environment for labour organisation, and had a negative impact on levels of union density. Paradoxically, membership is lower amongst those whose terms, conditions and job security are under greatest threat and therefore who arguably need unions the most. As we discuss in Chapter 2, Visser argues that there are various scenarios for unions going forward—they will either revitalise, or be replaced or marginalised, or solely focus on their current membership in big industries, formal employment relationships and in the public sector.

Trade unions are increasingly focussing their efforts on rebuilding union capacity from the grassroots and taking more robust and combative approaches to defending the interests of their existing members and extending their reach into new areas of the labour market. However, it could take years to build union density outside of workplaces where unions are currently organised. Even so, there are signs that workers increasingly want a voice at work and are willing to tackle poor employment practices with or without the support of traditional unions. Social media platforms such as Organise in the UK, have developed to enable the mobilisation of collective views and can cause huge embarrassment and overturn policies in large organisations. Peer to peer organising networks enable workers who need support and advice to help tackle or change employment practice to reach out to those experienced in unions or social justice movements. Workers are also turning to new independent unions, which are organised around specific occupations and have an ability to respond with agility, using different tactics and embracing more democratic structures—providing a different, albeit sometimes unpredictable, solution. This creates an exciting but also a fragmented and uncertain employment relations environment.

1.4 The Case for Collective Voice

After more than four decades when the collective regulation of employment was portrayed as a drag on businesses' performance and economic growth, the case for collective voice and union representation is being made in some surprising places. For example, the Organisation for Economic Co-operation and Development (OECD)—a forum representing the interests of 37 democracies with market-based economies—has generally promoted a free-market and arguably neo-liberal solution to economic problems and challenges. However, it has highlighted the positive impact of collective bargaining, seeing it as a mechanism for gaining the collective opinions of workers, enabling them to shape solutions to fundamental collective workplace challenges.

> "Collective bargaining and workers' voice are key labour rights, as well as potentially strong enablers of inclusive labour markets. As the digital transformation, globalisation and demographic changes are re-shaping the labour market, collective bargaining is well placed to design solutions to emerging collective challenges. Yet, its capacity to deliver is threatened by the weakening of labour relations in many countries, the flourishing of new—often precarious—forms of employment and the progressive individualisation of employment relationships".
>
> "…despite undeniable difficulties, collective bargaining and workers' voice remain important and flexible instruments that should be mobilised to help workers and companies face the transition and ensure an inclusive and prosperous future of work. The need for co-ordination and negotiation mechanisms between employers and workers is heightened in the changing world of work. Whether considering key issues such as wage inequality, job quality, workplace adaptation to the use of new technologies, or support for workers displaced by shifts in industries, collective bargaining and workers' voice can complement public policies to produce tailored and balanced solutions."
>
> "Negotiating Our Way Up: Collective Bargaining in a Changing World of Work" (OECD, 2019)

Even investment firms are beginning to make a very compelling argument for worker organisation. Trillium Asset Management, which claims to pursue "investment strategies and services that advance humankind towards a global sustainable economy, a just society, and a better world" cites research claiming a correlation between union membership and job satisfaction, with unionised workers reporting lower levels of stress, anxiety, depression or loneliness. Unionised workers are also more likely to speak up about health and safety issues, leading to better safety performance. Trillium also cites research which has shown that high union density and collective agreements lead to higher productivity. And, unions decrease the racial wealth and gender pay gap, while empowering workers, especially marginalised groups to build psychologically safer workplaces.

> "Sustainable economic growth cannot be built on abuses of power or the exploitation of workers. Profit should not supersede basic worker and human rights. For a healthy society and healthy economy, we believe there must be a balance of power and interests – and unions offer an important check to the enormous power of company executives compared to individual workers".
> "The Investor Case for Supporting Worker Organising Rights" (Trillium Asset Management, 2022)

In other words, organised workers can help organisations tackle some of the key fundamental problems in the workplace—mental health, engagement, safety, productivity and equality—thereby creating healthier societies and economies. They also balance the power of CEOs versus individual workers. Collective voice was a recurring theme for the Institute for Human Rights in Business, in its top ten business and human rights issues for 2024. It states that radical change for both production-based and office-based employees and workers requires solutions shaped by the voice of the workforce. As work is increasingly redesigned, it will be important to develop "collective empowerment and new partnerships between workers and employers" (IHRB, 2024).

In the US, trade union organisation and influence has been progressively eroded since the early 1950s, and trade unions face significant hostility from major corporations such as Starbucks, Amazon, Apple and Tesla. However, at the time of writing in 2024, governments in the US, UK and across the EU see trade unions as playing a central role in improving skills, increasing job quality and driving economic growth. The promotion of trade union membership and collective bargaining is a clear challenge to the attempts of some US corporations to actively resist worker organisation. However, this can quickly change based on the priorities of a new president and as a result of other global political and economic turbulence around the world. Whatever happens, collective employee voice must continue to be a high priority for organisational leaders and HR professionals.

1.5 Where Are the Leaders with Experience of Collective Voice?

Collective voice is arguably the most effective mechanism to enable organisations to have structured dialogue with their employees on a range of issues. It helps organisations to understand the views of their employees efficiently and regularly, through independent channels of influence. This collective voice will be most effective if it is endorsed as a positive strategic choice by the board and executive team, with a clear sense of direction for line managers and HR teams.

A General Secretary of a UK trade union, who we interviewed for this book, makes a clear case for the positive benefits of a strong union at times of change and uncertainty, arguing that leaders need to invest in building a long-term relationship with unions based on respect.

> **The case for strong unions**
>
> "A strong union is more useful during change; it is an effective bargaining partner that can speak truth to the membership. But employers have a clear stake in what relationship they want to foster. There is no basis for wanting a union to be an honest broker and critical friend, if the employer adopts a strategy that opposes that. A union with low density is more likely to engage in postures that are more about membership growth than the issues of the day. The risk is that issues become inflated to drive profile rather than measured resolution. Equally, employers determined to keep a union marginalised and treating them on sufferance, will deservedly experience the corresponding conflictual employee relations. It sounds trite but you get the unions you invest in. It is better to invest in a respectful long-term relationship than one based on short-term opposition. If that is the choice, it is likely that other business strategies are similarly short-termist".

But experience in collective employment relations at leadership level in organisations and within HR declined along with trade union membership. The rise of Human Resource Management (HRM) and a unitarist perspective of the employment relationship, cast trade unions as agitators and troublemakers. Conflict has become seen as a simple consequence of misunderstanding and miscommunication. In this context it is not surprising that employment relations became increasingly marginalised within HR functions, organisational practice and wider managerial discourse and debate.

However, this has created a dearth of understanding—employment relations talent is now worryingly scarce, and experience is low at a time when union confidence is high and bargaining power in some sectors has shifted in unions' favour. Many UK and global organisations with long standing union relationships do not have robust talent pipelines of employment relations professionals, or line managers who feel confident working with unions. Within these unionised companies, outside of a small group of individuals, there is little understanding of what unions are, how they work, why they do what they do, what motivates union representatives and how to work with them effectively. This lack of understanding ultimately creates suspicion and distrust and makes it far more difficult to build positive relationships and resolve organisational conflict. Unions may be present in the organisation, but relationships can be antagonistic; they are tolerated but their value to the organisation and the wider economy is unseen by leaders.

In the first two decades of the twenty-first century, managing collective employment relations and working with unions became an HR sideshow. HR professionals were less likely to study collective employment relations during their professional development. Enthusiasm for the specialism therefore waned and often felt like a 'dying art'. Vacant roles were hard to fill. The HR professional who can give the board or executive team a different perspective, can influence leaders to undertake joint problem solving with union representatives, or encourage leaders to spend time understanding a different perspective, was often sidelined or lost. But things have begun to change. In 2022, the UK's CIPD stated that employment relations was the most prized specialist HR skill (Peters, 2022) and increasingly, unionised employers are happy to pay a premium for those with experience of working with unions. Employers are seeing that working with unions and understanding collective employee voice is a critical skill they need to develop.

1.6 Collective Voice—A Strategic Advantage

In the past, collective employment relations has been characterised as 'smoke and mirrors', a tactical game of cat and mouse. However, for the reasons we have already outlined, the rules of employment relations have either been forgotten or seem irrelevant to new generations of leaders, HR practitioners and union representatives. The problem this creates is that in an increasingly volatile world of work, changes to existing agreements, working practices and ways of doing things are inevitable. However, we no longer have the skills, knowledge or know-how to negotiate change effectively. Instead, management proposals for reform are seen as an attack on the terms and conditions of workers, while unions are stereotyped as 'dinosaurs', resistant to change. The parties to employment relations are locked into positions and focus on winning and losing—voices get louder and threats are made, issues are escalated, and procedures invoked.

In some organisations, strained relationships between managers and union representatives lead to issues being escalated to the top of the organisation. Formal meetings are characterised by lateness, little preparation and a focus on trivial issues, rather than the key challenges facing the organisation and its employees. Minimal trust between the parties leads to a lack of local problem resolution. Everyone loses faith in the process and thinks engagement with union representatives is a waste of time. We want to move away from that, and we can. The traditional approach to collective employment relations is stuck in the past and incapable of dealing with today's workplace issues. We need a new way of seeing collective employment relations to motivate a new generation of employment relations professionals. We need people who see value in listening to different perspectives, people who apply creative thinking and help solve workplace challenges alongside trade union and employee representatives. Their aim will be to build inclusive cultures, listen to employee voice and experience, manage conflict constructively, challenge leaders to think differently, and build agreements and trust between leaders and their employees. With this approach, collective voice can become a strategic advantage.

1.7 A Strategic Approach to Collective Employment Relations

In this book, we argue that organisational leaders reconsider collective employment relations and its benefits, recognising collective employee voice as valid, positive and constructive in the workplace, critical to organisational success, with wider benefits to society and the economy. We advocate giving workers a voice in solving problems that affect them. This requires a focus on building skills and developing behaviours that build trust not division. Setting a clear employment relations strategy and investing in building relationships will provide the foundation for positive employment relations. Understanding different perspectives put forward by unions on behalf of employees and adopting skills such as empathy, adaptability and patience, rather than power and pressure, will help build lasting and sustainable agreements. This, in turn, requires a genuine focus on collaborative problem-solving skills. The book describes how leaders can and must evaluate the effectiveness of this strategy, enabling the identification of good practice

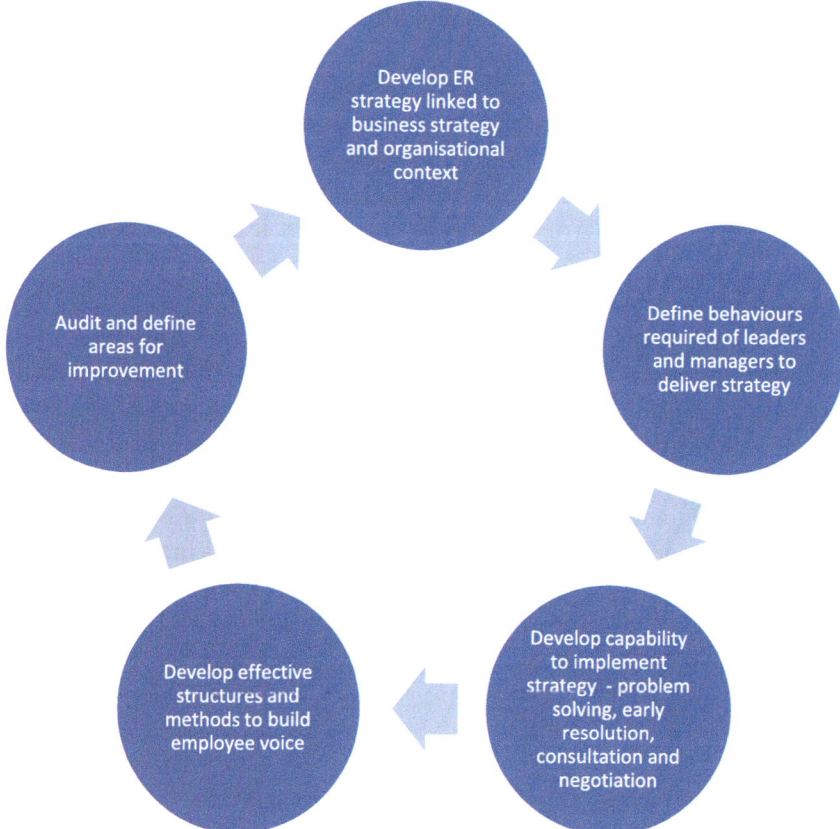

Fig. 1.1 A strategic approach to employment relations

and areas for improvement. This continuous improvement mindset regularly asks both parties to make small improvements to how they are working with each other rather than wait for disruption or dispute. Our approach is set out in Fig. 1.1 and also acts as a structure for this book as we take readers through developing strategy, defining behaviours, building capability, designing methods and structures for employee voice, and evaluating the effectiveness of the strategy.

1.8 A New Agenda for Employment Relations Practice

We need to rethink what good employment relations professionals do, how they make a difference and start to develop enthusiastic professionals who can meet the challenges of today's workplaces. This is not a job about policy and process; it is about culture, leadership and engagement. The key skills are building trust, listening, resolving conflict and reaching agreements. This is what great collective employment relations professionals can expect to do:

- **Managing change and uncertainty.** Employment relations is fundamentally about the effective management of change and managing differences of opinion on issues of relevance to workers in their daily lives. Its' value is in helping parties to find solutions which provide good work, flexible work, make people feel valued, enable upskilling and improve the quality of working lives.
- **Building healthy workplace cultures**. Employment relations is all about understanding the perspectives of a diverse group of people—leaders, union representatives, employees and employee networks. Employment relations professionals can impact the culture of an organisation by coaching others to value the importance of listening to different opinions before making decisions. If, through all organisational layers, employee views are encouraged, listened to and acted upon, leaders become better leaders, representatives take more responsibility and employees feel valued.
- **Finding creative solutions to conflict.** In employment relations, a big part of the role is to resolve problems, conflict and disagreements. Unresolved, these issues can impact employee well-being, organisational performance and productivity. There is something hugely rewarding about working through problems and reaching a positive, often creative solution, when at one point it may have looked like there was no potential solution, and in doing so helping the organisation and individuals to move forward.
- **Building trust and negotiating agreements.** The most effective employment relations specialists are curious, they spend time getting to know employee and union representatives, build trust, and understand fully why something isn't or is working. Without this curiosity and understanding different perspectives, agreements are unlikely to be reached. The employment relations specialist aims to build the most effective agreement, regardless of whose idea it was.

- **Managing risk**. Poor employment relations is very often a top ten risk in any organisation. Those organisations that take a strategic approach will foster a positive workplace climate, manage risks more effectively and reduce disruption to their business.
- **Minimising cost.** The cost of conflict such as disputes and overtime bans is high, as is the damage caused to brands and employee engagement. Rebuilding relationships after conflict can take years. Despite this, very little investment is made in employment relations in many large organisations. We ask organisations to spend less on contingency planning for disputes and more on strategic planning, specialist resources or leadership development in critical skills. We advocate spending more on prevention and less on reaction.

1.9 Rationale and Structure

We believe that there is an urgent need to reignite an enthusiasm for collective employment relations and realise the benefits for both organisations and employees of taking a serious, considered, conscious and systematic approach to employment relations, developing crucial skills, investing in problem solving and challenging the way we have been told collective employment relations has to be conducted. Today's challenges require a fresh approach and that is what we aim to set out in this book. This also relies on unions being effective and adapting to meet the needs of today's workers and organisations. The union leaders that we spoke to as part of the book are aware of the need for change and modernisation as the following quote illustrates.

> "The union movement can't just talk about strikes and disputes. They need to lead on how they enable good work, help manage better change and help on issues such as AI. They need to be capable of conflict where it is justified but not lead with that messaging".

Overall, the fundamental mission of this book is to help practitioners from both parties in the employment relationship to (re)build good relationships, based on listening to each other, solving problems together, strengthening trust, negotiating agreements, creating and sustaining good jobs and making work better.

First and foremost, this is a practical book providing case studies, insights from interviews with a range of HR/employment relations leaders and trade union leaders, and practical tools and resources to help today's practitioners working in unionised workplaces. It is based on what works effectively in workplaces. The book draws extensively from experience in the UK, supplemented by examples from Europe, the US and beyond. The approaches, the key principles and the behaviours that we discuss are applicable to different countries, systems and contexts. The techniques in the book are relevant to any unionised organisation—those with established unions or those looking at recognising a union for the first time.

The book is structured and written to be accessible and engaging while also rooted in robust and established theoretical frameworks and drawing on critical contemporary academic research. Contemporary case study material is used to illustrate specific issues and is drawn from a range of different contexts. Each chapter has a series of reflective activities which will act as a check on knowledge, and a focus for debate and discussion. Each chapter closes with a summary, review questions and a list of references for further reading.

The book is divided into five parts. Part I is entitled *Introduction and Context* and is made up of two chapters. This introduction sets out the rationale for the book and some of the main principles we will be discussing, including an encouragement to organisations to adopt a strategic approach to employment relations. In Chapter 2, the reader is introduced to the political, economic and social context that shapes employment relations, along with key concepts to help understand the contemporary employment relations environment.

Part II is focussed on *Strategy and Implementation* and is made up of three chapters. Chapter 3 discusses different ER strategies and the factors that influence an organisational strategy and introduces ways to evaluate this strategy. Chapter 4 describes different operating models that can be implemented alongside roles and accountabilities to build an effective employment relations team. In Chapter 5, the behaviours required to implement the ER strategy are described with specific emphasis on how to build relationships based on trust.

Part III is entitled *Working with Unions and Collective Voice*. In Chapter 6, we explore how to build effective processes and structures for constructive collective employee voice. Chapter 7 focuses on negotiation, identifying practical steps which can be taken to improve how negotiation is structured and managed. The chapter also looks at some of the frameworks to help practitioners and students reflect on their own style and the style of others. Chapter 8 explores joint problem-solving with unions, which requires high levels of trust and commitment and can bring huge positive organisational benefits.

Part IV deals with *Managing Conflict*. Chapter 9 explores strikes, the path to a dispute and the different roles played by the parties. In chapter ten, we focus on how conflict impacts the relationship between unions and employers, and the practical steps which can be taken to rebuild relationships are explored, including the use of team mediation.

Part V is entitled *Evaluating ER Strategy* and in chapter eleven we explore why organisations should consider formally evaluating their approach to employment relations and the different approaches that organisations can take. The book concludes by exploring the challenges facing practitioners in the future and setting out an agenda for positive and constructive employment relations.

References

Brinkley, I. (2023). *CIPD Good Work Index 2023: Survey Report*. Chartered Institute of Personnel and Development.

Guggenberger, P., Maor, D., Park, M., & Sion, P. (2023, April 26). *The State of Organizations 2023: Ten Shifts Transforming Organizations*. [Online]. McKinsey and Company. https://www.mckinsey.com/capabilities/people-and-organizational-performance/our-insights/the-state-of-organizations-2023. Accessed 29 Nov 2023.

IHRB. (2024). *Top 10 Business and Human Rights Issues 2024*. [Online] Institute for Human Rights and Business. https://www.ihrb.org/library/top-10/2024-top-10-business-and-human-rights-issues. Accessed 08 Mar 2024.

McRae, E. R., Aykens, P., Lowbaster, K., & Shepp, J. (2023, January 18). *9 Trends That Will Shape Work in 2023 and Beyond*. [Online]. Harvard Business Review. https://hbr.org/2023/01/9-trends-that-will-shape-work-in-2023-and-beyond. Accessed 24 Sept 2023.

Newman, D. (2022, 23 March). *Microsoft's 2022 Work Trends Index: Exploring Hybrid Work and a Workforce in Transition*. [Online] Forbes. https://www.forbes.com/sites/danielnewman/2022/03/23/microsofts-2022-work-trends-index-exploring-hybrid-work-and-a-workforce-in-transition/?sh=70c43c95c1a0. Accessed 30 Oct 2023.

OECD. (2019). *Negotiating Our Way Up: Collective Bargaining in a Changing World of Work*. OECD Publishing. https://doi.org/10.1787/1fd2da34-en. Accessed 20 Nov 2023.

Peters, R. (2022). *People Profession 2022: UK and Ireland Survey Report*. Chartered Institute of Personnel and Development.

Stark, E., Carnahan, B., & Kerr, J. (2023, March 28). *How to Tell if a Potential Employer Has a Burnout Culture.* [Online] Harvard Business Review. https://hbr.org/2023/03/how-to-tell-if-a-potential-employer-has-a-burnout-culture. Accessed 2 Feb 2024.

The Policy Institute. (2023, September). *What the World Thinks About Work.* [Online] Kings College London. https://www.kcl.ac.uk/policy-institute/assets/what-the-world-thinks-about-work.pdf. Accessed 1 Nov 2023.

Trillium Asset Management. (2022). *The Investor Case for Supporting Worker Organizing Rights.* https://www.trilliuminvest.com/whitepapers/the-investor-case-for-supporting-worker-organizing-rights. Accessed 19 Nov 2023.

Visser, J. (2019). *Trade Unions in the Balance, ILO ACTRAV Working Paper.* International Labour Organisation. [Online]. https://www.ilo.org/wcmsp5/groups/public/---ed_dialogue/---actrav/documents/publication/wcms_722482.pdf. Accessed 24 Nov 2023.

2

Context and Concepts in Contemporary Collective Employment Relations

Abstract The practice of employment relations is inevitably shaped by the political, economic and social context. The nature and conduct of employment relations within developed economies has changed radically over the past five decades. We have witnessed the decline in trade union membership and organisation, the erosion of collective bargaining, reductions in the incidence of industrial action and the rise of Human Resource Management (HRM). This chapter examines this new terrain and introduces key concepts which help the reader to understand the contemporary employment relations environment and the profound challenges this has created for management and unions. The chapter provides a foundation for the rest of the book and a rationale for a strategic approach to the management of employment relations which foregrounds collective voice.

Keywords Trade unions · Voice · Employment Relationship · Engagement · Representation · Human Resource Management · New technology

2.1 Introduction

Employment relations does not exist in a vacuum. It is shaped by the perspectives of organisational and union leaders, managers, workers, trade union representatives, Human Resource (HR) practitioners and politicians. How these key parties behave and the decisions they take also reflects the dynamic context in which they work. Options and actions are constrained by the legal framework, which varies from country to country and are affected by political and cultural factors. For example, in the US and the UK, a broad commitment to free markets has created a relatively hostile environment for trade unions. This is not necessarily true of other countries in Northern Europe and Scandinavia, in which antipathy to unions and collectivism is not hard wired into societal values. Instead, governments have created legislative frameworks that support and promote collective representation. Nonetheless, in the last five decades a series of factors has progressively eroded the influence of trade unions and challenged the wider case for collective employment relations. Manufacturing and other industries which have traditionally been highly unionised have declined, while employment in services has grown. This has been accompanied by a steep rise in the employment of women, and a growth in part-time, temporary and freelance employment, with the emergence of zero-hours contracts and platform working. The globalisation of economic activity has increased the mobility of labour and capital, further undermining union bargaining power. In 2019, only 16% of workers in countries within the Organisation for Economic Co-operation and Development (OECD) were union members and fewer than a third of workers were covered by collective bargaining (OECD, 2019a, 2019b). However, union decline has been mirrored in growing income inequality and employment insecurity, exacerbated by the long-term impacts of the global banking crisis of 2008/9, the Covid-19 pandemic and rapid technical change. In this new environment there are growing signs of workplace discontent and a fresh focus on worker organisation and mobilisation. This chapter examines the challenges facing management and unions in navigating this new and uncertain terrain.

2.2 Collective Employment Relations—Trust, Voice and Engagement

The rationale for employment relations is rooted in the nature of the employment contract. While an employer can determine hours of work, it is much less easy to quantify the amount of effort that an employee will expend or the creativity they might bring to a task. Similarly, while an employer can impose rules regarding expected conduct and behaviour, they cannot anticipate all the ways in which these rules can be broken or bent. Employment contracts are always incomplete and open-ended, creating a gap which is filled by a constant process of negotiation and renegotiation. Therefore, this type of 'relational contract' requires channels of worker voice, through which employers can communicate with their employees and involve them in decision-making, negotiate change and resolve conflict. If workers feel that they are being heard, they are more likely to feel that they are being managed fairly. This leads to greater trust, which provides the foundation for engagement (Purcell et al., 2009; Saks, 2006).

> **Important**
>
> "A rule is a complex social institution not just a few sentences in a rule book. It can comprise beliefs, ideologies, and taken-for-granted assumptions as well as formal provisions of rights and obligations" (Edwards, 1995: 13).

However, one cannot view the employment relationship as one between an individual employee and their employer. The employment relationship has a core collective component because, in all but the smallest of organisations, the ability of an employee to fulfil the expectations of their employer depends on the actions of their colleagues. Moreover, there are practical problems in employers managing exclusively through individual channels. First, direct voice is difficult to create at strategic levels of larger organisations. Senior managers cannot deal directly with every employee in a meaningful way. Second, enabling direct employee voice and consequently building trust depends on skilled and effective managers but there is abundant evidence that managerial quality is a major problem for organisations (Townsend et al., 2022).

Purcell (2014) argues that collective representation is critical to building a sense of informational and interactional justice and therefore trust. Representatives can efficiently summarise and synthesise the concerns of workers and provide a channel through which managers at all levels can discuss, consult and negotiate change. Furthermore, Purcell and Hall (2012) argue that the strongest voice effects are found in organisations in which there are multiple (union and non-union) voice mechanisms.

> **Exercise 2.1: Engagement and involvement in decision-making**
>
> "Employee engagement is best seen as an outcome of managerial activity to build perceptions of trust, fairness and organizational justice…these are the antecedents of engagement and are closely related to the employees' perceptions that they have an effective voice, their opinions are sought, and they are listened to, and their views are treated with respect" (Purcell, 2014: 244).
>
> Thinking of an organisation you know, to what extent do employees and their representatives trust managers and HR? Are employees and their representatives involved in decision-making?

2.3 Trust and Voice—A Question of Perspective?

The role played by trust and voice within employment relations practice will vary depending on the values and beliefs of the main parties. These are important because they shape our understanding of the actions of employees, union representatives, managers and HR practitioners. For example, if you believe that employers and employees have shared interests, but that trade unions constrain organisational performance, you will try to limit union activity rather than work collaboratively.

These different perspectives, or frames of reference, are reflected in a widely used framework developed by Alan Fox (1966, 1974). This is illustrated in Table 2.1 which maps unitarist, pluralist and radical perspectives against a range of key concepts. This, in turn, implies different approaches to the management of employment relations. The management of contemporary workplaces has tended to be influenced by unitarist perspectives which emphasise shared values and see conflict as an irrational sign of dysfunction. However, this has a direct impact on organisational strategies, which prioritise direct voice over collective representation. For example, one out of every five managers would rather consult directly with their staff as opposed to trade unions (van Wanrooy et al., 2013).

Table 2.1 Frames of reference

	Unitarist	Pluralist	Radical/Marxist
Interests and goals	Employer and employees have shared interests in organisational success	Stakeholders have varied and conflicting interests, but these can be reconciled through negotiation	Interests of capital and labour are diametrically opposed
Trust	Trust is assumed- based on shared interests	Trust needs to be built - reflects perceptions of fairness and justice	Mistrust implicit in management-labour relations
Voice	Direct - focus on communication and information	Emphasis on collective voice via consultation and bargaining	Worker voice viewed as management tool to control labour process
Conflict	Conflict is dysfunctional - result of miscommunication or agitation	Conflict is inevitable but can be minimised or resolved.	Conflict is inevitable and can only be resolved by transforming capitalist employment relations

Adapted from Budd and Bhave (2008)

In contrast, the politics of trade unionism has its roots in a more radical view of the world and economic organisation, which sees the interests of labour and capital as implacably opposed. This is frequently tempered by the practical realities of representing their members, whose main interest is often in protecting or improving pay and working conditions. In fact, survey evidence from the UK suggests that most workers feel that they share the values of the organisations they work for (van Wanrooy et al., 2013). In reality, organisations contain a plurality of perspectives and attitudes. Although workers see the benefits of co-operation with their employer—this brings security, stability and the prospect of advancement—there is also a fundamental conflict as it is in the employers' interests to control costs and the behaviours of their employees.

2.4 The Rise and Fall of Collective Voice

For most of the twentieth century, the defining feature of employment relations in developed economies was increasing trade union membership and influence. Trade unions, as we know them today, are fundamentally a product of industrialisation and developed to improve the pay and conditions of workers often employed in dangerous workplaces, working excessive hours and for limited reward. In essence, trade unions were a direct response to the imbalance of power inherent within the employment relationship. In the UK, there were around two million union members at the start of the twentieth century but by 1979 this had increased to more than 13 million (Newson, 2023). In the same year in the US, there were 21 million members compared to fewer than a million in 1900 (Congressional Research Service, 2023).

> **Exercise 2.2: The contemporary relevance of trade unions**
>
> "Strong, responsible unions are essential to industrial fair play. Without them the labor bargain is wholly one-sided. The parties to the labor contract must be nearly equal in strength if justice is to be worked out, and this means that the workers must be organized and that their organizations must be recognized by employers as a condition precedent to industrial peace."
>
> Louise Brandeis, US Supreme Court Justice, 1916–1939
> Louis Brandeis made this argument in 1934, in the middle of the Great Depression in the US. To what extent is this relevant to the contemporary workplace?

Growing union membership meant greater influence, which in turn led to an increase in the scale and scope of collective bargaining over wages and conditions. This was often accompanied by, or related to, wider legislative and regulatory change as employers and governments responded to demands for greater worker voice and tried to contain and resolve workplace conflict. However, the specific response varied from country to country, often linked to social, cultural and economic factors. For example, Hall and Soskice (2001) argued that liberal market economies such as the UK, US and Canada tended to have relatively limited institutional support for collective voice and low levels of employment protection (see Table 2.2). Employers in these countries often developed structures of representation and bargaining reluctantly, in order to contain and accommodate union power.

In contrast, in more coordinated economies, the focus on longer-term investment complements employment relations institutions which provide greater job security, promote structured employee voice and underpin sectoral collective bargaining. Although this means that labour costs are higher, and employers have less discretion and authority, these "beneficial constraints" (Streeck, 1997) arguably stimulate investment, embed engagement and improve business performance. Recent research from the OECD argues that there is a positive link between collective bargaining and productivity (OECD, 2019a, 2019b), as organisations are forced to increase productivity to compete rather than simply rely on driving wages down. This also tends to reduce income inequality (Darvas et al., 2023), which can restrict economic

Table 2.2 The political economy of employment relations

	Financial systems	Inter-company relationships	Employment relations	Countries
Liberal market economies	Focus on share price. Reliance on equity markets for borrowing and emphasis on short-term profit maximisation.	Market relationships based on formal contracts. High levels of competition and limited collaboration.	Emphasis on free labour markets. Low levels of employment protection. Unilateral management authority. Limited institutional support for unions/representation. Adversarial employment relations.	Australia, Canada, Ireland, New Zealand, UK, US.
Co-ordinated market economies	Long-term financing and less reliance on equity markets. Performance less focused on balance sheet.	High levels of collaboration and key role for industry associations. Significant information sharing and co-operation – relational contracting.	Relatively high levels of employment protection and job security. Management authority constrained by worker representation at all levels. Institutional support for collaborative employment relations	Austria, Belgium, Denmark, Finland, Iceland, Germany, Japan, Netherlands, Norway, Sweden, Switzerland.

Adapted from Hall and Soskice (2010)

growth, particularly in advanced countries and potentially have a range of negative societal impacts—increasing discrimination, conflict and populism (Cingano, 2014; Piketty, 2014).

However, the broad trend in recent years has been declining union membership and with it an erosion of union power. As Fig. 2.1 shows, within OECD economies, there was a gradual but sustained contraction in union density between 2000 and 2019, even in countries with significant institutional support for worker representation.

This decline is even more pronounced if one looks at the data over a longer timeframe. Between 1980 and 2020, union density in the UK, US and Australia more than halved, while it reduced by more than 40% in France (OECD, 2024). There is no single explanation for union decline, however de-industrialisation, the shift to services and the fragmentation of employment have combined to create a more hostile terrain for union organisation. The globalisation of production and consumption has also shifted the balance of bargaining power away from labour. Multinational corporations can use the threat of investment or disinvestment to negotiate preferable terms and conditions with trade unions and persuade governments to offer conducive environments for profit maximisation (Greer & Hauptmeier, 2016; Wright et al., 2020).

The situation in less developed economies is a little more positive for trade union organisation (see Fig. 2.2). But even among developing economies in West and East Africa, and Asia, where one might expect trade unions to be growing, the overall trend is downwards. It could be argued that a key factor

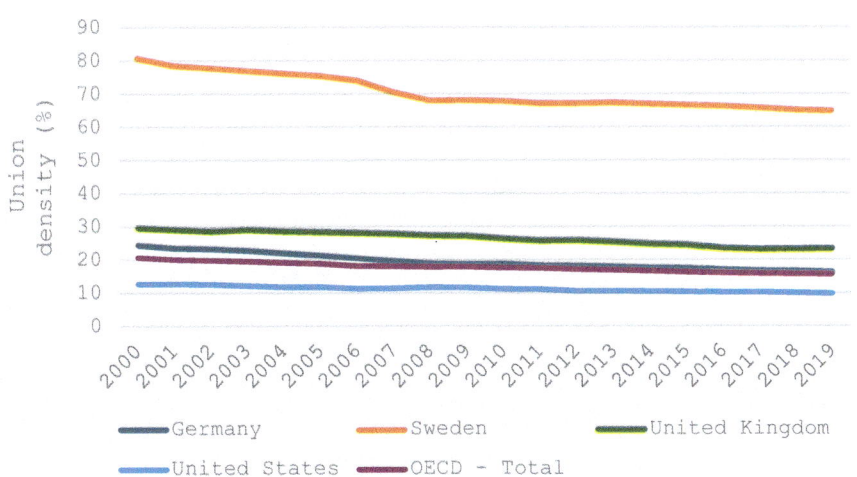

Fig. 2.1 Union Density (OECD), 2000–2019 (*Data Source* OECD)

here is technological change and the growth of digitalisation—this means that industrial and economic development is not necessarily driven by the growth of large, labour-intensive manufacturers, which have tended to have a higher propensity to unionise.

In addition, the unionisation gap between workers aged between 16 and 24, and those between 55 and 64, increased significantly during the 2000s (Visser, 2019). This potentially represents an existential threat to trade unions. However, this does not appear to have been driven negative views among young people of the notion of trade unionism or what trade unions do. Instead, the real problem appears to lie in the insecurity and precarity faced by young people entering the labour market. While this creates a basis for activism, unlike previous generations, they find themselves in organisations with little, if any, union presence. Moreover, where unions are present, their structures and agendas often appear inaccessible and irrelevant for younger workers (Hodder & Krestos, 2015).

> **Case study 2.1: Union trajectories—decline, replacement and renewal**
>
> Visser (2019) suggests that the challenges we have discussed in this chapter create several trajectories for trade unions.
>
> - **Marginalisation**—the progressive decline of trade unions continues. Intensifying globalisation creates an increasingly hostile environment for union organisation. This is exacerbated by increasingly liberal government

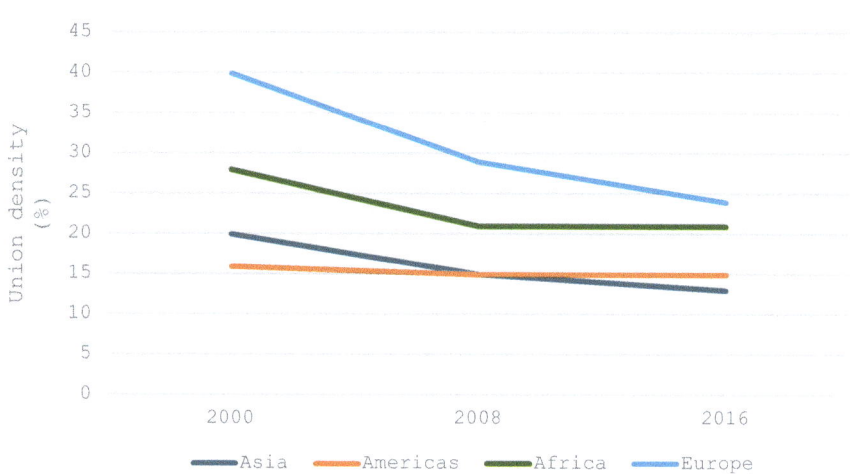

Fig. 2.2 Global Union Density, 2000–2016 (*Data Source* International Labour Organisation)

approaches as they compete for investment. Automation erodes traditional areas of union strength and unions fail to grasp the potential of new technology.
- **Dualisation**—unions focus on defending and reinforcing areas of existing strength within larger organisations and the public sector. Organising revolves around workplaces where access is relatively easy while the harder to reach areas of the economy are abandoned, creating a greater distinction between unionised and non-unionised workers.
- **Replacement**—conventional unions give way to alternative forms of voice and representation. These may be rooted in legislation, such as wages councils, or through employer initiatives such as staff associations and employee fora. In addition, we may see the development of community-based organisations and new, less organised forms of grassroots resistance and representation.
- **Revitalisation**—unions focus on developing grassroots organisation. This may involve the development of less hierarchical and more agile and accessible structures, using new technology more creatively. Bargaining agendas will be refreshed and embrace issues of equality and identity.

Key questions

1. Which trajectories above reflect the current position of unions in your organisation and/or your country?
2. Can unions move towards a trajectory of revitalisation? If so, how?
3. What are the implications of these trajectories for managing employment relations?

2.5 The Implications of Employee Silence

For some employers and governments, declining union membership has been seen as a positive development. From this perspective, reduced union power removes a barrier to the operation of the free market and an obstacle to change. It even signals an era of industrial harmony and shared values. However, the gap left by unions has not been filled by alternative mechanisms of representation contributing to a wider silencing of workers' voices, which has several worrying implications.

2.5.1 Disengagement

If union decline had ushered in a new era of co-operative employment relations, we would expect to see this reflected in increased employee engagement. However, the available data suggests otherwise. Figure 2.3 presents

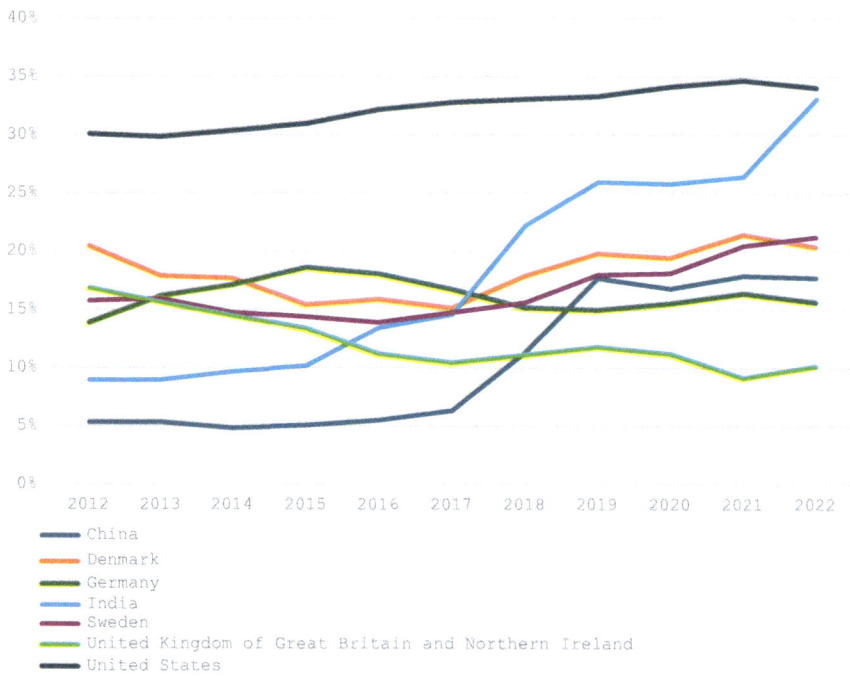

Fig. 2.3 Employee Engagement—% actively engaged, 2012–2022 (*Data Source* Gallup)

data collected by Gallup (2023), which creates an overall engagement score for workers in different countries from a battery of 12 questions. From this, Gallup calculates the percentage of workers that are actively engaged (thriving and enthusiastic about their work), not engaged (psychologically unattached to work and employer), and actively disengaged (resentful and undermining the performance of others). As one can see, there are relatively few actively engaged employees according to Gallup—in the US, this is relatively high at 34% compared to a global average of 23%—engagement is particularly low in the UK, just over 10%, and this has fallen steadily over the past decade.

In 2022 fewer than one-third of US employees strongly agreed that 'at work, my opinions seem to count' (Gallup, 2023). Moreover, this had remained largely unchanged since 2007.

2.5.2 Covid-19 and Changing Attitudes to Work

Assumptions that union decline heralded a new age of industrial harmony and shared values were also brought into question by increasing inflation and interest rates in the wake of the Covid-19 pandemic and Russia's invasion of Ukraine in 2022. For many workers, rising prices and increasing rents and mortgage payments created a growing sense of grievance. Tightening labour markets and rising living costs increased the bargaining power of trade unions—and their ability to negotiate improved wages and conditions demonstrated their relevance to working people. In the UK, 2023 saw groups of workers not known for their industrial militancy, such as barristers, hospital consultants and nurses, taking industrial action.

There was also evidence of a wider sense of discontent as employers found it increasingly difficult to recruit and retain key staff. In the immediate aftermath of the pandemic, frontline workers—in healthcare, hospitality, education and retail—were changing jobs, retiring early or moving to part-time work. This phenomenon was labelled 'the Great Resignation' with voluntary quit rates in the US in 2021 reaching the highest yet recorded (Klotz, 2022). A number of causes were suggested—the pandemic provided an opportunity for workers to rethink their careers and work-life priorities. In addition, front-line workers had traumatic experiences in hostile working environments. Although there is some evidence that turnover has returned to pre-pandemic levels, it does not necessarily signal a return to normality.

In 2023, PWC surveyed more than 50,000 workers across 46 countries (PWC, 2023). They found that 26% of workers were looking to change their job (compared to 19% in 2022). This appeared to be driven by work overload, a lack of fulfilment and growing financial pressure. This was also leading an increasing proportion of workers to look for a pay rise (42%, up from 35% in 2022). The desire to look for alternative work was even more pronounced among Generation Z, reflecting a more general trend questioning the role and importance of work. According to the World Values Survey (The Policy Institute, 2023), the proportion of people in the UK who think that 'it would be a good thing if less importance was placed on work' has increased from 26% in 1981 to 43% in 2023. This mirrors similar changes in other developed economies—25% to 41% in Canada and 30 to 45% in Germany.

Given these changing attitudes to work, it is perhaps not surprising that support for trade unions appeared to gather pace. For example, survey evidence from Gallup in the US, gathered in 2024 (Gallup, 2024) (see Fig. 2.4), suggested that approval for trade unions had increased from 52% in 2011 to 70% in 2024.

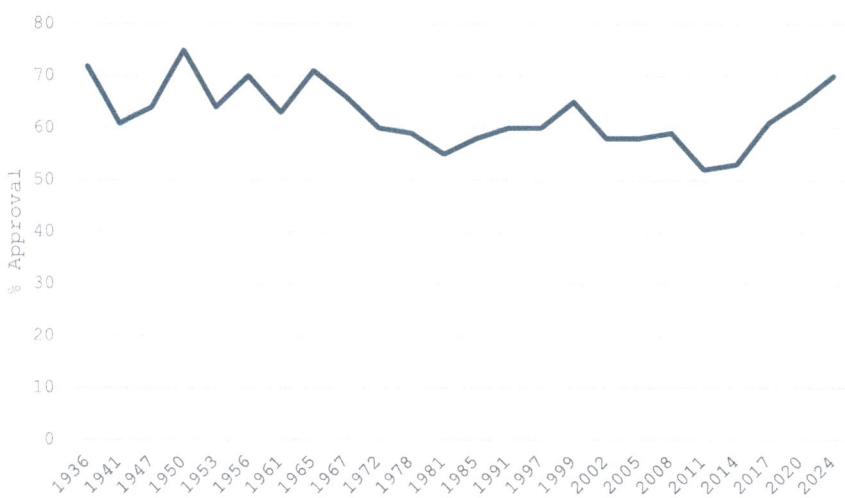

Fig. 2.4 Approval of Trade Unions, USA (*Data Source* Gallup)

Moreover, this support was also reflected by growing activism and widespread attempts to unionise in companies such as Amazon and Starbucks. In both the US and the UK, government support for the potential benefits brought by trade unions and collective bargaining became key issues in general election campaigns in 2024.

Employment Relations on the Ballot?

"The right of workers to come together and form a union is under attack. We must unrig the rules that block workers from having the union they want and update our labor laws to make it more possible. We must change labor law so that it is easier for unions and employers to enter into multi-employer agreements establishing minimum workplace standards related to wages, benefits, and working conditions." US Democratic National Committee, Party Platform 2024 (DNC, 2024).

"Labour will stop the chaos and turn the page to create a partnership between business and trade unions, by implementing 'Labour's Plan to Make Work Pay: Delivering a New Deal for Working People' in full—introducing legislation within 100 days…This will include banning exploitative zero hours contracts; ending fire and rehire; and introducing basic rights from day one to parental leave, sick pay, and protection from unfair dismissal. We will strengthen the collective voice of workers, including through their trade unions…These changes will improve the lives of working people across the entire UK." UK Labour Party, Election Manifesto, 2024 (Labour Party, 2024).

At the time of writing, we don't know whether the increased prominence of the case for trade union organisation, representation and bargaining will deliver substantive and sustained change. Nonetheless, it points to a growing need for employers to respond in a positive way to the clear demand for a collective voice.

2.5.3 A Growing Gulf in Perspectives

The erosion of trade union organisation has also been accompanied by the increasing domination of unitarist perspectives among management and people professionals. The power of trade unions ensured that employment relations was at the core of the development of the HR profession. However, the influence of Human Resource Management (HRM) has seen HR practitioners become much more closely aligned with business performance (Legge, 2005). This is illustrated by the dominance of business partnering models (Keegan & Francis, 2010) which embed practitioners in the business, working side-by-side with senior managers to deliver organisational strategy (Ulrich, 1997). Consequently, HR practitioners are less likely to play a more impartial, mediating role between employees, unions and managers.

> **Important**
>
> In practice, employee relations is increasingly seen as a second-tier function, subservient to HR and largely concerned with procedural and legal compliance and with very little connection with wider collective issues (Saundry, Fisher and Kinsey, 2021).

Saundry, Fisher and Kinsey have argued that employment relations has become marginalised and ghettoised within the HR profession. Their research found that employment relations tended to be handled lower down the HR hierarchy or in specialist units which were separate from the main, strategic HR function. This is understandable from a unitarist view of the world in which trade unions are an irrelevance and conflict is simply a function of miscommunication. However, such an approach risks organisations simply not having the knowledge, expertise and experience to respond to re-energised trade unions and employees who are increasingly prepared to challenge authority.

The dominance of unitarist perspectives among HR practitioners, managers and employers is reflected in their attitudes towards trade unions. Figure 2.5 shows an exercise that we conducted with just over 50 students from our development programme—all of whom were HR practitioners working in employment relations. They were asked to write down the three words which best described their view of trade unions. On the positive side words like negotiate, represent and mediate were prominent, but the most common word was challenge, with protect, strike and block also widely cited.

The view of trade unions as blockers and disruptors not only underlines a misunderstanding of the role of trade unions but fails to appreciate that the attitudes, tactics and strategies of trade unions cannot be separated from managerial behaviour.

As traditional industries have declined, the organisations that have replaced them are more likely to have cultures in which trade unions are seen as disruptive and inimical to the wider goals of the organisation. This can most commonly be seen in companies which have developed in the last three or four decades when trade union organisation has been at a low ebb. The case below looks at possibly the most well-known example of this—Amazon.

> **Case Study 2.2: Amazon—the Earth's best employer?**
> From its inception, Amazon refused to recognise or engage with trade unions. In 2018, its chairman, Jeff Bezos, said "we don't believe we need a union to be an intermediary between ourselves and our workers". Since then, it has taken a robust approach to fighting any attempts at union organisation. In 2021, the Retail, Wholesale and Department Store Union forced a vote among 6000 Amazon workers at a warehouse in Bessemer, Alabama. The

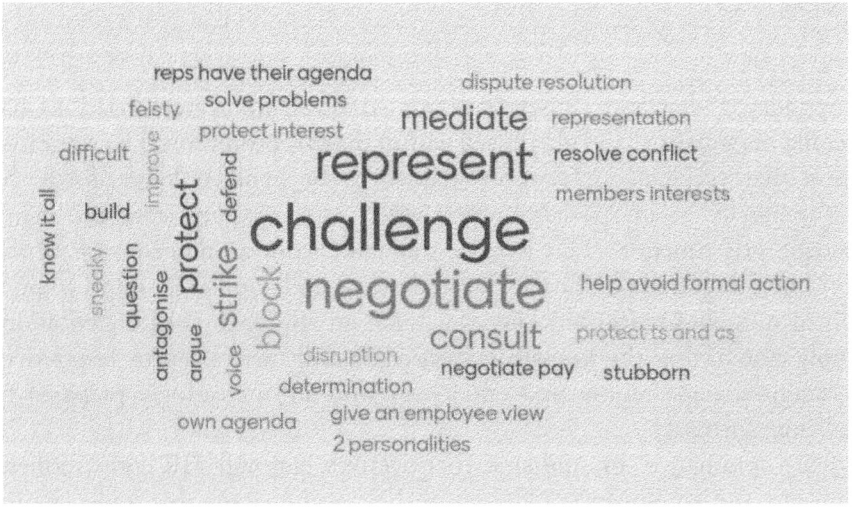

Fig. 2.5 What three words best describe trade unions?

fact that this vote took place at all, in a part of the US which has traditionally been hostile to union organising, points to a rising demand for union organisation within Amazon and other non-union organisations, in the wake of the Covid-19 pandemic. Amazon used a range of tactics to defeat the organising drive. These included setting up a dedicated website, which told workers that paying union dues may result in them being unable to afford to eat lunch or pay for their children's school equipment. Unions also accused Amazon of removing and prohibiting pro-union materials, creating a culture of surveillance, and holding meetings where employees were forced to listen to anti-union messaging. Eventually, workers at Bessemer voted 1798 to 738 against unionisation.

Following the vote, Jeff Bezos wrote to shareholders as follows:

"Does your Chair take comfort in the outcome of the recent union vote in Bessemer? No, he doesn't. I think we need to do a better job for our employees…it's clear to me that we need a better vision for how we create value for employees—a vision for their success. If you read some of the news reports, you might think we have no care for employees. In those reports, our employees are sometimes accused of being desperate souls and treated as robots. That's not accurate. They're sophisticated and thoughtful people who have options for where to work. When we survey fulfilment center employees, 94% say they would recommend Amazon to a friend as a place to work.

Employees are able to take informal breaks throughout their shifts to stretch, get water, use the rest-room, or talk to a manager, all without impacting their performance. These informal work breaks are in addition to the 30-minute lunch and 30-minute break built into their normal schedule…Performance is evaluated over a long period of time as we know that a variety of things can impact performance in any given week, day, or hour. If employees are on track to miss a performance target over a period of time, their manager talks with them and provides coaching…We terminate the employment of less than 2.6% of employees due to their inability to perform their jobs…The fact is, the large team of thousands of people who lead operations at Amazon have always cared deeply for our hourly employees, and we're proud of the work environment we've created…

Despite what we've accomplished, it's clear to me that we need a better vision for our employees' success. We have always wanted to be Earth's Most Customer-Centric Company. We won't change that. It's what got us here. But I am committing us to an addition. We are going to be Earth's Best Employer and Earth's Safest Place to Work."

Key questions

1. How would you explain the approach taken by Jeff Bezos and Amazon in terms of the theoretical perspectives discussed earlier in the chapter?
2. Is Amazon's anti-union strategy sustainable?
3. What would be the challenges and potential benefits of adopting a more co-operative approach towards trade unions?

In April 2022, the Amazon Labor Union won the right to negotiate at the company's Staten Island warehouse which employs 8000 workers. Amazon is also facing other organising campaigns, including in the UK. However, there is little sign of the company adopting a less hostile approach to trade unions. It is tempting for organisations to convince themselves that union activists only represent a small minority of workers and that unions are agitators acting against the interest of the organisation and its employees. But continuing to thwart legitimate employee voice runs the risk of undermining organisational performance and customer reputation. An alternative approach is to embrace the desire of workers to be organised and try to develop high trust management-union relationships.

2.6 The Challenge of Contemporary Employment Relations

As trade unions have grappled with the challenge of declining membership, they have increasingly turned to new strategies focussed on grassroots union organising (Holgate, 2015; McAlevey, 2020; Simms & Holgate, 2010). The organising approach seeks to empower members and encourage them to take responsibility for representing their interests. Through the development of a culture of self-organisation, unions hope to create a more active base. A crucial aspect of organising is the development of a new generation of local leaders capable of re-energising workplace organisation. Organising also implicitly rejects accommodation and partnership with employers, and a shift to more robust responses to local concerns, revolving around campaigns which seek to mobilise workers and collectivise their grievances. Unions hope that this will increase bargaining power and deliver better terms and conditions, which in turn will provide a firm basis for sustainable increases in union membership.

> **Case Study 2.3: Trade union organisation—building from the bottom up.**
>
> *The following is an extract from a conversation with a General Secretary of a trade union in the UK. The union has around 500,000 members working in a wide range of roles within the public and private sectors.*
>
> "Our strategy is really pretty simple. We focus on the workplace, listening to members, helping them build their own campaigns, identifying leaders and developing our future leaders.. I don't particularly want or need politically-minded people. I need people who have decent values…who you would want to represent you if you had a problem, whoever workers themselves identify…the person who is that organic leader, that's what you're seeking to identify.

> We have just started this journey...we have to look at how we train and develop people...we have put a huge effort into changing the culture in the union...in new leadership, more women, younger leaders. We need to get the vast bulk of our people in a space where they listen to members and can build good industrial campaigns...our absolute focus is going to be on campaigning and organising excellence. We have a structure to how we approach campaigns. We train our people in the emotional element of campaigning because emotion always wins.
>
> I think a lot of the debate around organising has been artificial...what works is listening to members, developing the leaders, running the campaigns and getting people into the union...You've got organisers who we are telling to go out and listen to the members and light fires and they're doing it...all we want to do is change the world one little bit at a time but change the world by listening to people rather than lecturing people."

Key questions

1. If you were an employer faced with an organising campaign being conducted by this union, how would you respond and why?
2. To what extent does the approach set out by the General Secretary provide a viable blueprint for union revitalisation?
3. What, if anything, do trade unions like this one need to do to win the support of the new generation of workers coming into the contemporary labour market?

Crucially, new trade unions have also started to emerge to fill gaps arguably left by conventional union organisation. They often represent more precarious workers 'employed' under non-standard contracts and focus on those engaged in platform working. These unions tend to be smaller in scale, occupationally focussed with less centralised and more autonomous structures. Consequently, they have the potential to be more agile and responsive to the needs of their members.

Organising, with its focus on campaigning and robust resistance, presents additional challenges to employers, who have arguably become used to more compliant trade unions with limited bargaining power. That said, it also raises questions for trade unions around how these relatively combative approaches can be balanced against the need to negotiate successfully to improve members' terms and conditions, particularly if the political and economic context reduces union bargaining power.

Many of the changes in the orientation of trade unions, as well as new areas of activism and militancy, are linked to developments in new technology. The rapid rise of Artificial Intelligence (AI) and other information-based automation has triggered a so-called fourth industrial revolution. There is little doubt that humans will no longer be needed for a large range of tasks which can be performed more accurately, more efficiently and/or more safely by machines and others will be deskilled (Brione, 2017). Analysis by the World Economic Forum suggested that while 85 million jobs would be lost due to AI, 97 million would be created. Similarly, a survey of leading economic researchers by the Centre for Economic Policy Research (CEPR) in 2023, found that most respondents felt that overall employment would be unchanged but there could be implications for the balance of work and leisure time, and income inequality (Ilzetzki & Jain, 2023).

> **Exercise 2.3: New technology and employment relations**
>
> "Risks of stress and anxiety arise if workers feel that decisions are being made based on numbers and data that they have no access to" (Moore, 2020).
>
> To what extent do you agree with this statement? How can employers, unions and worker representatives work together to eliminate or minimise these risks?

The way in which work is managed is also likely to change as AI and other technologies provide opportunities to control activity more quickly and directly. If AI is used to increase surveillance and intensify work, this could have significant negative impacts on the health and well-being of workers. This could also increasingly blur the work/home boundary. In addition, the loss of autonomy and control could lead to heightened stress and anxiety. However, the existing limits of technology could also lead to job creation and an increasing demand for some skills which are currently low paid and undervalued. More specifically, social skills or an awareness of shifting social contexts are difficult to replicate (Frey & Osborne, 2013). The capabilities needed to manage people effectively—to persuade, influence and negotiate—are essentially human. Therefore, it could be argued that these skills may become even more important in an age of AI, where there is potential for significant conflict as it begins to transform organisational experience. Given the challenges of new technology, it is not surprising that new modes of employment, made possible by technology, have become a particular focus for union organisation and activism.

Case Study 2.4: Platform working—new technology, voice and representation

Employment relations academic Kurt Vandaele (2018) conducted a review of the implications of platform working for trade unions, published by the European Trade Union Institute in 2018. He suggested that there were three main responses to the challenges presented by platform work.

Grassroots unions and co-operatives—new grassroots trade unions, such as the Independent Workers' Union of Great Britain (IWGB) in the UK and Freie Arbeiterinnen- und Arbeiter-Union (FAU) in Germany, which represent precarious workers more generally, have been active in representing platform workers. In addition, specific occupational-based unions or guilds have been established, sometimes linked to existing traditional trade unions. These provide a range of services and support for members but also pursue active litigation strategies, often funded through crowdsourcing. In addition, one response has been for platform workers to unite to develop co-operatives offering platformed services—for example Riders x Derechos in Spain.

Traditional trade unions—some traditional European unions are attempting to gain recognition from digital platforms. The GMB in the UK entered into a voluntary partnership agreement with Deliveroo, which included certain bargaining, consultative and representative rights. In Germany and Austria there have been attempts to establish works councils. The IG Metall union has set up a website through which platform workers can share their experiences, rate employers and make this information public. In parallel they have established a voluntary code of conduct for platforms pledging to ensure certain labour standards. In Denmark, a platform offering cleaning services (Hilfr.dk) entered into a collective agreement with Danish union 3F.

Quasi-unions—this relates to the development of organisations which are essentially labour market intermediaries for freelance and contract workers, but which position themselves as co-operative associations with specific aims to provide security and support for their members. The best example of this is Société Mutuelle pour Artistes (SMart), which was set up in Belgium and now claims to have 100,000 members (mainly freelance creative workers) across eight countries. SMart provides insurance, legal assistance, guarantees payments and provides administrative support—it claims in essence to act as both employer and employee.

Key questions

1. What do you think are the main employment relations challenges created by the development of platform work?
2. Do you think that traditional trade unions can adapt to this new context?
3. To what extent do these new ways of working require a new approach to employment relations?

It is impossible to hold back technological advance. However, the way that this is implemented is crucial. In particular, the extent to which information is democratised will determine whether these changes improve or degrade experiences of work. An absence of worker voice will make it more likely that technology is not introduced and applied in a way that protects or enhances experiences of work. Moreover, from an employers' perspective, this approach has the potential to create negative consequences and currents of conflict and resistance in the longer term. If change is negotiated and workers are involved in the decisions over AI and automation, the outcome is more likely to be both positive and sustainable.

2.7 Conclusion

The nature of collective employment relations has been fundamentally changed by rapid and far-reaching changes in the nature of work and peoples' attitudes to it. The prevailing wisdom has pointed to a progressive erosion of collectivism and therefore the collective institutions of employment relations. However, political and social contexts are dynamic and there are some tentative signs of younger workers, denied the security and stability of their parents, creating new ways of defending and furthering their interests. We should also be cautious about assuming that technological change will benefit employing organisations—it may be just as likely that new (and different) groups of workers will possess the scarce (human) skills that could be the foundation for greater bargaining power in the future. The purpose of employment relations revolves around the reconciliation and mediation of the varying interests of employers, managers, workers, trade unions and governments. For many years this meant the development of pluralist institutions and practice which supported negotiation and dispute resolution. Consequently, the key parties developed skills, expertise and know how that enabled them to build trust and to contain and resolve conflict. However, the rise of HRM and the undermining of trade union influence in certain nations not only reduced the need for those institutions but also eroded the employment relations skills base. The danger is that this creates a vacuum in which distrust and conflict can flourish. If this is to change then it is crucial that managers, HR practitioners and union representatives understand each other, the positions they take and their fundamental interests and needs.

Questions

1. To what extent has the development of HRM undermined the role of employment relations in contemporary organisations?
2. You work in an organisation with no experience of recognising trade unions, but which is facing a sustained union organising drive. What are the main benefits of union recognition and developing a strategic plan for building positive employment relations?
3. Does Generation Z offer new hope for organised labour?
4. What are the implications of the growth of AI and similar technologies for the future of collective employment relations?

References

Brione, P. (2017). *Mind Over Machines: New Technology and Employment Relations*. Acas Research Papers, 02/17.

Budd, J., & Bhave, D. (2008). Values, Ideologies, and Frames of Reference in Industrial Relations. In P. Blyton, E. Heery, N. Bacon, & J. Fiorito (Eds.), *SAGE Handbook of Industrial Relations*. Sage.

Cingano, F. (2014). *Trends in Income Inequality and its Impact on Economic Growth*. OECD Social, Employment and Migration Working Paper No. 163. Organisation for Economic Co-operation and Development.

Congressional Research Service. (2023). *A Brief Examination of Union Membership Data*. [Online]. https://crsreports.congress.gov/product/pdf/R/R47596. Accessed 14 Jun 2024.

Darvas, Z., Gotti, G., & Sekut, K. (2023). *Collective Bargaining Is Associated with Lower Income Inequality*. Analysis 04/2023, Bruegel.

DNC. (2024). *Democratic Party Platform 2024*. [Online]. https://democrats.org/where-we-stand/party-platform/. Accessed 27 Aug 2024.

Edwards, P. (1995). *Industrial Relations—Theory and Practice in Britain*. Blackwell.

Fox, A. (1966). *Industrial Sociology and Industrial Relations*. HMSO.

Fox, A. (1974). *Beyond Contract: Work*. Power and Trust Relations.

Frey, C., & Osborne, M. (2013). *The Future of Employment. How Susceptible Are Jobs to Computerisation?* Oxford Martin Programme on Technology and Employment.

Gallup. (2023). *Employee Engagement*. [Online]. https://www.gallup.com/394373/indicator-employee-engagement.aspx. Accessed 16 Oct 2023.

Gallup. (2024). *Labor Unions*. [Online]. https://news.gallup.com/poll/12751/labor-unions.aspx. Accessed 17 Dec 2024.

Greer, I., & Hauptmeier, M. (2016). Management Whipsawing: The Staging of Labor Competition Under Globalization. *ILR Review, 69*(1), 29–52.

Hall, P., & Soskice D. (2001). *Varieties of Capitalism: The Institutional Foundations of Comparative Advantage*. Oxford University Press.

Hodder, A., & Krestos, L. (Eds.). (2015). *Young Workers and Trade Unions—A Global View*. Palgrave Macmillan.

Holgate, J. (2015). Community Organising in the UK: A 'New' Approach for Trade Unions? *Economic and Industrial Democracy, 36*(3), 431–455.

Ilzetzki, E., & Jain, S. (2023). *The Impact of Artificial Intelligence on Growth and Employment*. [Online]. Centre for Economic Policy Research. https://cepr.org/voxeu/columns/impact-artificial-intelligence-growth-and-employment. Accessed 13 Oct 2023.

Keegan, A., & Francis, H. (2010). Practitioner talk: the changing textscape of HRM and emergence of HR business partnership. *International Journal of Human Resource Management, 21*(6), 873–98.

Klotz, A. (2022, June 3). *The Great Resignation Is Still Here, but Whether It Stays Is Up to Leaders*. [Online]. OECD Forum. https://www.oecd-forum.org/posts/the-great-resignation-is-still-here-but-whether-it-stays-is-up-to-leaders. Accessed 17 Feb 2024.

Labour Party. (2024). *Labour Party Manifesto 2024*. https://labour.org.uk/change/kickstart-economic-growth/#making-work-pay. Accessed 27 Aug 2024.

Legge, K. (2005). *Human Resource Management*. Palgrave Macmillan.

McAlevey, J. (2020). *A Collective Bargain: Unions, Organizing, and the Fight for Democracy*. ECCO.

Moore, P. (2020). *Artificial Intelligence in the Workplace: What Is at Stake for Workers?* [Online]. https://www.bbvaopenmind.com/en/articles/artificial-intelligence-in-workplace-what-is-at-stake-for-workers/. Accessed 12 Oct 2023.

Newson, N. (2023). *Trade unions: Members and relations with the government*. House of Lords Library. [Online]. https://lordslibrary.parliament.uk/trade-unions-members-and-relations-with-the-government/. Accessed 12 Sep 2024.

OECD. (2019a). OECD Employment Outlook 2019: The Future of Work. *OECD Publishing*. https://doi.org/10.1787/9ee00155-en

OECD. (2019b). *Negotiating Our Way Up: Collective Bargaining in a Changing World of Work*. OECD Publishing. https://doi.org/10.1787/1fd2da34-en

OECD. (2024). *OECD Data Explorer*. Trade Union Density

Piketty, T. (2014). *Capital in the 21st Century*. The Belknap Press of Harvard University Press.

Purcell, J. (2014). Employee Voice and Engagement. In C. Truss, R. Delbridge, K. Alfes, A. Shantz, & E. Soanne (Eds.), *Employee Engagement in Theory and Practice*. Routledge.

Purcell, J., & Hall, M. (2012). *Voice and Participation in the Modern Workplace: Challenges and Prospects*. Acas Future of Workplace Relations discussion paper series. Acas.

Purcell, J., Kinnie, N., Swart, J., Rayton, B., & Hutchinson, S. (2009). *People Management and Performance*. Routledge.

PWC. (2023). *Hopes and Fears Global Workforce Survey 2023*. [Online]. PWC. 20/6/2023. https://www.pwc.com/gx/en/issues/workforce/hopes-and-fears.html. Accessed 2 Oct 2023.

Saks, A. (2006). Antecedents and Consequences of Engagement. *Journal of Managerial Psychology, 21*(7), 600–619.

Saundry, R., Fisher, V., & Kinsey, S. (2021). Disconnected Human Resource? Proximity and the (Mis)management of Workplace Conflict. *Human Resource Management Journal, 31*(2), 476–492. https://doi.org/10.1111/1748-8583.12318

Simms, M., & Holgate, J. (2010). TUC Organizing Academy 10 Years On: What Has Been the Impact on British Unions? *International Journal of Human Resource Management, 21*(3), 355–370.

Streeck, W. (1997). Industrial Citizenship Under Regime Competition: The Case of the European Works' Councils. *Journal of European Public Policy, 4*(4), 643–664.

The Policy Institute. (2023, September). *What the World Thinks About Work*. [Online]. Kings College. https://www.kcl.ac.uk/policy-institute/assets/what-the-world-thinks-about-work.pdf. Accessed 11 Dec 2023.

Townsend, K., Bos-Nehles, A., & Jiang, K. (Eds.). (2022). *Research Handbook on Line Managers*. Edward Elgar Publishing.

Ulrich, D. (1997). Human resource champion: The next agenda for adding value and delivering results. *Harvard Business Review, 76*(1), 124–34.

Vandaele, K. (2018). *Will Trade Unions Survive in the Platform Economy? Emerging Patterns of Platform Workers' Collective Voice and Representation in Europe*. ETUI Research Paper—Working Paper 2018.05. https://doi.org/10.2139/ssrn.3198546

Van Wanrooy, B., Bewley, H., Bryson, A., Forth, J., Freeth, S., Stokes, S., & Wood, S. (2013). *Employment Relations in the Shadow of Recession: Findings from the 2011 Workplace Employment Relations Study*. Palgrave Macmillan.

Visser, J. (2019). *Trade Unions in the Balance, ILO ACTRAV Working Paper*. International Labour Organisation. [Online]. https://www.ilo.org/wcmsp5/groups/public/---ed_dialogue/---actrav/documents/publication/wcms_722482.pdf. Accessed 24 Nov 2023.

Wright, C. F., Wailes, N., Lansbury, R. D., & Bamber, G. J. (2020). Beyond Varieties of Capitalism, Towards Convergence and Internationalisation. In G. J. Bamber, R. D. Lansbury, N. Wailes, & C. F. Wright (Eds.), *International and Comparative Employment Relations: National Regulation, Global Changes* (6th ed., pp. 341–361). Routledge.

Part II

Strategy and Implementation

3

Creating an Effective Employment Relations Strategy

Abstract A collective employment relations strategy aligned to the business strategy, and the organisation's values and purpose, is critical in helping an organisation achieve its goals. The strategy that an organisation chooses is often rooted in the perspectives of organisational leaders and is shaped by the political, economic, social and technological context. This chapter focuses on employment relations strategies and makes the case for organisations to consciously articulate their approach to employment relations. We use practical examples to illustrate the different employment relations strategies adopted by organisations and link these to some key theoretical perspectives. Consequently, we explore the key factors that influence an organisation to review its approach to employment relations before focussing on how to bring the strategy to life through a practical implementation plan.

Keywords Strategy · Implementation plan · Capability · Behaviours · Structures · Evaluation

3.1 Introduction

In this chapter we discuss employment relations strategies which clearly and consciously set out the objectives of an organisation in relation to its relationships with trade unions and employee representatives. An employment relations strategy aligned to the business strategy, and the organisation's values and purpose, is critical in helping an organisation to achieve its goals. Strategic choice is often rooted in the perspectives of organisational leaders and is shaped by the political, economic, social and technological context.

Strategies can be designed to avoid and suppress union organisation. They can also be collaborative and co-operative, reflected in genuine partnership working. In chapter one we set out our view that attempts to undermine and constrain union organisation rarely have positive outcomes for organisations or employees. However, if organisations are going to develop constructive and mutually beneficial relationships with unions, establishing a clear strategic direction is the first step before organisations set out a practical implementation plan to bring the strategy to life. A well-executed employment relations strategy guides leaders on how to work with its unions, how to listen, how to lead and who to involve and engage. In this chapter, we set out how to build the case for a strategic approach, describe the key components of an effective strategy and explain the main steps in planning its implementation. In the chapters that follow each of these steps is discussed in detail.

> **Exercise 3.1: Does your organisation have an employment relations strategy?**
>
> Find out if the organisation in which you are currently working has a written employment relations strategy. If there is a strategy, what are its main goals and key components? If you can't find a written strategy, how does your organisation manage employment relations in practice?

3.2 Why Have an Employment Relations Strategy?

In our experience, many organisations do not have a clearly articulated employment relations strategy. Most large organisations will have a Human Resource (HR) or a people strategy and it may say something about working with unions or employee voice but it is unlikely to be detailed or explained. There will be a way of working with unions or employee representatives but if asked, 'why do we work this way', the answer is likely to be 'because that's the way we have always worked with our unions'. Managers may be left to work with their representatives without sufficient guidance or rationale on why or how.

We have found that organisations often have various strands to their approach to employment relations but how they all fit together has not been thought through to maximise benefits to the business and to employees. In many cases, they have simply developed over time as the organisation has reacted to short-term challenges created by the changing contexts we discussed in the previous chapter. Too often, organisational leaders do not really understand why their employee forum exists or what they should talk to their unions about. In part this is because they rarely see it as being of wider strategic importance. It is therefore likely that the employment relations practitioners will face significant barriers in persuading others of the need for an employment relations strategy and therefore will need to build a strong business case to secure the necessary resources and support.

> **Building the case for a strategic approach to employment relations**
>
> **Voice**—employees want to have a voice at work. There is strong evidence that employee voice is a key building block of trust and engagement. Positively tapping into the potential of working people and creating a culture which encourages them to speak up and contribute fully at work is a core organisational responsibility.
>
> **Reputation**—without structured channels for voice, employees are likely to raise concerns in other, often more public and damaging ways. Reputation is increasingly important—investors are sensitive to public perceptions of good governance and ethical business practices. Current and potential employees want to work for organisations with positive values and an open and honest culture. Without these in place, organisations are likely to lose key talent.
>
> **Risk**—without an employment relations strategy, it is unlikely that many work-related risks are being managed proactively or coherently.
>
> **Conflict**—organisational reputation can be damaged by conflict which can incur significant costs. Even in the absence of strikes and industrial action, poor employment relations can have negative impacts on well-being, engagement and productivity.
>
> **Change**—employment relations is integral to the smooth deployment of organisational change, whether this is related to the increasing use of AI and its impact on jobs, or how to deal with the complexities of hybrid working.

3.3 What Determines the Strategic Approach Taken by an Organisation?

Figure 3.1 illustrates the factors that shape employment relations strategies. Walton and McKersie (1991) identify five different 'relationship patterns' that employers can adopt or develop with trade unions. To some extent, these patterns are influenced by context. For example, organisations operating within a legal framework which supports collective representation will be more likely to accommodate or co-operate with unions. The product and labour conditions faced by employers may also be important—high levels of competition may prompt organisations to adopt more conflictual approaches to try to reduce costs. The nature of the product may also reflect the risk associated with employment relations and particularly the impact of industrial action—the higher the risk the more likely it is that organisations will try to mitigate that risk by engaging with trade unions. In addition, the perspectives of owners and senior managers will influence strategy—where unitarist perspectives are dominant, organisations will tend to try to fight or contain attempts to unionise. This may also have deep historical roots which can define organisational culture and therefore attitudes towards employment relations. However, as Kochan et al. (1984) have argued, these contextual influences are not deterministic—while they may shape strategy, organisations have agency and are able to make choices about the nature of the relationships they want to develop in order to achieve wider organisational goals.

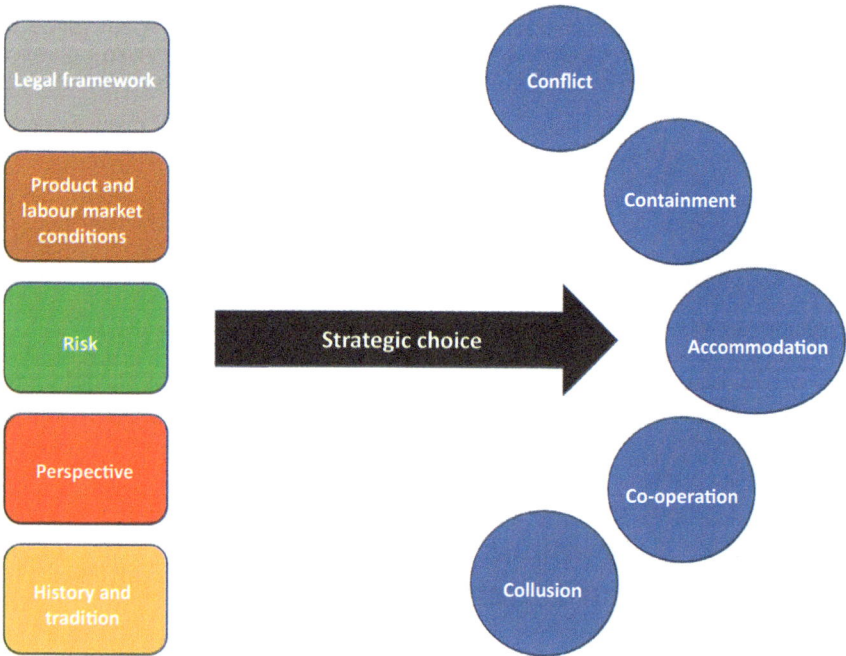

Fig. 3.1 Strategy—context and choice

3.4 Attitudes and Relationships

Walton and McKersie's (1991) research in this area shows the link between different patterns of employment relations and attitudes towards union representatives. Where organisations are hostile to unions but also enjoy a significant degree of bargaining power, employment relations are likely to be characterised by conflict. The employer will adopt a competitive approach where its ultimate aim is to weaken or destroy any attempts at union organisation. It completely denies the legitimacy of the union as a voice of the employees and instead foregrounds direct communication. The union, its representatives and supporters are seen as agitators—they are distrusted and even hated.

In certain situations, in which trade unions have significant bargaining power, it may be impossible to avoid or suppress union organisation—the employer is then left with a range of choices, which will ultimately reflect the dominant perspectives within the organisation. It may be forced to grudgingly accept a degree of representation, but the relationships will still be adversarial, antagonistic and based on distrust. The employer's intention will be to contain the growth of union organisation, which implies making few, if any, concessions as this will be seen as a sign of weakness. Engagement with the union will generally be limited to what the organisation is compelled to do through law or regulation. Consequently, even where employers are hostile to trade unions, they may be forced to adopt a strategy of containment if the regulatory framework is conducive to union organisation or other forms of representation. In the longer term, the employer will seek to minimise union influence and take advantage of changing conditions to disengage completely.

A relatively common relationship pattern is accommodation—in essence this reflects an acceptance by management of unions as the status quo. Therefore, it is often seen in organisations in which there is a long history of union organisation, and this is seen as the 'way it is and always has been'. Neither party has a great incentive to risk the disruption of changing this relationship. Allowances are made and management and unions treat each other with courtesy but trust is limited as, although representation is seen as legitimate, this is only due to tradition and is fundamentally superficial. This also means that the scope and ambition of bargaining is limited to pay and conditions.

A much more positive path is co-operation, which stems from a belief that progressive employment relations can have concrete mutual benefits. Rather than simply 'dividing the pie', the parties believe that by working together they can 'increase the size of the pie' by improving performance and building engagement. This requires and creates a deep sense of trust between the parties—relationships are built by working together. The parties also have a clear understanding of the constituencies they serve and the challenges they face. Crucially, this also widens the bargaining agenda and provides employment relations with a strategic intent, extending into areas of corporate strategy, equality, diversity and inclusion, employee well-being and organisational performance. This is not to say that conflict doesn't arise—we would argue that it's inevitable—however, conflict is less likely and the web of relationships that this approach creates enhances the capacity of the parties to resolve problems.

Finally, there is the potential for the relationship between management and unions to develop into one that resembles collusion. Walton and McKersie argue that this creates a degree of intimacy between the parties, creating a 'sweetheart relationship'. This is not necessarily a healthy relationship as it is subject to 'symmetrical blackmail', i.e. where the relationship is maintained because of the fear of the damage that the other could do. This type of relationship is also unstable as it runs the risk of union representatives becoming distanced from their members and ultimately being voted out, or from managers losing the trust of their colleagues and leaders as they are seen to be losing sight of organisational interests. This leads to an important lesson for managers and HR practitioners—it is important that they maintain and respect a distance between themselves and union representatives and acknowledge the need for representatives to prioritise the interests of their members.

> **Important**
> "Whether or not the employer sees fit to nurture the union organisation, reflects a strategic choice, conscious or otherwise" (Brown & Oxenbridge, 2004: 156)

> **Exercise 3.2: Relationship patterns and attitudes**
> Which of the relationship patterns described above most closely resembles those in your own organisation or one with which you are familiar. To what extent is this also reflected in the different attitudinal dimensions? If you were to try to move towards a more co-operative relationship approach, what could you do to encourage a change in attitudes and behaviours?

3 Creating an Effective Employment Relations Strategy 51

The use of strategic choice is also illustrated by the way in which organisations, working in the same sector and operating under the same legal and regulatory framework, adopt very different approaches to employment relations. In Case study 3.1 below, we explore different approaches to employment relations taken by four UK retailers.

Case study 3.1: Different approaches to employment relations in four UK grocery retailers

Tesco: Tesco employs 330,000 people (mainly in the UK) in almost 5,000 stores, with a turnover of nearly £60 billion. From the 1950s onwards, Tesco has recognised the shopworkers' union USDAW. In 1998, Tesco and USDAW signed a partnership agreement which *"lays out the principles and processes for how we work together, engage, listen and respond to colleagues, improve terms and conditions, and solve problems together."* Emma Taylor, Head of People at Tesco, argues that *"the success of our partnerships with unions like USDAW is built upon honesty and respect – we are one of the few major retailers to have a full collective bargaining agreement in place with their respective union, with USDAW being the sole recognised union for colleagues working in our UK stores"* (Taylor, 2022).

Marks and Spencer: Marks and Spencer has 1,064 stores in the UK and 406 worldwide. It employs around 65,000 people and has a turnover of around £12 billion. It has traditionally had a paternalistic approach to its staff and avoided unionisation by ensuring job security and good terms and conditions, and providing channels for direct voice. It does not recognise trade unions in the UK for its retail or warehouse staff and has a long-established employee forum for these employees, and for those in head office functions. In October 2022, in response to the possibility of store closures and redundancies, Paddy Lillis, the USDAW General Secretary called for Marks and Spencer to recognise USDAW: *"We again urge M&S management to abandon their long-held resistance to allowing USDAW to represent the staff. It is simply unjust that the company have made the decision not to engage with a trade union. The staff are telling us they want USDAW to represent them not the in-house staff association. It should be their choice."* (USDAW, 2022).

Asda: Asda runs just over 600 stores in the UK, employing 145,000 staff and has a turnover of around £20 billion. Between 1999 and 2021 it was owned by US retail giant Walmart. Asda recognises the GMB union for its retail employees in England, Scotland and Wales, but does not negotiate on pay. However, it does conduct collective bargaining with the GMB for warehouse and distribution workers in the UK. Asda conducts full collective bargaining with its retail workers in Northern Ireland who are members of USDAW.

John Lewis: The John Lewis Partnership has around 80,000 employees in the UK working in 32 department stores and 329 supermarkets. It has a turnover of approximately £12 billion per year. It has never recognised trade unions but has a long-standing structure of non-union employee representation. Each employee is known as a 'partner' and normally gets a share of the annual profit. Employees' views are represented by partnership representatives who are elected to a national Partnership Council. John Lewis claims that it is *"the largest employee-owned business in the UK...We are to all intents and purposes a social enterprise; the profits that we make are reinvested into the business...Our Constitution requires us to make sufficient profit to keep the Partnership going, not create the highest amount possible, and to put our customers and our Partners ahead of profit"* (John Lewis Partnership, 2020). Between 2020 and 2023, there were a series of store closures and redundancies, and staff did not receive their annual profit share in two of the three years.

Key questions

1. How would you describe the employment relations strategy of each retailer?
2. What factors have determined the difference in approach to employment relations in these organisations?

Organisational attitudes to risk and the potential consequences of conflict and disruption are also critical factors in determining the approach to employment relations. For example, the potential cost of industrial action to a company which distributes perishable food items or one which provides passenger transport services is extremely high in both lost sales and brand damage. In these companies, employment relations is a regular item on the corporate risk register, monitored closely by the risk team and audit committee. Therefore, these organisations have a greater incentive to invest in building effective methods of conflict resolution, employ skilled employment relations professionals and build the capability of internal teams. This is illustrated by the extract of an interview that we conducted with an HR director from a European airline.

Employment relations strategy in a European airline

"We don't have a written down specific employment relations strategy for the entire airline. In the UK, the approach is part of the wider people and engagement strategy, alongside other elements of employee voice. We tend to develop behaviour standards and relationship agreements as part of our recognition agreements. This sets out how we run meetings, when we share strategy, how we exchange communication and how we resolve conflict. This is more prevalent in the UK and it works well in Germany too.

In the EU, the collective bargaining framework means we tend to be more reactive, waiting for the other airlines ("flag-carriers") to negotiate first and we follow. In Europe, our leaders have worked with trade unions more regularly throughout their career and unions are more widely understood and accepted. There is always a level of caution between managers and representatives, since their objectives are never wholly aligned, although this varies across European countries. Our approach to employment relations depends on the social and legal framework and environment. However, we are increasingly sharing employment relations models across parts of the business to get more visibility across Europe.

The key factors which influence our approach to employment relations are:

Attitude to risk—airlines are risk averse so tolerance to risk is low. Disruption has a huge impact on passengers on the day and flights can continue to be disrupted for days. Customers don't tend to come back if their flight is disrupted. We have to balance our attitude to risk with the imperative for change and shareholder value.

Different leadership styles—specific business leaders and HR individuals have a huge impact on the employment relations approach taken. Leaders move on and the style can change.

The sector—airlines and aviation are traditionally unionised—pilots, cabin crew, engineering—so that plays a part too. It is inevitable that our industry will work with unions.

The business agenda—the need to manage change, remain competitive and react to competition in the industry means that industrial dispute or challenge can seem inevitable and then the tolerance of risk becomes a factor again.

Style and tone of the union—if the union representatives are intransigent, resistant to change and have higher bargaining power, this will influence the nature of the relationship. There is not just one approach that works in every situation. Every situation is different depending on the relationships you have with your representatives and those that have existed in the past.

Broader engagement approach—the balance between individual and collective engagement is important and will influence our overall strategy.

Social-legal framework—each individual country has its own legal set-up which dictates the approach we need to take. Germany is different to France, for example, and both are different to the UK."

Strategic decisions made by organisations lead to specific actions. If it is decided that an organisation should work with trade unions, there are still choices to be made about which unions to recognise and the precise nature of that relationship or those relationships. For example, an organisation may decide to work more closely with unions that they see as more open to co-operation and collaboration. It is also important to decide the scope of bargaining and negotiation, and whether to develop parallel mechanisms of employee voice alongside union channels. Of course, these decisions will themselves affect relationships and may need to be negotiated. In contrast, if an employer commits to a strategy of union avoidance, it needs to think about how this will be maintained and develop alternative ways of engaging and communicating with its staff. These decisions also have implications in terms of costs and resources.

In Case study 3.2 (below) we explore how the strategic direction of the organisation would affect how consultation over restructuring is conducted.

Case study 3.2: Managing change

You work as head of employment relations in an organisation which has invested a lot in its values, which are based around respect, dignity, trust and inclusivity. However, much less attention has been given to developing its employment relations strategy. The organisation has recognised a trade union for many years. Union density is around 60%, and 80% of employees are covered by a collective agreement. Union membership is concentrated among employees with long service rather than newer employees.

Relationships with union representatives are formal and respectful but you are not encouraged by the leadership team to share too much business information with them. Overall, you would describe the approach to unions as containment. Your dialogue is normally about low-level 'hygiene' issues and representatives don't seem interested in strategic matters. The company has not invested in the relationship or built skills amongst the union representatives or managers to help them understand each other's roles or perspectives.

The company is now considering an extensive restructuring, involving reduced headcount, which is critical to sustainability and future success. You are responsible for consulting with your union representatives, and you also need to involve senior and operational managers in the process so they can explain the business case and rationale for change. You have no idea how the union will respond, and you are concerned about the competence of your management team in dealing with representatives.

You know how important it is to manage this restructuring as well as possible. Employees will be very anxious about what this means for their jobs, and it is vital that the process used demonstrates the core values of the organisation.

Key questions

1. What are the limitations of the existing union containment strategy in this situation?
2. What would be the benefits of a more collaborative approach to the restructuring process?
3. How would you implement a more collaborative approach?
4. In the longer run, how do you change and/or develop the employment relations strategy of the organisation?

3.5 Employment Relations Strategy in Practice

An employment relations strategy determines the best way to capture and manage 'employee voice'. It will fit the organisational culture, leadership style and values, while giving clarity to managers and employees in how to consult and engage. This could be with unions, without unions, via employee representatives, or a mixture of the two. It may be supplemented by networking groups which employees join based on shared identities, communities and interests. For some organisations, this is likely also to be supplemented by internal social media channels enabling real time data collection and pulse surveys to understand employee sentiment at key points in time.

> **Amazon–challenging the system?**
>
> Amazon has a consistent strategy wherever it operates, aimed at union avoidance and active resistance to attempts at organisation. However, this is more challenging in a country like Germany where co-determination and collective bargaining is woven into the fabric of its industrial relations system. While Amazon has been able to resist (so far) attempts by the Ver.di trade union to secure a collective agreement covering its workers, it cannot avoid the legal duty (under the German Works Constitution Act) to elect works councils in organisations with more than five workers. Therefore, it has tried to use works councils as a means to bypass trade unions by, for example, actively supporting non-union candidates in works council elections. Nonetheless, Amazon works councils have been able to win important improvements to working conditions (Kassem, 2022).

The strategy should align to the organisational strategy, culture, purpose and values, ideally spanning three to five years. The strategy need not be complicated, but it must reflect the key challenges that the organisation is facing and expecting in the future. It also needs to consider whether the current employment relations climate, behaviours and structures will enable or block its objectives. As well as outlining the strategic approach, it may have a tactical element which enables the organisation to react to the environment in a pragmatic and flexible way. For example, an overall strategy might aim to develop a collaborative partnership with trade unions. However, in the face of rising inflation, the union may adopt a more conflictual stance on the annual pay round. Therefore, the strategy will need to provide some guidance on how the organisation responds to conflict. In Fig. 3.2, we have set out a simple strategic approach which describes the challenges for the organisation, both in the immediate and longer term. In the second box, the vision for employment relations is set out, with the final box describing how it intends to deliver the strategy.

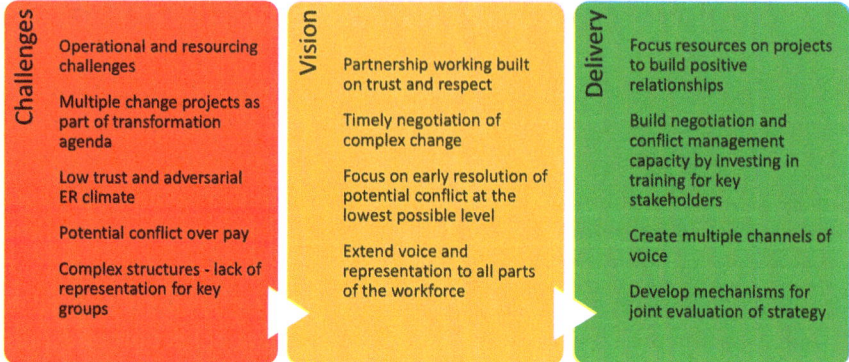

Fig. 3.2 Employment relations strategy

Case study 3.3: Strategic employment relations in financial services

This case is based on an interview with the Colleague Relations Director of a large financial services organisation.

The organisation employs around 68,000 people and recognises two trade unions for collective bargaining purposes, with significant membership density concentrated in one of the unions. The organisation has a dual strategy of operating parallel channels of union and direct employee voice. Therefore, it has a listening strategy, undertaking regular pulse surveys to understand views across the workforce and to 'do the right thing by all their colleagues'. The employment relations strategy is embedded in the three to five-year corporate strategy. This is the big picture, which is also influenced by external events such as the economic climate, cost of living, world events and the broader industrial relations climate. The employee/colleague relations team "interprets this and gives it meaning".

The Colleague Relations Director believes that the unions play a very important role in the business, and this is shown in an extensive recognition agreement. The relationship is particularly important during times of change, enabling the company to consult and negotiate change through existing channels and structures. Without the union, the company would have to develop something new each time change was on the agenda. She believes that the interests of the organisation and the unions are like a Venn diagram, with overlapping and separate aims. The overlapping area of joint interests relate to skills, job and terms and conditions. It is useful, she says, to think about those joint and separate interests and the external factors before every discussion with the unions on significant issues. This is why the employment relations strategy is never static. Unions change their approach, and the business has to adapt to that. You need to start from a set of principles about what you are trying to achieve. You will never agree on everything, and you need to accept this.

Our interviewee believes that everyone who works with their unions needs to understand the strategy and be aligned behind it. This minimises confusion, reduces the risk of misinterpretation and ensures consistency. The strategy applies across the different levels of the organisation—a macro level for the Group; divisional plans; and a tactical/micro level. Whatever level someone is working at, they need to be able to explain the rationale for any change or decision in their conversations with the unions. It is important to be clear whether discussions with the unions are negotiations, consultation or information. If it is a negotiation, the company needs to know what happens if they can't agree and what is the dispute resolution process. If it is a consultation, they may have to 'agree to disagree' at some point. Getting clarity here on the 'labels' enables risks to be better managed.

The Colleague Relations Director talks about the key behaviours she adopts and expects from those working with her. These include negotiating with authority, credibility and integrity, choosing your words carefully and not misleading. "If you lose your integrity, it is almost impossible to get it back and the unions will not trust you when you need them to. You can't be erratic but must be thoughtful in your dealings with people and think about how to respond," she says. As a company, there are choices about whether to accept a position or not and these decisions will need to be made. She subscribes to the ethos 'that everyone leaves the pitch feeling as though they have won'. If you are not able to do this, it is important to be strategically aware and think about how to manage the risk of that.

Key questions

1. Why is it important to anchor the employment relations strategy in the business strategy?
2. How does an organisation align its leaders around the employment relations strategy?
3. How would you describe the behaviours in this case study and why are they so important to constructive employment relations?

3.6 What Factors Influence a Change in Approach to Employment Relations?

Several issues can lead an organisation to review or make a strategic change in employment relations. These can include increased competition, new organisational or union leadership, and/or change in political environment. We have worked with companies who have faced different events which have shaped their employment strategy, and two examples are discussed below.

Acquisition or a change in ownership can trigger a change in strategy. One organisation that we worked with had a strategy of union avoidance from its inception—it engaged directly with its employees via an employee forum and had developed a number of ways of directly listening to its employees. It then acquired a heavily unionised company, which led the parent company to conduct a review of its strategy. The acquisition meant that the company now embraced a mixed model of employment relations involving direct listening, an employee representative forum and collective bargaining. The strategic review led to an increased focus on improving the effectiveness of the employee forum, keeping pay and benefits competitive and ensuring the business listened regularly to employee sentiment and acted on it. It also set out a plan to improve its capability in industrial relations and established governance across HR to make sure that everyone working on employee voice was better aligned across the business. Finally, more robust risk management processes were put in place to understand and improve the management of employment relations risks. Its overall aim was to manage the mixed model of employment relations, while also minimising the risk that union recognition in one part of the business would spill over into another.

> **Exercise 3.3: An alternative approach?**
>
> The organisation in the above example could have adopted two alternative strategies. First, it could have tried to move away from working with the union in its newly acquired subsidiary. Second, it could have promoted union organisation across its existing operations. Why do you think it did not opt for either of these options? What would be the challenges and risks of adopting these approaches?

In a second example, two companies in the energy sector merged. Both companies recognised unions for some of their employees and the relationships were relatively constructive, however, levels of union membership varied. Following the merger, a new divisional structure was formed which brought two very disparate groups of employees together—those working in power stations who were heavily unionised and those working in a call centre, who were largely non-unionised and not represented by a union. A review was conducted to look at what the merger meant for the trade union role and employee voice. The decision was made to establish a new employee consultative forum for employees in the recently established division which would be made up of union representatives and newly elected employee representatives. Both parties received training for the new forum alongside management representatives. The unions were initially reluctant to take part in the new forum alongside employee representatives but when they saw that the new forum did not undermine their role, they agreed to take part. These mixed forums are now a long-established mechanism of employee voice in this company.

> **Exercise 3.4: A different strategy?**
>
> The organisation in the above example could have adopted a different strategy. It could have decided to keep its unionised and non-unionised workforces separate in terms of consultation and engagement. Why do you think it did not choose this option? What are the challenges, opportunities and risks of adopting the approach it took?

Another common trigger for reviewing and renewing an organisation's employment relations is industrial action. This can reveal the need to reset relationships which may be damaged. In chapter ten, we describe the actions taken by a company and its unions to develop a new strategy in the wake of a high-profile dispute.

3.7 Building an Implementation Plan

Once the strategy is agreed, organisations should consider the practical steps needed to put it into practice. However, this can be difficult as it will often require those involved to change the way they work and can represent a challenge to dominant perspectives and interests. Consequently, strategy implementation can meet with significant resistance. The questions that we discuss below will help employment relations practitioners to build an accurate picture of the current situation and steer a clear route to their eventual destination.

3.7.1 Guiding Principles

Would a set of employment relations principles help as a guide for managers and union representatives?

A set of guiding principles explains the high level strategy in a clear and succinct way. They define what the organisation stands for in terms of employment relations and can be shared internally and externally. The sample below is drawn from an organisation with a dual strategy of both recognising trade unions and operating channels of direct employee voice. The principles provide clarity for the leadership team and union representatives, and help employees to see that they have a voice regardless of which part of the business they are in.

> **Example of Guiding Principles**
> - The collective voice of our employees is via our employee forum
> - We expect colleagues to have their say in how the business is run via our business-wide network of employee representatives and engaged line managers
> - We practise a culture of listening and taking action amongst our line managers and leaders
> - We commit to involving our employee representatives in business decision-making
> - We work with, accept and respect unions in parts of the business where they are recognised

3.7.2 Governance and Risk

What are the internal governance structures for employment relations?
How do we ensure we are complying with existing corporate governance requirements?
How and where are risks reported, managed and mitigated?

It is important to identify the specific meeting where the overall employment relations picture can be discussed and where employment relations information, insight and data can be shared with the organisation's senior leaders. It is likely that in some larger organisations, the audit committee will ask for updates, and employment relations or HR leaders will need to provide robust analysis of the current risks and mitigation plans. Employment relations risks should be a standing agenda item at HR leadership team meetings.

3.7.3 How Employment Relations Fits into the Wider HR Team

What type of HR operating model is needed to deliver the strategy?
Is a specialist employment relations team needed or will employment relations be a core priority of HR business partners?

It is important to understand who within the HR function is responsible for the delivery of the employment relations strategy and we discuss HR/employment relations operating models in chapter 4. Whichever model is adopted, it is important to clarify roles, scope and reporting lines to ensure clean oversight and alignment. Some organisations have developed an employment relations Community of Interest for all those involved in any industrial relations and employment relations activity to build capability, share best practice and provide support.

> An employment relations 'community of interest' brings together people across the organisations who interact with key union representatives on a regular basis. It can include HR, employment relations leaders and health and safety teams. They share examples of good practice or discuss challenges to get advice and guidance. This works particularly well in organisations with multiple divisions and locations or those in matrix-type organisational structures. It helps with alignment, consistency and risk management, ensuring that good employment relations is not undermined by silo working. It also provides moral support and aids problem solving.

3.7.4 Key Relationships—Managers and Union Representatives

What and where are the key relationships?
Who needs to be working well with each other and why?
What is the succession plan for managers and leaders in unionised areas?
Are there key representatives who are relied on who are due for election or retirement? What risks does this pose?

There are always some key roles where it is critical for there to be a good working relationship between organisational leaders, operational managers, HR and union representatives. Consider where these are and what happens when these key people move on. In some cases, long standing relationships with union representatives are the basis of co-operative and collaborative working. If that relationship is broken up, then trust has to be built from scratch. Therefore, identifying core relationships and regularly reviewing them is critical.

> **Tip**
>
> When a new manager moves into an area which has specific employment relations issues or if a new union representative is elected, think about how you can begin to build high-trust relationships. Line managers have the biggest impact on day-to-day employment relations. Target those in the organisation who have the most critical interfaces with union representatives and invest in their employment relations and leadership capability.

3.7.5 Behaviours and Capability

What behaviours and capabilities from leaders, managers and employee representatives are necessary to deliver the strategy?
What are the current gaps in behaviour and capability?
How can we encourage constructive behaviours and build employment relations capacity?
Is employment relations competency considered in recruitment and selection decisions for key unionised areas?

This is a critical part of the implementation plan—if those involved in operationalising the employment relations strategy do not have the necessary skills and/or behaviours, the strategy will fail. Therefore, an honest assessment in terms of existing employment relations capacity is crucial. Employment relations specialists can then work with learning and development specialists and operational managers, to build a learning package to bridge any skills gaps. In addition, organisations should build employment relations competency into the recruitment and promotion process for managers and leaders who are going to work in unionised areas.

> **Tip**
>
> In our experience, training sessions which involve HR, managers and union representatives can get the parties to 'walk in each other's shoes'—this can help to shift perspectives and build trust.

3.7.6 Formal and Informal Meetings

Are formal and informal mechanisms used to resolve problems?
Are joint meetings effective in managing change and resolving problems?
What changes need to be made to these meetings to help the organisation deliver the strategy?

In our experience, reviewing the effectiveness of meeting structures is a useful exercise to undertake with union representatives, leaders and managers and we discuss this in more detail in later chapters. It is critical that these meetings are focussed on the right topics, at the right level, with the right people. Ideally, issues should be resolved as close to the source as possible and through informal discussion. However, if matters are being escalated regularly and problems are not being resolved, it is time to review the effectiveness of the meetings.

> **Tip**
> Asking your union representatives and your leaders how meetings could be more effective is a useful exercise. It may be that the terms of reference need updating, the agendas could be better managed, time could be spent solving problems outside of the formal meeting, or actions could be followed up and closed more quickly.

3.7.7 Conflict Management

How is conflict dealt with and what happens when conflict arises?

How competent are key players in conflict resolution and problem solving?

Conflict is an inherent part of the employment relationship—even in organisations with constructive employment relations. Therefore, a key part of delivering an employment relations strategy is to ensure that there are processes in place for conflict resolution. Conflict resolution and problem-solving skills should also be a core element of management training and development.

> **Exercise 3.5: Strategic priorities, challenges and barriers**
> Think about the questions under each heading in terms of the organisation that you work for or one with which you are familiar. In developing a new employment relations strategy for the organisation, what would be your key priorities and what would be the main barriers to successful implementation?

3.7.8 Developing a Tactical Change Plan

The output of the process of questioning and discussion outlined above is a tactical change plan, designed to help the organisation to deliver the strategy it has articulated. Setting out a step change plan with prioritised, achievable goals is more likely to be acceptable to senior leadership and avoids disruption to the organisation. This has been described in some organisations as

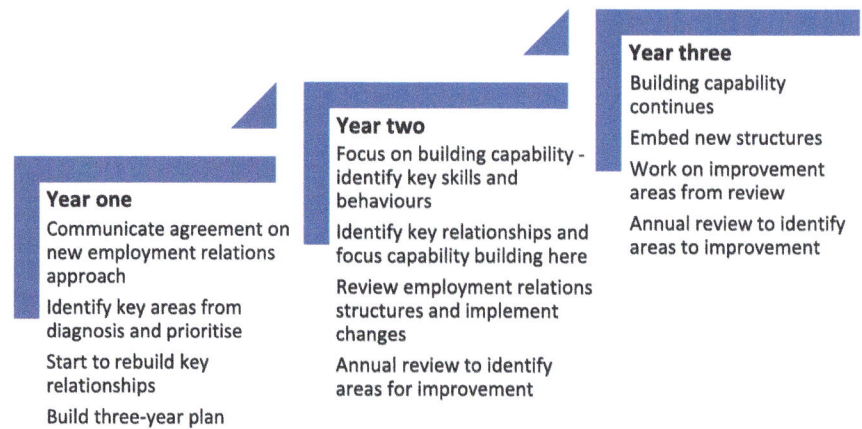

Fig. 3.3 Step change plan for implementation of employment relations strategy

'evolution rather than revolution' or a 'marathon not a sprint'. These small steps can give both parties confidence that the plan is workable and enables trust to be built as goals are met. Figure 3.3 gives an example of the type of high-level step plan that can be used in organisations. It assumes some diagnosis has taken place of the current employment relations strategy and an agreement has been reached to make improvements to the employment relations climate.

3.7.9 Evaluate Effectiveness and Identify Improvements

Regular evaluation is necessary to see if the strategy is working and where improvements can be made. In chapter eleven, we look at some practical examples of how organisations can annually evaluate the effectiveness of their employment relations strategy.

> **Tip**
> Measure your employment relations climate regularly and do not let it deteriorate so far that you need to invest in totally rebuilding the climate and the trust. This will take years.

3.8 Conclusion

The cost and risks of employment relations requires organisations to take a strategic and conscious approach to the relationship they wish to have with their unions and employees. Strategic approaches to employment relations are influenced by many factors such as leadership, sector, history and events such as merger or acquisition. Whichever strategy is chosen, it will come alive in the behaviours that are displayed, the structures that are in place and in the agreements that are made. A clear and practical implementation plan is required to bring the strategy to life. We will explore these elements in the rest of the book: effective behaviours and capability; robust structures for dialogue; clarity on how conflict will be managed; and evaluation of the entire strategy, to see its impact and areas for improvement. In our experience, risk and conflict increase without a clear strategic direction. Avoiding and fighting unions rarely has good consequences for organisations or employees. A strategy of collaboration and engagement has many positive consequences if time and effort is taken to build this approach.

> **Questions**
> 1. What factors determine the type of strategy an organisation has and what does this tell you about your organisation's approach to employment relations?
> 2. What arguments would you make to convince a sceptical CEO or HR director of the need to develop a strategic approach to employment relations?
> 3. What can HR and employment relations leaders do to bring the strategy to life on a day-to-day basis?
> 4. What are the main barriers and obstacles in delivering an effective employment relations strategy?

References

Brown, W., & Oxenbridge, S. (2004). The Development of Co-operative Employer/Trade Union Relationships in Britain. *Industrielle Beziehungen: Zeitschrift Für Arbeit, Organisation und Management, 11*(1/2), 143–158.

John Lewis Partnership. (2020). *Our Business Partnership Model*. [Online]. https://www.johnlewispartnership.co.uk/content/dam/cws/pdfs/Juniper/ARA2020/JLP-Business-Model-2020-ARA.pdf. Accessed 17 Nov 2023.

Kassem, S. (2022). (Re)shaping Amazon Labour Struggles on Both Sides of the Atlantic: The Power Dynamics in Germany and the US Amidst the Pandemic.

Transfer: European Review of Labour and Research, 28(4), 441–456. https://doi.org/10.1177/10242589221149496

Kochan, T., McKersie, R., & Cappelli, P. (1984). Strategic Choice and Industrial Relations Theory. *Industrial Relations: A Journal of Economy and Society, 23*, 16–39. https://doi.org/10.1111/j.1468-232X.1984.tb00872.x

Taylor, E. (2022). *Investing in Our Colleagues—How We Work Collaboratively with Unions.* [Online]. https://www.tescoplc.com/blog/investing-in-our-colleagues-how-we-work-collaboratively-with-unions/. Accessed 27 Nov 2023

USDAW. (2022, October 22). M&S Staff Are Deeply Concerned by Today's Confirmation of More Store Closures—Usdaw Renews Their Call for Recognition [Online]. https://www.usdaw.org.uk/About-Us/News/2022/Oct/MS-staff-are-deeply-concerned-by-todays-confirmati. Accessed 13 Oct 2023.

Walton, R. E., & McKersie, R. B. (1991). *Behavioural Theory of Labor Negotiations: An Analysis of a Social Interaction System* (2nd ed.). ILR Press.

4

Building Employment Relations Teams

Abstract The appropriate organisation design for an employment relations team will be influenced by the external environment, the type of organisation including its strategic approach to employment relations, whether the team has a global or national remit and how it fits within the wider Human Resources (HR) function. In this chapter we discuss the purpose and structure of the employment relations team, the key roles within the team and the activities the team undertakes. We explore the variety and scope of employment relations roles in organisations, using case studies to explore key themes around organisational design and implementation. This will help those who are considering the management of collective employment relations for the first time and establishing a new team. It also provides important guidance to practitioners who need to make changes to an existing operating model.

Keywords Employment relations teams · Organisational design · Organisation structure · Roles · Accountabilities

4.1 Introduction

The maintenance of good employment relations has been a central part of the development of the people profession. As trade union membership and influence increased, organisations attempted to develop capacity to manage the consequent challenges, and in particular, contain and resolve industrial disputes. This initially took the form of personnel departments which had a focus on developing and implementing policy and managing workplace conflict (Storey, 1992). Importantly, they maintained a broad responsibility for all aspects of people management. As we discussed in Chapter 2, the development of Human Resource Management (HRM) triggered significant changes to this relatively interventionist approach. Crucially, HR practitioners sought to develop what they saw as a more strategic orientation devolving day-to-day issues to operational managers. In principle, this allowed HR to develop great specialist expertise and adopt a closer focus on business objectives and goals (Francis & Keegan, 2006).

These changes were reflected in the way that organisations developed and structured their HR teams. In particular, operating models revolved around the idea of strategic HR business partners often embedded within operational business units and focussing on helping senior leaders to deliver strategic objectives and goals. What were seen as more basic and transactional HR activities could be outsourced or standardised, while specialist areas of HR expertise were increasingly centralised (Ulrich & Brockbank 2005). These changes have had important implications for the management of collective employment relations. Some commentators have argued that a focus on business performance has come at the expense of more traditional employment relations concerns (Francis & Keegan, 2006; Harris, 2007). While this may be an oversimplification, the popularity of the HR business partner (HRBP) model has blurred accountability, relationships and ownership of union relationships.

Changes in the nature and organisation of work have also created a range of new dilemmas for the HR profession. As we discussed in Chapter 2, organisations have become increasingly complex with more diverse employee groups with different interests and attitudes to work. For example, employment relations often involves consideration of human rights, equality, diversity and inclusion, as well as more conventional labour management issues. Traditional employment contracts are often supplemented (and in some cases have been replaced) by atypical work forms (contractors, outsourced providers and platform workers). Managing this mix of workers requires distinct forms of employee voice and arguably less reliance on a single channel such as consultation and negotiation with trade unions. Moreover, many employers have prioritised direct channels of voice and adopted more hostile approaches to unionisation. Unions themselves are adapting and placing increased emphasis on new forms of organising, but they have not yet been able to fill the representation gap that has emerged. These challenges are likely to intensify as technology such as Artificial Intelligence (AI) changes work and our relationships within it, requiring employment relations and HR teams to (re)think how they operate and structure themselves.

4.2 Organisation Design and Employment Relations Strategy

Organisational design enables the organisation to integrate processes, people, management systems and structure. It aligns the form of the employer closely to the strategy that it is trying to achieve, improving the probability that the collective efforts of the organisational teams will be successful. Irrespective of the context, we advocate the clear articulation of an employment relations strategy aligned to organisational strategy and values. With a clear strategy, the next stage is to consider the size, shape and purpose of the employment relations function who, along with leaders and managers, will implement this strategy. It will also consider processes that will connect relevant stakeholders and the skills, capabilities and accountabilities of those in the team and wider organisation. If an organisation has a strategy of union avoidance, this is likely to lead to a very different structure, accountabilities, capabilities and way of working on a day-to-day basis compared to an organisation wishing to work more collaboratively with its unions. An organisation wishing to work with its unions in a mature relationship will require a greater quantity and quality of communication and a defined level of competence, capability and interpersonal skills amongst its leaders, managers and HR practitioners.

Organisations will also take into account issues such as the appetite for risk from the external environment at the time of review and in the future, and therefore the resources required to manage that risk. They may also consider the current relationship with their unions and what is required to maintain this when they look ahead to changes required within the organisation. Another key consideration is how the relationship with unions is managed and whether this is centrally or locally. Many organisations find it useful to establish some design principles which can guide decisions about team size and structure. These design principles are used and referred back to as the organisation design develops to ensure that they are still being adhered to. After that there will be consideration given to the processes and activities that need to be carried out, the roles required to carry out these activities, building into a high-level organisational shape.

Naomi Stanford describes organisational design as "a step-by-step methodology which identifies dysfunctional aspects of workflow, procedures, structures and systems" (Stanford, 2015: 5). We have taken the five design principles from Stanford and overlaid an employment relations perspective which draws out some practical, specific points from this model of organisational design for a collective employment relations environment. This is outlined in Table 4.1. Once the design principles have been established, there are some key decisions for the organisation to make to help bring the operating model to life. These decisions about issues such as centralisation, devolution and specialisation are relevant if the organisation is undertaking a review of the existing operating model due to changes in the external context or the identification of internal challenges.

4.3 Different Models for Delivering Collective Employment Relations

There is no "one size fits all" organisational structure for an employment relations team. Like any organisational design, the range of variables is wide, and the influence of culture and strategy will vary enormously. However, there are some consistent structures which commonly appear in a range of organisations and industries. These may vary in their scope depending on how much consultation or collective bargaining is delegated to line managers in a devolved model, and ownership of the relationship with the trade union. Some of the most common operating models are set out below with a short commentary on the features of each.

4.3.1 Stand-Alone, Centralised Employment Relations Centre of Excellence

In organisations with a history of engaging with trade unions and high levels of membership and density, some employers opt to create a specialist team to set the strategy and support day-to-day employment relations. The function reports into the CEO/COO rather than through HR, reflecting the strategic importance and the impact which disruption will cause. This creates a direct level of control for the CEO over collective employment relations activity

Table 4.1 Organisational design for collective employment relations

Design principle	Design implications	Employment relations perspective
Organisational design is driven by the organisational strategy, purpose, environment and operating model.	The strategy is vital to define the 'what', but the 'how' is a critical factor. The combination of these factors helps to identify the day-to-day activities.	Without an intentional strategy, the approach to employment relations will be difficult to manage. The purpose, context and operating model will inform how employment relations is brought to life through day-to-day interactions and relationships with employees and/or unions.
Organisational design requires systems thinking – how do the different elements and connections fit together?	Poor designs result in poor outcomes. Therefore, teams need to identify and understand all organisational elements and their interdependencies.	To design effective employment relations, it is important to try to align all organisational elements. What are all the mechanisms for employee voice? Do we understand all the channels where feedback is captured? How is this data fed into decision-making and governance structures?
Organisational design takes strong, thoughtfully used, future-orientated mindsets and methods.	The future is unknowable. But it is imaginable and not entirely unpredictable. Some defined structures and number of roles are necessary, but equally, it is important to have underpinning principles for the design and advocate problem-solving capabilities.	Employment relations structures and processes need to be flexible and adaptable to respond to changes in the organisation and the introduction of new technology. Working remotely during the pandemic meant moving collective meetings to online forums. Organisations with effective ways of working and clear principles managed this well and used joint workshops to identify future challenges.
The design process involves social interactions and conversation as much as formal planning.	The purpose of this book to help encourage these ways of working, not just in a design context. Involving those working in the area in the design process is critical. Involving those who know the most in the team provides a wide cross-section of participants.	Engaging senior leaders, line managers and union/employee representatives, in the design process will help establish the interfaces needed and create opportunities to build relationships. Joint problem-solving is a good approach for a design process.
Organisational design is a fundamental continuing business process, not a one-off repair job.	What works in one time and environment, does not work in another. Organisations need to consider the signals that the design isn't working and have regular processes/stages at which to review it.	From formal annual reviews of how employee/union engagement is working to short interventions after each collective meeting to test progress and behaviours, it is possible to identify issues and make small (and large) changes to how employment relations is managed.

Source: Stanford (2022)

and provides visibility of issues at board level. There is also clarity on the type of relationship the organisation wants with its people and trade unions. In an international context, there may be a central team with country/region specific experts who work with the relevant business leaders but who are aligned to the overall organisation-wide approach or strategy.

Fig. 4.1 Centralised employment relations operating model

While this can ensure consistency of approach, there can be a risk that there will be duplication between employment relations and HR, leading to conflict between their goals and objectives. The key interface between HR and employment relations is at director level, leading to a potential for silo working. Also, leaders may not wish to take accountability for the relationships with unions and may not feel confident, preferring to leave it to 'experts'. An example of such a team is set out in Fig. 4.1.

4.3.2 HR-Led Employment Relations Centre of Excellence

As a result of the decline in trade union membership since the mid-1980s and increased direct communication with employees, some organisations have structured their employment relations teams within the wider HR function. In theory, the collective employment relations expertise remains but there are also additional elements of the role which may divert the focus from union relationships, and which may mean some members of the team do not have deep employment relations skills. The focus on collective employment relations is diluted by other projects and objectives. This means there may be a greater range of activity for the team to be involved in but as a result, strategic focus on collective issues is impacted by day-to-day activities. There may also be less direct visibility at board level due to the wider role of the HR director. An example of this type of team is shown in Fig. 4.2.

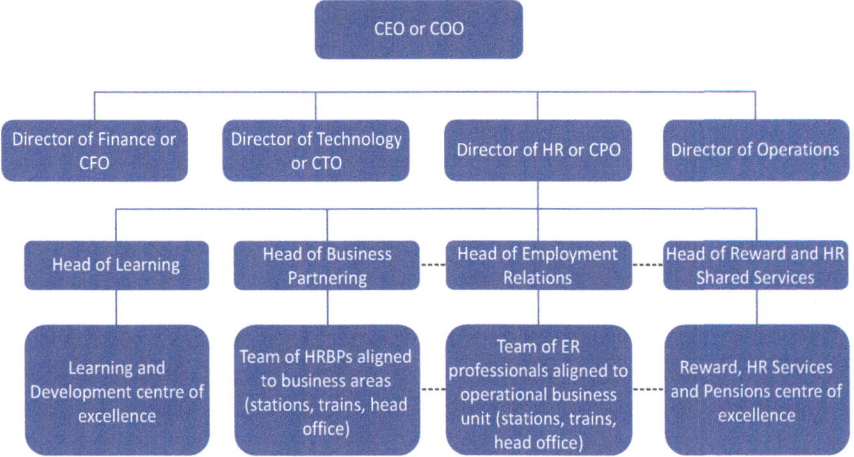

Fig. 4.2 Specialist employment relations function within HR

4.3.3 Employment Relations Embedded Within Business Partnering

The popularity of the HR Business Partner model has seen employment relations accountabilities delegated to the HR team or an individual with responsibility to support a specific team or unit. The attraction of this model has been the ability of the HR practitioner to 'partner' with the teams they are working with, and design strategies and plans which help them to achieve their goals. By being embedded alongside managers and leadership teams, they can align more closely with the goals and objectives of the business.

In this model, the HRBPs will include employment relations within their remit. At first glance, this could be seen as a positive move—as the HRBP is positioned as a strategic role, this could reflect employment relations being seen as a priority. In a collective employment relations context, this may mean greater ability to craft a bespoke approach and to build a relationship which addresses the profile and nature of employees at a certain site. Trust can be built if there is autonomy and ability. It also may mean that problems are identified, and potentially resolved, at an early point. However, for this to work, the HRBP and the managers and/or leaders they work with need to develop and maintain a sophisticated employment relations skillset. Moreover, where there are multiple business units, competing pressures and no overarching strategy, it can mean that there is a lack of accountability and consistency which can damage wider collective relationships.

4.3.4 Devolved Employment Relations

At plant level in manufacturing, it is common that the facility manager is responsible for collective employment relations. In a unionised context this means they own the relationship, manage negotiations and direct the HR or employment relations expertise locally. This model requires the leaders to have maturity and experience in this field, something which has declined over the last 20–30 years. Where this has worked successfully, mature leadership teams have recognised the position and interests of the trade union and worked with them on a shared vision. They are able to solve local issues and have clarity over what requires escalation outside of the plant. The accountability of managers and union representatives can often be limited with collective bargaining or changes to policy handled by central teams, depending on the business model.

4.3.5 A Mixed Employment Relations Model

Some complex organisations have implemented alternative approaches to collective employment relations for different employee groups, locations or business sectors. This, in turn means that the HR operating model will be adapted and designed to meet the needs of the different employee groups. For example, where there is no trade union or method of collective voice, the HR team may focus on a direct listening strategy under the function of a colleague engagement or colleague experience team. Within the same organisation or group of companies there may also be employees who are unionised and undertake collective bargaining. The HR team will therefore require some specific skills in working with unions with a varying level of employment relations experience needed in different roles and within different teams.

Outsourcing and global supply chains can add complexity to the role of the employment relations team. An organisation may have a range of third-party suppliers, providing key outsourced activities. The employment relations climate in that industry and the suppliers' relationships with its unions and its ways of working have the ability to impact the service, reputation and brand of the primary organisation. The host organisation HR team will therefore also need to have some clear oversight and governance in place to understand risk to the business, but the team will not require specific employment relations expertise or skills. The operating model in HR needs to reflect the varying degrees of control and influence implied by these arrangements.

> **Exercise 4.1: Choosing the right employment relations operating model**
>
> Thinking about your own organisation or an organisation you are familiar with, consider the following questions to help you decide the most appropriate employment relations operating model:
>
> - How does your employment relations strategy influence your organisation design?
> - What sort of relationship do you want with your employees (and increasingly workers and contractors) and what relationship do you want with your trade unions?
> - How critical is the management of collective employment relations for your organisation and how much control can you have?
> - What level of resource are you prepared to invest in this field?
> - What other role or functions come within the scope of employment relations? What is the level of skill and capability in collective employment relations of this wider team?

4.4 Employment Relations Accountabilities and Skills

The employment relations climate is influenced by a range of key organisational positions including the CEO, the union representatives and operational managers. In Table 4.2, we summarise the key roles that impact employment relations with their corresponding accountabilities and skills.

The employment relations strategy and organisational design principles set out above will clarify what the team needs to do at a high level, where accountability sits, how the team will work together to achieve it, and what capabilities and behaviour are required skills. However, the specific activities undertaken by employment relations teams can vary, depending on the type, complexity and size of the organisation, and the volume and nature of work.

It is important to define the role and scope of the employment relations function and the specialists working within it. There are a wide range of activities to choose—this choice both reflects the organisation's employment relations strategy and its main priorities. In the example below, we provide some of the typical activities undertaken by employment relations specialists.

Table 4.2 Roles, accountabilities and skills

Role	Accountabilities	Skills	Specific example
CEO	Endorse the strategy and set the tone. Engage with key representatives and communicate effectively. Clarity on values. Decision maker.	Listening. Sharing the vision. Creating the right environment and role modelling behaviours for effective employment relations.	Provide a clear sense of direction. Honesty about challenges.
Employment relations specialist or lead HR role	Manage the process, ensure there is a platform for relationships, speak truth to power and share their knowledge and understanding of the union perspective and motivation.	Understanding different perspectives and the historical perspective. Storytelling and communication. Influencing leaders and representatives.	Finding common ground and alternative ways to look at problems. Openness to alternative ideas and problem solving. Creating the structure and process to facilitate discussions.
Line manager	Own the operational changes proposed and explaining the reasons. Promote the role of the team in problem solving and involve representatives.	Day-to-day support and guidance and pastoral care. Escalation of issues where required. Liaison with reps on local issues and welfare. Balancing operational priorities with employment relations considerations.	Support staff during times of uncertainty or change, work closely with union reps, ensure there is feedback into the proposals.
Representatives	Seek feedback and ideas from team. Structure the points collated into meaningful feedback. Highlight issues and solutions. Ensure understanding of proposals.	Challenge, communicate to constituency, create framework for difficult messages. Support members/teams. Provide independent view.	Sharing the reason for change, communicating the next steps, ensuring there is independent two-way communications about concerns and issues.

Scope of Employment Relations Activity

- Set employment relations strategy, standards and policies, and support and/or manage the governance which brings this to life.
- Manage collective relationships directly or through supporting the organisation to engage with employees and unions effectively.
- Maintain and develop channels of direct employee voice and monitor employee engagement
- Develop and implement organisation-wide employment relations projects, change programmes, tools and processes, in consultation with key business units, that enable consistent delivery of core business activity.

> - Ensure effectiveness of organisation-wide employment relations programmes and provide expert advice and consultancy support to the business units and Shared Services.
> - Provide corporate glue from an employment relations perspective—drive coherence, consistency and a 'one company' approach.
> - Identify external trends, champion and facilitate the sharing of internal and external good practice across the organisation and use data and management information (MI) to inform how the employment relations strategy is delivered and evaluated.

At the time of writing, we conducted a review of employment relations roles advertised across Europe to try to get a sense of what organisations were looking for from their employment relations specialists. These revolved around five broad areas as outlined below.

4.4.1 Building Relationships

Relationship building was a key theme in the advertised roles. Operational employment relations activity sat with the employment relations team and its role was to develop high-trust relationships with all stakeholders and consequently secure positive organisational outcomes. Role descriptions covered responsibility for a wide range of subject areas such as wellbeing, inclusion, and communications. One organisation assigned responsibility for creating the 'ideal work environment' in the role. Some organisations were explicit in the primary role of collective bargaining whilst others placed the emphasis on engagement, voice and involvement.

4.4.2 Collective Engagement

The core of many employment relations roles was the development and management of the strategy towards collective groups. This included European Works Councils, trade union forums and employee involvement groups. The level of ownership and management of these channels strongly emphasised the strategic importance of such roles, described as building 'powerful relationships', 'trade union management' or 'driving collaboration' to provide employee voice and involvement. However, these roles typically sat one or two levels down in the HR hierarchy.

4.4.3 Subject Expertise and Advice

There was a strong emphasis on the provision of specialist employment relations skills and knowledge. This was often linked to risk and legal compliance and there was an emphasis on management and resolution of individual conflict. There was also a demand for broader skillsets in managing relationships with trade unions, employee fora and works councils, management of change and employee engagement. In addition, there was a clear demand for employment relations specialists to play a role in building capability through training and development.

4.4.4 Supporting HR Business Partners and Other Departments

A common task in many of the advertised roles was providing support to other functions in HR, in particular HRBPs. This reflects the dominant operating models used in many organisations, which remove and relegate employment relations from strategic level HR roles.

4.4.5 Management of Change

Negotiating and managing change was a key theme within the posts that we examined. This reflected the overlap between the management of any change programme and the collective mechanisms in place to involve employees in such decisions and negotiate positive outcomes. Change programmes sit with the employment relations team, particularly collective consultation and negotiation over redundancy, restructuring and acquisition.

4.5 Developing Specific Employment Relations Accountabilities

Whilst there is some overarching consistency in the roles analysed above, they tend to focus on employment relations specialists and HR professionals. However, as a result of the devolution of people management, day-to-day employment relations activity can be the responsibility of operational and line managers. As we have already argued, there is considerable evidence that many managers lack the skills and confidence to manage employment relations issues in general and find dealing with union representatives particularly daunting (Saundry et al., 2016). This potentially leads to a blurring of the lines of responsibility for dealing with employment relations and can leave managers dependent on employment relations and HR teams (McCracken et al., 2017).

An example of how this can be structured is outlined in Table 4.3. This shows how one large international organisation described the various levels of employment relations skills and capability required by different groups within the organisation. This was designed to help everyone understand their accountabilities, provide clarity on their scope and ensure they had the right training and support to help them deliver. The employment relations function itself had responsibility for strategic level work, which included liaising with senior union officials and delivering the employment relations strategy. At a tactical level, senior departmental managers have key responsibility for the day-to-day management of employment relations. This involves working with local union representatives and resolving basic issues. In this example, the indirect responsibility was where there was low membership, but employees were covered by a collective agreement. Managers needed to know the context but did not deal with unions on collective issues.

This approach highlights the importance of employment relations skills at all levels of the organisation, and sets out a clear agenda for skill development and capability building. If managers do not feel capable or confident, they will simply refer issues back to the employment relations specialists who will quickly become overloaded and overwhelmed. Therefore, the role of line managers within employment relations is crucial but frequently overlooked. The next case study highlights an attempt to integrate line managers into employment relations activity.

Table 4.3 Defining employment relations capabilities

Strategic level Employment Relations	Tactical level Employment Relations	Indirect responsibility for Employment Relations
Has responsibility for the employment relations function and strategy within a department (usually leads the local engagement). Interacts and works with senior representatives and full-time officers on a regular basis.	Interacts with employment relations in every (or most) elements of the day-to-day job. This manager has regular communication and responsibility for working with local and other reps in the organisation.	Manages staff covered by a collective agreement. Requires knowledge of employment relations and relevant policies and procedures.
<ul><li>Develop local employment relations strategy to support business plan initiatives.</li><li>Lead and facilitate positive industrial relationships at a local level in order to deliver operational essentials and business plan/ targets.</li><li>Owns employment relations structures and agreements and aligns these to business plan requirements.</li><li>Lead an effective employee communication strategy that generates a positive/constructive employment relations climate capable of dealing effectively with critical business and people priorities within own business.</li></ul>	<ul><li>Maintain knowledge of collective agreements and employment relations developments (i.e. meetings, agreements) in order to manage own department.</li><li>Apply collective agreements to resolve day-to-day issues raised by representatives.</li><li>Establish and maintain effective working relationship with local employee/union representatives to maintain productive working environment</li><li>Establish effective departmental employee communication channels to influence positive/constructive employment relations enabling effective and timely change and/or resolution to operational and/or people issues.</li></ul>	<ul><li>Understand collective agreements, including legal and statutory requirements that apply to the department to maintain a positive working environment.</li><li>Keep informed of employment relations developments that might be relevant to the management of own department.</li><li>Interpret employment relations dynamics that drive change/culture in own business area to help generate realistic and practical plans and targets.</li></ul>

> **Tip**
>
> It is essential to clarify the specific employment relations accountabilities for each role and level within an organisation to avoid confusion or duplication and give clarity on scope and escalation.

Case study 4.1: Line manager lifecycle—empowering line managers

The manager lifecycle (see Figure 1 Case Study 4.1) reflects a conscious attempt to ensure employment relations skills are considered from the start of the recruitment process for critical line manager positions. These skills will form part of the advert and search process. Skills in this area are assessed at interview and prioritised as part of the induction process. This helps to ensure that new managers have the right skills and experience for the environment as well as the right expectations of what work will be like and how they will need to operate.

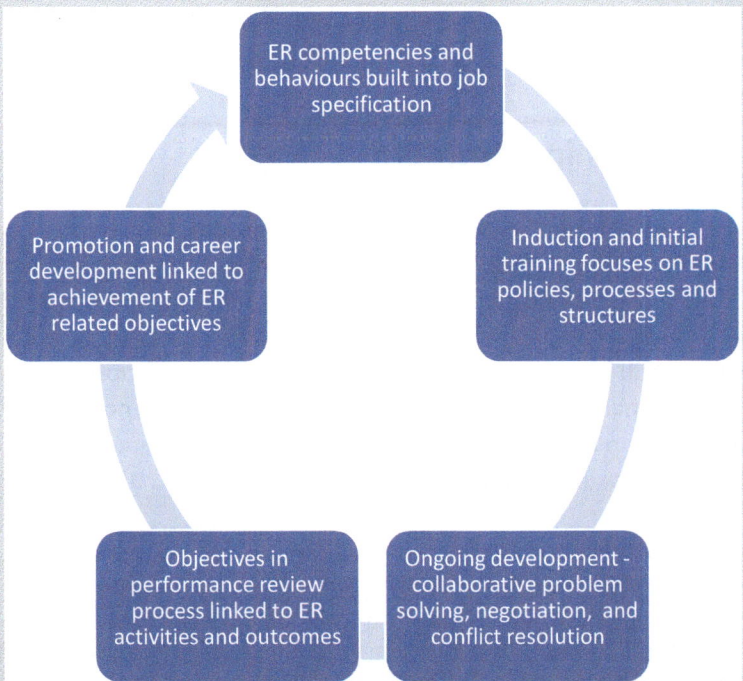

Figure 1 Case Study 4.1 Line manager lifecycle

As their career develops, managers receive specific learning and development interventions in this area and their performance is considered in light of how they deliver, as well as what is delivered. The focus on behavioural impact is critical given the importance of trust in unionised environments. This is underpinned by an intentional strategic approach which is cascaded to departmental and team level and informs planning and development as well as future recruitment activity.

Having a transparent standard is critical to set expectations with leaders and also with other stakeholders such as representatives and external trade union partners. Being open about the approach you expect leaders to take is important to build trust. But it also creates clarity in terms of the culture which is desired and rewarded. This constitutes an express attempt to create a

> positive relationship between managers and unions, and to help improve levels of trust.
>
> **Key questions**
>
> 1. Thinking about your own organisation, or one with which you are familiar, do managers have the skills and confidence to deal with employment relations issues?
> 2. What are the main training needs of these managers in terms of employment relations?
> 3. How could you apply the lifecycle approach to build the capabilities of line managers?

4.6 Overcoming Problems

Designing and implementing new operating models can be challenging. There are two common problems. First, in some cases there is an overlap between the roles of HRBP and the employment relations specialists. HRBPs work with business leaders within a defined area of the business and will be responsible for all aspects of HR including employment relations. It is important to define what sits in the remit of the business partner and what sits with the employment relations specialist. In our experience, there is frustration if the latter only gets involved when something goes wrong.

> **Tip**
>
> To help work out the roles of HRBPs and the employment relations team, it can be helpful to hold a session where you define the roles clearly, working through examples together to delineate who does what in these common scenarios.

Second, the operational responsibility for managing employment relations risk often sits with the employment relations team. They will own the comprehensive risks for issues that they manage, for example a breakdown in the relationship or a dispute at an organisational level. However, it can be the case that the team cannot mitigate or reduce the risk as the ownership of the relationship with the unions sits with the HRBP or manager. Therefore, managers or HRBPs may be less concerned about creating a positive employment relations climate as they are unlikely to 'carry the can' for failures, problems or conflict. However, if the line managers own their risks and are held accountable, they are more likely to build a positive employment relations climate.

> **Tip**
> Consider carefully where employment relations risks sit. If they sit in the employment relations team, the team needs to have influence with operational and senior leaders and have the resources to be able to manage risks effectively.

4.7 Conclusion

This chapter has discussed some of the key areas for practitioners to consider when setting up or reviewing the employment relations function and how it supports the delivery of the organisational strategy. It has also discussed different organisational structures and the roles within them. The critical roles are played by leaders and managers with support from the employment relations team, so how and when these roles interact is also a fundamental consideration to reduce duplication or confusion. The employment relations roles will vary enormously depending on the size of the organisation, its industry, its risks and its plans for the future. In the next chapter, we will discuss constructive employment relations behaviours and how important it is for organisations to develop and nurture positive behaviours which support their stated strategy.

> **Questions**
> 1. Summarise the differences you would expect to see in the structure, role and accountabilities of employment relations teams in those organisations with trade unions and those without trade unions?
> 2. Assess the benefits and potential disadvantages of integrating the employment relations function within the HR business partner role.
> 3. How does the employment relations strategy of the organisation influence the organisation design of the employment relations team?
> 4. What factors would lead an organisation to review its employment relations team design?

References

Francis, H., & Keegan, A. (2006). The Changing Face of HRM: In Search of Balance. *Human Resource Management Journal, 16*(3), 231–249.

Harris, L. (2007). The Changing Nature of the Human Resource Function in UK Local Government and Its Role as Employee Champion. *Employee Relations, 30*(1), 34–47.

McCracken, M., O'Kane, P., Brown, T. C., & McCrory, M. (2017). Human Resource Business Partner Lifecycle Model: Exploring How the Relationship Between HR Business Partners and Their Line Manager Partners Evolves. *Human Resource Management Journal, 27*(1), 58–74.

Saundry, R., Adam, D., Ashman, I., Forde, C., Wibberley, G., & Wright, S. (2016). *Managing Individual Conflict in the Contemporary British Workplace*. Acas Research Papers, 02/16.

Stanford, N. (2015). *The Economist Guide to Organisation Design: Creating High-Performing and Adaptable Enterprises* (2nd ed.). Economist Publications.

Storey, J. (1992). *Developments in the Management of Human Resources*. Blackwell Publishing.

Ulrich, D., & Brockbank, W. (2005). The Business Partner Model: 10 Years On—Lessons Learned. *HRM Magazine*, November 2015.

5

Constructive Behaviours for Effective Employment Relations

Abstract A positive employment relations climate is not simply dependent on articulating a coherent strategy and developing a complementary operating model with robust structures. These conditions enable people to interact, negotiate agreements and resolve conflict. However, success is ultimately dependent on the skills and attitudes of leaders, managers, Human Resource (HR) practitioners and union and employee representatives. This chapter explores the behaviours and capabilities that are needed for effective employment relations practice. In particular, it discusses the skills, techniques and processes that practitioners need to build trust, sustain relationships and find lasting solutions to problems. It highlights the importance of focusing on the interests of key stakeholders and moving away from position-based, adversarial approaches.

Keywords Behaviours · Trust · Capability · Interests · Conflict

5.1 Introduction

Effective employment relations require management and unions to be able to consult, negotiate and work together to solve complex problems. This depends on the ability of key stakeholders to discuss issues openly, honestly and in confidence. Trust creates a safe space in which organisational leaders, HR practitioners, and union representatives can float suggestions and explore solutions. Without this, parties often retreat to conventional and adversarial positions. A key ingredient in building and maintaining trust is a recognition and understanding of the perspectives of the 'other side'. However, as we discussed in Chapter 2, there has been a growing perception gap in recent years. HR practitioners and leaders are less likely to see unions as legitimate, while trade union representatives increasingly view HR practitioners as an extension of management, with little interest in the welfare of workers. To bridge this gap, the parties in the employment relationship need to focus on mutual interests rather than hard and fast positions. In this chapter, we seek to explain how practitioners can develop collaborative practices that emphasise constructive problem-solving, and which provide a firm foundation for sustaining positive employment relations.

5.2 Trust, Mistrust and Employment Relations

Trust is the main building block of collaborative working and conflict resolution. It allows representatives and HR practitioners to explore issues that would be difficult to discuss publicly or could be sensitive in nature. This opens up a wider range of potential outcomes for mutually beneficial resolutions. This can create a virtuous circle whereby trust is developed, which in turn provides the basis for addressing and potentially working though more difficult, deep-rooted and complex problems (see Fig. 5.1).

It is tempting to think that trust is a natural state in employment relations and that mistrust develops as a result of miscommunication or conflict between the parties. In reality, trust must be built and, in many organisations, the starting point for representatives of management and unions is one of scepticism. If leaders and HR practitioners have a predominantly unitarist perspective, they will see union representatives as a threat to organisational harmony—or they may expect that union representatives will share their values, goals and objectives. Such a simplistic approach is likely to undermine the conditions for trust to develop. HR practitioners often have a conception of 'the good union rep' as someone who is co-operative, flexible and organisation-focussed. This tends to lose sight of the main function of trade unions—to represent their members and provide a challenge to unilateral management authority. All parties have constituencies that they need to serve. In order to retain credibility, representatives must show their members that working closely with management can deliver positive outcomes. At the same time, HR practitioners and managers may need to persuade sceptical leaders of the benefits of co-operative working with trade unions.

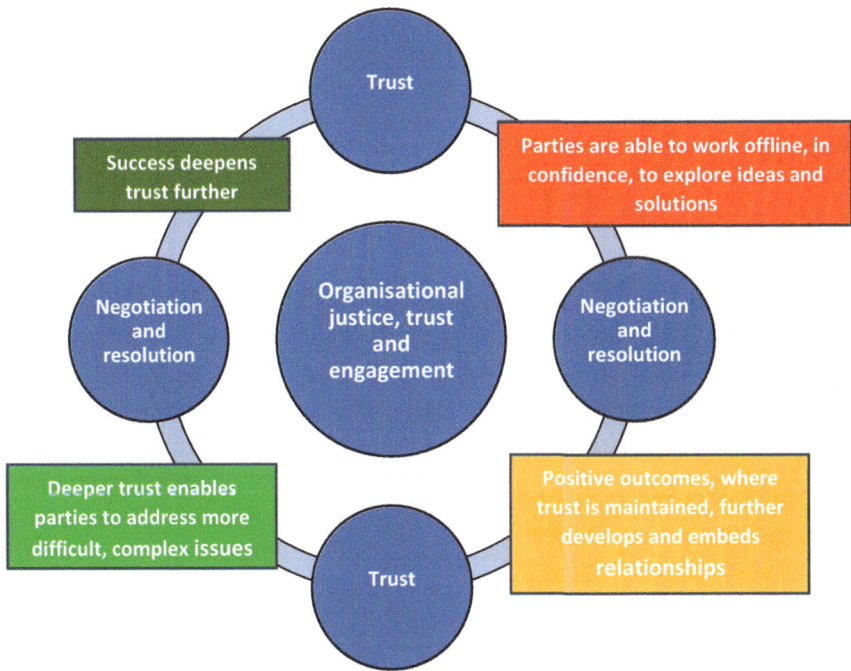

Fig. 5.1 Trust and resolution—a virtuous circle

> **Tip**
>
> If you are a manager or an HR practitioner, it is important to remember that it is in your interests for representatives to have credibility with their members. If they can deliver for their members, any agreements that you negotiate will be more likely to stick.

The perception gap between HR and union representatives can foster distrust and make co-operative relationships more difficult to forge. In the same way that high-trust relations can create a virtuous circle, low trust can feed a vicious spiral, whereby defensive and adversarial attitudes create conflict which in turn further undermines management-union relationships.

Exercise 5.1: Trust in employment relations

Think about the key individuals that you work alongside—this could be a member of the leadership team, HR practitioner or a union representative. Taking each relationship in turn, would you characterise this as high- or low-trust? Write down the reasons for this and identify actions that you could take to improve the relationship.

Trust is central to wider patterns of employment relations. Walton and McKersie (1991) suggest that the extent of trust is a function of the motivation of the organisation and whether it accepts the legitimacy of the trade union and its representatives (see Table 5.1). Not surprisingly, if an organisation is seeking to destroy or weaken the union, relationships will be characterised by distrust. However, if the organisation wants to develop co-operative relationships, this involves accepting the legitimacy of the unions and building extended trust. Moreover, trust will be evident through 'friendly' relationships between leaders, managers and union stakeholders.

Exercise 5.2: Relationship patterns and attitudes

Which of the relationship patterns in Table 5.1 most closely resembles those in your own organisation or one with which you are familiar. To what extent is this also reflected in the different attitudinal dimensions? If you were to try to move towards a more co-operative approach, what could you do to encourage a change in attitudes and behaviours?

Table 5.1 Attitudes and relationships

Attitudinal Dimension	Relationship Pattern			
	Conflict	Containment/aggression	Accommodation	Co-operation
Motivation	Competitive – destroy or weaken		Hands off	Preserve relationship
Legitimacy	Denial	Grudging acceptance	Status quo	Complete
Trust	Extreme distrust	Distrust	Limited trust	Extended trust
Friendliness	Hate	Antagonism	Neutral courtesy	Friendliness

Source: Walton and McKersie (1991)

5.3 Behaviours for Building Trust

As we argued in the previous section, trust is not automatic. Leaders, HR practitioners, managers and union representatives need to work hard to build and sustain positive relationships, often in very challenging contexts. Although having the right structures and processes in place is important, the way in which the parties behave is key to creating a positive and constructive dialogue. Brown and Oxenbridge (2004) highlight the need for senior leaders to explicitly acknowledge the legitimacy of representation and the benefits of collective voice. Moreover, this should be reflected in the active participation of representatives at all levels of decision-making and governance. However, trust is also built through the day-to-day interactions between the parties at a micro-level.

Key behaviours

- **Active listening and curiosity**—avoid assumptions and preconceptions. Get to know the 'other side' and draw on their experience and expertise.
- **Understanding and empathy**—try to understand the perspectives of others and the context they are working in. Put yourself in their shoes to see things from their point of view.
- **Treating with respect and recognition**—recognise the legitimacy of all parties and acknowledge the value of their contribution.
- **Inclusivity**—recognise, involve and give weight to a diversity of voice, opinion and interests.

5.3.1 Questioning and Listening

One of the main barriers to building trust is that leaders, managers, union representatives and HR practitioners come into relationships with preconceptions and negative expectations. For example, managers may stereotype union representatives as being inflexible or 'difficult'. At the same time, representatives sometimes assume that managers and HR practitioners have no interest in the welfare of workers or issues such as fairness and equity. It is important to break down these barriers by getting to know the people that you are going to be working with. In particular, HR practitioners and managers need to ask questions, listen and show curiosity. This will not only give them a greater understanding of the actions and behaviour of union representatives but also recognises their legitimacy and experience.

> **Tip**
> Trade union representatives often have more experience and knowledge of the organisation (particularly policies, procedures and agreements) than managers or HR practitioners. Tapping into this know-how will show respect and help to build trust. Asking a trade union representative for advice or help should not be seen as a sign of weakness.

5.3.2 Respect and Recognition

One of the main stumbling blocks to developing trust is a sense that leaders don't respect the role that union representatives play. This can be seen in patronising attitudes and behaviours and a failure to acknowledge their experience and expertise. Furthermore, if organisational leaders demonstrate disrespect, this can reinforce attitudes among managers and HR representatives. For example, we have noticed a tendency for newly qualified HR practitioners to assume that they are more knowledgeable than union representatives who have been working in the role, the industry and the organisation for many years.

> **Tip**
> Constructive behaviour starts at the top of the organisation—leaders need to visibly demonstrate that they recognise, respect and value the role played by union and employee representatives.

It is crucial to recognise the legitimacy of the union representative and their potential contribution to the organisation. Trade union representatives are generally elected. Therefore, they have a degree of legitimacy that managers and HR practitioners do not have. The importance of the role that unions play can be recognised by keeping representatives closely involved in both individual and collective issues. Ideally this needs to go beyond a simple invitation to a formal consultative meeting. Instead, informing unions of any relevant announcements or proposals before they become public is critical. However, communication alone is not enough—the key to building trust is to involve unions in the decision-making process in a clear and transparent way. We explore this in more detail in the next chapter.

> **Recognising the role of unions in practice**
>
> 1. Give union representatives a heads-up of any important announcement or proposals
> 2. Make sure there are no surprises—don't go direct to staff before consulting with unions
> 3. Where possible give them the opportunity to have an input in the decision-making process
> 4. Make sure that this input is meaningful and not just 'window dressing'
> 5. Pick up the phone to alert the representative about a potential problem regarding one of their members
> 6. Ask for their advice—show appreciation for their input

5.3.3 Understanding and Empathy

Many of the assumptions that the key parties in employment relations hold about each other are based on a lack of understanding. This means that they can fall back on caricatures and tropes. Therefore, it's important to understand the other party as a person—for example, why did they become a union representative or decide to go into HR. This, in turn, requires some time to develop a social and friendly relationship—one that isn't forged in formal meetings. This type of interaction has two benefits: first you can get a handle on their interests and needs, and second, it starts to build trust.

> **A typology of union representation**
>
> *The traditionalist*—this representative is steeped in the union and may have been in the role for some time. They will almost always have been in the organisation longer and know how it works much better than the HR practitioners and managers they deal with. They will know policy, procedure and collective agreements back-to-front. They may seem old-fashioned, and it may be difficult to gain their trust and respect, but they are often very influential.
>
> *The politician*—some representatives are drawn to the role through ideology and political conviction—they are often less experienced and see issues in principled terms. They are less likely to be pragmatic and open to negotiation. Managers and HR practitioners are seen in oppositional terms and collaboration is viewed negatively.
>
> *The axe-grinder*—negative personal experiences can persuade some workers to take on a more active role in the union. This can cut two ways—these representatives are often dedicated and want to give something back if they felt that the union supported them in the past. However, they can also have an 'axe to grind', which can mean that their perspective on issues can be skewed.

> *The organic leader*—most representatives take on the role because they simply want to help their colleagues. Their primary motivation is not political or ideological—they have a sense that people need to be supported and that fair play is crucial. Because they often come to the role with few preconceived ideas, their attitude to their employer will be quickly shaped by the way they are treated.

While these categories are simplistic, they show that union representatives have a range of motivations which shape their attitudes and responses. In recent years, long-standing union representatives have increasingly been replaced by less experienced activists, who sometimes have a more ideological perspective. They may be less willing to engage with management and unlikely to simply adopt the conventions and rules of the employment relations 'game'. In addition, as we discussed in Chapter 2, unions have progressively moved away from partnership approaches to strategies that revolve around grassroots organising. This change in orientation is challenging for managers and HR practitioners who often equate 'good' union representatives with co-operative attitudes. This is why managers and HR practitioners need to understand the history and traditions of the trade union they are negotiating with. Trade unions are political organisations, so it is crucial to develop an understanding of how that shapes the specific positions the union might take. Again, this has a dual purpose, it helps to inform your approach and strategy but demonstrating an understanding of the union will also help to build much needed credibility. The same is true for trade union representatives—understanding the context within which managers and HR are operating is extremely important and will help to deepen relationships.

> **Case study 5.1: The importance of trust—A tale of two organisations**
>
> The following vignettes are taken from a study conducted by Jones and Saundry in 2016, that explored the roles adopted by HR, managers and representatives in trying to manage and resolve workplace conflict.
>
> **Organisation one**—the following quote comes from a manager working in private services, a sector with relatively low levels of union organisation. However, in this case there was a strong steer to engage positively with trade unions. The manager made it a priority from day one to build high-trust organisations with the union.
>
>> When I came into the operational role the most important thing was to engage the union and for them to understand that actually I'm not this ogre of a manager who's just going to run all over you and make life hard for your staff and it's taken me a long time to get that trust and

understanding. What I always do, which is key, is if you're making any changes just tell the union and when someone comes knocking on [their] door they'll say, we know about it, we haven't got a problem with it.

Organisation two—in this organisation a low-trust culture had developed over a period of time. There was a lack of respect between managers and union representatives. Managers adopted an adversarial approach because they felt that the main union representative was unpleasant and aggressive while the main union representative felt that he and his members were neither given proper recognition nor listened to. Therefore, he adopted conflictual positions to defend their interests. The following quote sums up this situation very succinctly:

> I think it was always a case of we didn't trust management. We would never enter into any kind of informal discussion because we were mindful that at some point in the future that would be used against us so we were always very formal…

Based on: Jones and Saundry (2012)

Key questions

1. Why do you think high-trust relations are so important to resolving conflict at work?
2. The actions of the managers in Organisation one seem very sensible but what barriers do you think this manager could encounter in engaging with union representatives?
3. If you were a new manager or HR practitioner in Organisation two, what would you to try to turn around the culture of low trust?

5.3.4 Inclusivity

Good employment relations relies on the parties being able to speak openly and honestly—this not only creates trust but encourages challenge and a diversity of opinion. However, it is quite easy to exclude individuals from discussions and meetings or create environments in which they feel unable to speak up. This is particularly the case within more formal meetings. The way that people behave within meetings can determine outcomes, and also shape the nature of long-term relationships (LeBlanc & Nosic, 2019). Moreover, bad behaviour can undermine the usefulness of meetings and erode credibility and trust.

> **Exercise 5.3: Inclusivity**
>
> Research conducted by Heath and Wensil (2019) based on 360 degree feedback from more than 1000 senior women executives found that:
>
> - Women often feel shut out of meetings and uncomfortable speaking up.
> - Women are more than twice as likely as men to be interrupted or talked over during group discussions.
> - These problems are particularly acute in male-dominated organisations.
>
> They also found that senior male managers from minoritised groups report similar experiences.
>
> To what extent do these findings reflect your own experiences? What would you do to increase the inclusivity of discussions and meetings?

Leaders arguably play the most important role in creating more inclusive environments. For example, Heath and Wensil (2019) argue that it is a leader's job to intervene if meetings are being dominated by an 'in group' and other voices are being excluded. If there are persistent 'dominators' and 'interrupters' it is important to step in and redirect the conversation back to the original speaker. Crucially, leaders need to model inclusive behaviours and avoid a temptation to dominate themselves.

5.4 (Re)structuring Attitudes

The attitudes and behaviours that the parties to employment relations bring with them into meetings, discussions and negotiations are complex and rooted in a range of different factors. The context, both institutional and organisational, will encourage and incentivise certain behaviours. For example, if the government is hostile towards trade unions, this is likely to be reflected in negative employer attitudes, which in turn are likely to be met with defensiveness and resistance by union representatives. Moreover, the ideology and perspectives of the parties will shape how they behave towards each other—the more these perspectives diverge the more likely there is to be conflict and antagonism. Attitudes are also shaped by experience—we argued earlier that trust can be built and reinforced by positive joint working. However, negative experiences can also create and embed a sense of grievance, resentment and resistance. The quotation below from a trade union representative interviewed as part of a research project into workplace mediation, suggests that his confrontational attitude to management was a response to how he felt managers had treated him.

> "There wasn't a partnership...It was a 'them and us,' batter the barricades the old-fashioned way. If there was a problem just hit it head on...we went in always with a big hammer, trying to get a bigger hammer than they had...I put round about, I think, at one stage, 20-odd grievances in a year and only lost one. I was at a point where management had wound me up that many times, I didn't care whose grievance it was. Sometimes I'd say I'd say I've got to go back and have a go at these people." (*Source* Saundry et al., 2011)

It is important to note that these experiences can also create negative organisational memories, with feelings of mistrust passed on to successive managers, HR practitioners or trade union representatives. Attitudes and behaviours can also be a function of personality, which can be particularly problematic. Although, in some cases, this may be rooted in personal experience of work, which can be addressed, in others the only course of action may be to 'manage' or find a way of working around that individual.

> **Managing on the frontline**
>
> **The following is an extract of an interview with an operations manager working in a large, highly unionised organisation. He explains how he developed as a manager and the importance of building good relationships with trade unions.**
>
> "Looking back at it, I think I was probably quite naive and quite young. I was just happy-go-lucky...I was very fortunate with one of my line managers at the time who was very good with her people leadership and what I was able to do is learn how she dealt with me...she gave me feedback and coached me and developed me...but formal training? I think we're very, very good in organisations in throwing people in the deep end but not really upskilling them to the level that they perhaps need to be.
>
> I think two key words describe how I felt about first dealing with unions. One is apprehensive. And one was probably nervous. Because when you're in some of those more difficult conversations, especially around restructure and potential redundancies, it's actually affecting people's wellbeing, it's affecting people individually and personally, isn't it? And I think there's very much a perception that the union representative is going to be there to fight you the whole time, and it's going to be a challenge. Whereas some of the time they just want to work with you.
>
> The relationship that I've built with our trade unions is definitely more engaged, it's more cohesive...and what they can also do is sometimes act as a bit of a filter...they will listen to their membership...they will bring items to the table either formally or informally that actually matter and need some resolution...they cut through some of the weeds and some of the noise. By talking to the union at an early point you're bringing them on the journey

> with you without them realising you're actually bringing them on the journey sometimes. They feel engaged. They feel part of that decision.
> If there are issues bubbling away, it gives you an opportunity to put the fire out.
> When I moved into this role, I had to build my own relationships and not being new into the business helped as well because I already knew some of the characters. But I took it upon myself very much to have early interaction with the unions over a cup of coffee and asking, 'how can we work together, what do you need from me'? I tried to set those rules of engagement early on and we've continued with those open lines of communication. So, we have a weekly session on a Wednesday morning where it's their opportunity to bring anything that's a burning issue—to talk about things, to try and resolve issues on an informal basis. We then have a monthly departmental forum where all of the union representatives from both unions are invited and then we have an organisation-wide forum for key representatives, which is chaired by the HR director on a quarterly basis…You have to be resilient [when union representatives adopt a more robust stance]. It's not a personal attack because they are dealing with the situation that they've got in front of them and you when you're in those formal environments, you deal with it in a formal way on both sides."

In most cases, it is possible to change the attitudes and behaviours of the individuals that you deal with on a regular basis. Walton and McKersie (1991) describe this as a process of 'attitudinal structuring'. This is set out in Fig. 5.2. The first group of tactics use cognitive balance theory which suggests that individuals prefer consistent beliefs and perceptions and prefer to conform rather than oppose. This demonstrates the importance of emphasising common interests—this could be personal, e.g. an interest in a hobby or shared background. In addition, it points towards focussing on mutual interests and successes, and showing respect for the experience, status and position of the other party.

You may naturally 'get on' with your opposite number—in this case you will probably not need to be 'tactical'. However, when met with difficult attitudes and behaviours, you need to try to find areas of mutuality on which a relationship can be based. This can even involve forging a common cause against other parties within the organisation, for example HR and union representatives may both be critical of organisational strategy. Working together to improve this can provide a basis for building trust.

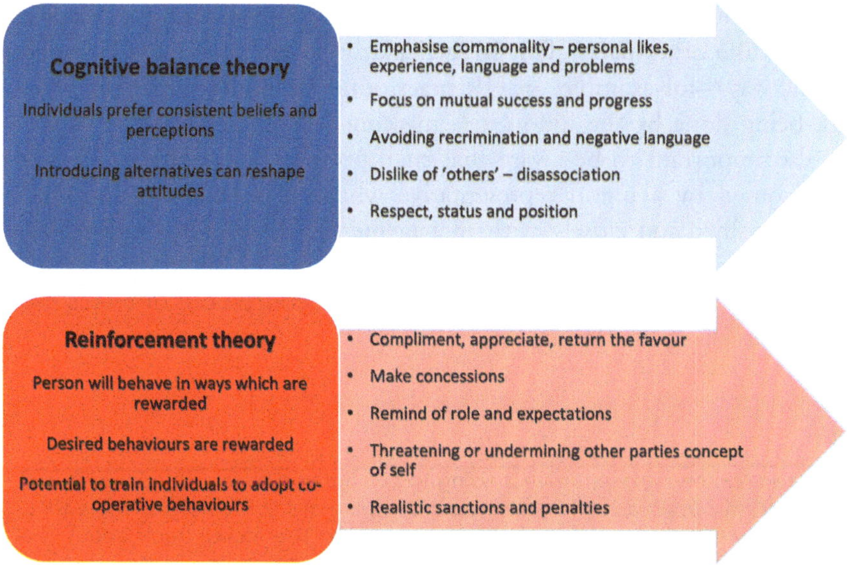

Cognitive balance theory

Individuals prefer consistent beliefs and perceptions

Introducing alternatives can reshape attitudes

- Emphasise commonality – personal likes, experience, language and problems
- Focus on mutual success and progress
- Avoiding recrimination and negative language
- Dislike of 'others' – disassociation
- Respect, status and position

Reinforcement theory

Person will behave in ways which are rewarded

Desired behaviours are rewarded

Potential to train individuals to adopt co-operative behaviours

- Compliment, appreciate, return the favour
- Make concessions
- Remind of role and expectations
- Threatening or undermining other parties concept of self
- Realistic sanctions and penalties

Fig. 5.2 Attitudinal structuring Based on: Walton and McKersie (1991)

> **Tip**
> Try to develop a social relationship with the people you are going to be negotiating with. This doesn't mean being 'best friends', but regular catch-ups when you don't simply "talk shop" are crucial in breaking down barriers and building trust.

Walton and McKersie also draw on reinforcement theory to identify several ways in which attitudes can be shifted. In essence this relies on the fact that desired behaviours should be rewarded and there should be realistic sanctions for misbehaviour. This suggests that it is possible to 'train' individuals to be more co-operative.

> **Important**
> What is good behaviour? From both a unitarist and a radical perspective, one might argue that collaborative and co-operative behaviours are problematic. However, throughout this book we take a clear (and arguably a pluralist) stance that the prevention and resolution of conflict creates better working experiences and more effective workplaces.

A crucial element of reinforcement is to show appreciation for the contribution of the other party. This is particularly powerful if it can be done in a public way—for example, an HR practitioner might highlight the positive work being done by the union in a meeting with senior leaders. However, it is also important to be aware that such positive praise might not always be welcomed by a union representative who might feel compromised by being identified too closely with management. This is why understanding the other party is so important. Nonetheless, in some situations, constructive behaviours can also be rewarded by concrete concessions or by reciprocal actions (returning the favour).

> **Tip**
> If a trade union representative is going to be able to sustain a co-operative and collaborative approach with management, they have to be able to show their members that they benefit from this approach. Therefore, think about the long-term returns of positive employment relations when considering possible concessions.

If positive reinforcement tactics are not successful, you might have to consider trying to penalise negative behaviours. The first stage in this is to remind the other side about their role and responsibilities—to appeal to their better judgement. If you are an HR practitioner, you might take this further by suggesting to the union representative that their actions may have a detrimental impact on the interests of their members. There is a clear danger, however, that this could inflame the situation, unless there is already a strong, trusting relationship. The ultimate step would be to threaten a sanction of some sort—for example withdrawal of co-operation, which once again runs the risk of escalation. Therefore, the use of more negative tactics needs to be very carefully thought through and used as a last resort, if at all.

> **Exercise 5.4: Punishing misbehaviour?**
> You are an HR practitioner involved in early, informal discussion about restructuring in your organisation with two union representatives. You have a very strong relationship with one of the representatives, but the other is quite new, and you have had little contact with them. At your meeting you stress the confidential nature of the discussions. Later that day, you are contacted by a local journalist with clear knowledge of the potential restructuring, which could only have come from one of the union representatives. How would you address this breach of trust?

5.5 The Power of Interests

One of the most useful tools in developing more collaborative behaviours, and building trust is the position, interests and needs framework, illustrated in Fig. 5.3. This reflects the idea that in conflict situations, we tend to revert to positions based on our conception of the fairness and merits of an issue. For example, in a high-pressure meeting over potential restructuring, the HR Director may hold a position that job losses are inevitable because of inflexibility on the part of the union over working practices. In contrast, the union's position may be that the real reason for job cuts is the emphasis placed by senior management on profit maximisation. This focus on positions is exacerbated by a tendency to attribute a problem to the behaviour of, and ascribe fault to, the other party. The problem with this, from an employment relations point of view, is that these positions are often very difficult to reconcile. Consequently, at the 'tip of the iceberg' in Fig. 5.3, there is an unbridgeable gap.

However, if one looks below the surface, there is a degree of mutuality and an area of overlapping interests. If we take the example above, the HR Director needs to find savings but also has an interest in maintaining the morale of the workforce and retaining key staff. At the same time, the union has an interest in providing its members with support and security

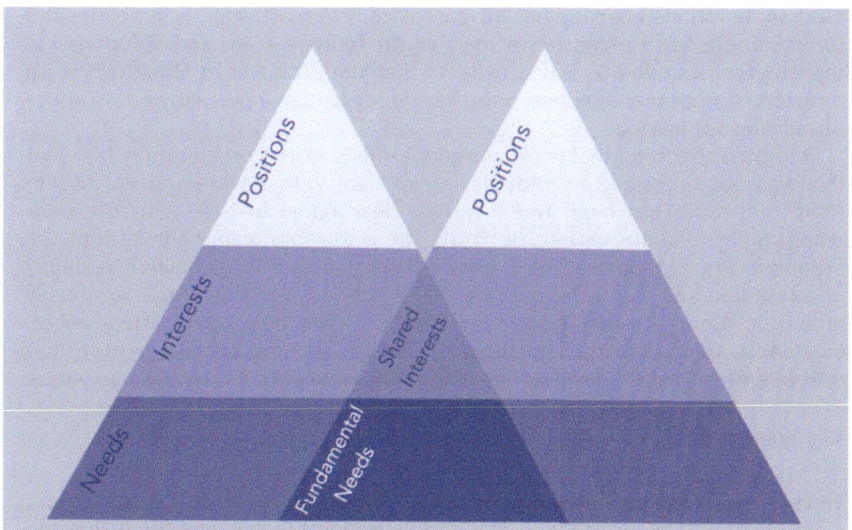

Fig. 5.3 Positions, interests and needs

in an extremely difficult situation. Therefore, both sides have an interest in minimising negative impacts on the workforce. If we dive even deeper, both parties have fundamental needs—these may be to be kept informed, to be respected, trusted and to secure a degree of fairness and justice. Overall, if we can shift the focus to interests and needs and away from adversarial positions, there is greater space to find a resolution and a collaborative way forward.

> **Case study 5.2: Searching for mutuality**
>
> Greytown Healthcare operates four hospitals and employs 3000 staff. It recognises three trade unions which represent different occupational groups—doctors, nurses and support and ancillary staff. While employment relations with the unions representing doctors and nurses is relatively good, those with the remaining union have deteriorated in recent years. Senior managers believe that this is due to the election of the lead union representative, David Smith. They claim that David is 'a militant' and 'a troublemaker'. He has a reputation for using social media and the press to voice criticisms of management. Moreover, managers and a number of the organisation's HR practitioners have experienced negative and disruptive behaviours in meetings. He is seen as being unnecessarily antagonistic and while it is possible to have reasoned discussions with other union representatives, this is impossible with David.
>
> David is 54 years old and has worked at Greytown as a hospital porter for 28 years. He has been a union activist for most of his working life but has never held an official post in the union. He did not have a good relationship with the previous lead representative and ran against her, arguing that she was 'too close to management'. He is popular with his members and since his election, union membership has increased. He is also active in local politics and community issues. He coaches a local youth football team and volunteers in the Greytown foodbank. David believes that the problems at Greytown are a function of poor management and that senior leaders have allowed a culture of bullying to develop.
>
> Recently, the Head of People resigned—many in the organisation feel that this was not unconnected with having to deal with David—and an interim Head of People has been hired with a clear remit to deal with the poor employment relations within the Trust. The leadership team believes that the organisation needs to take on David—they argue that his behaviour is simply unacceptable and that he should be side lined and marginalised. Traditionally union representatives are given very generous paid time off to attend meetings and engage with their members. However, senior managers believe that one way of forcing David to adopt a different attitude is to cut this allowance.
>
> **Key questions**
>
> 1. Using the positions, interests and needs framework—identify the positions, interests and needs of David, the interim Head of People and the leadership team.
> 2. Are there any areas of potential common interest between the parties? If so, what are these areas?

3. If you were advising the interim Head of People, what actions do you think they should take to address this issue and improve employment relations within the organisation?

5.6 Changing Behaviours in Practice

So far in this chapter, we have identified the behaviours that are consistent with building high-trust relationships between HR, managers and representatives. We have also explored how these behaviours can be shaped and attitudes restructured. Much of this discussion has focussed on what individuals can do to change their own behaviours and also foster improved behaviour from their colleagues. However, it can also be argued that organisations can play a key role in providing frameworks that support behavioural change.

Although organisational leaders may not necessarily be involved in the day-to-day management of employment relations, they can play a key role in modelling the behaviours of recognition, understanding and empathy which we highlighted earlier in the chapter. Conversely if senior leaders show little respect for trade union and employee representatives. It is likely that these attitudes will be mirrored by more junior colleagues. While some leaders will grasp the importance of providing a positive example, others may need to be persuaded and coached to display a more constructive approach. Given the dominance of unitarist perspectives among managers and leaders, this may not be straightforward. Therefore, it will be the role of HR practitioners to build a convincing case for change and to try to build references to employment relations into strategic goals and related leadership frameworks.

A framework for collaborative behaviours

One organisation that we worked with made a determined effort to change the behaviours of its leaders and managers to ensure they were able to lead on the implementation of the new employment relations strategy. The strategy aimed to build more collaborative relations with unions and encourage managers to resolve issues locally with their representatives. To do this, there was reference to collective employment relations in the organisation's new Leadership Framework. Under a heading of "Working Together as one team", the leadership framework outlined a key goal as "consulting and engaging trade unions in a genuine and timely way". Leaders were then expected to define some specific personal objectives designed to achieve this goal. These included:

- Building effective and constructive relations with trade union representatives
- Consulting and involving trade unions in strategic plans
- Owning local issues, seeking to resolve locally wherever possible

In this case, managers were paid a bonus depending on achieving their targets so constructive employment relations were now linked directly to the performance of the manager and their individual reward. In the same way, collaborative behaviours can be built into competency frameworks which in turn determine reward, progression and development. Constructive employment relations can also be included within assessment centres for "key talent". For example, organisations could develop specific case studies, role plays and exercises to test the approach and behaviours of those identified as likely to be future leaders. In this way the behaviours needed for constructive employment relations can be embedded into the leadership of an organisation. Moreover, this would also underpin the link between employment relations strategy and organisational success. Of course, some organisations may not have sophisticated systems for talent identification and management, but even including employment relations competencies into job specifications can make an important difference.

Succession planning for good employment relations

Organisations can ensure that demonstrating collaborative employment relations behaviours becomes part of succession planning conversations for key leadership positions. We find that organisations often recruit people into roles with significant employment relations responsibility, without the necessary experience or training. HR practitioners can address this problem by redesigning succession planning processes to ensure that potential leaders receive mentoring from those with significant employment relations experience and are provided with suitable learning and development opportunities.

Therefore, while individuals can develop their own behaviours to forge high-trust relationships, this is likely to be more difficult without a supportive organisational context. In this sense, constructive behaviours are not simply crucial in delivering good employment relations they are a critical part of employment relations strategy itself.

5.7 Conclusion

Poor employment relations and high levels of conflict can often be traced back to low levels of trust. Crucially, organisational memory can be pervasive and mistrust is almost always grounded in poor behaviours or perceptions of mistreatment and injustice. Therefore, these negative and adversarial attitudes can be deep rooted and difficult to break down. The first step in addressing this is trying to understand the perspectives of the other side—too often HR practitioners and organisational leaders dismiss challenge from trade unions as illegitimate. At a simple level this means really listening to the concerns of union representatives rather than trying to impose solutions. Using their experience and knowledge to inform decision-making is not only likely to lead to better outcomes but will start to create a virtuous circle of trust and resolution. But individual HR practitioners and managers may find it difficult to build high-trust relationships unless the same constructive behaviours are modelled by organisational leaders. If trade union representatives feel that they are respected and recognised at the top of the organisation, management and unions will find it easier to move away from positions-based, adversarial employment relations towards a focus on common interests and collaborative problem-solving.

> **Questions**
> 1. Thinking of your own organisation or one that you are familiar with, how would you describe the behaviours of leaders, unions, managers and HR? In what ways could trust be built and employment relations improved?
> 2. Many HR practitioners are too quick to label trade union representatives as 'good' or 'bad'. To what extent do you agree with this statement and why is this counterproductive to effective employment relations?
> 3. Find an example of a well-publicised industrial dispute. Think about this using the concept of positions, interests and needs. How could more constructive approaches could have been adopted by the parties?

References

Brown, W., & Oxenbridge, S. (2004). The Development of Co-operative Employer/Trade Union Relationships in Britain. *Industrielle Beziehungen: Zeitschrift Für Arbeit, Organisation und Management, 11*(1/2), 143–158.

Heath, K., & Wensil, B. (2019). To Build an Inclusive Culture, Start with Inclusive Meetings. Online. *Harvard Business Review.* https://hbr.org/2019/09/to-build-an-inclusive-culture-start-with-inclusive-meetings. [Accessed on 26/1/2024].

Jones, C., & Saundry, R. (2012). The Practice of Discipline: Evaluating the Roles and Relationship between Managers and HR Professionals. *Human Resource Management Journal, 22*(3), 252–266.

LeBlanc, L., & Nosic, M. (2019). Planning and Leading Effective Meetings. *Behavior Analaysis in Practice, 12*, 696–708.

Saundry, R., McArdle, L., & Thomas, P. (2011). *Transforming Conflict Management in the Public Sector? Mediation, Trade Unions and Partnerships in a Primary Care Trust*. Acas.

Walton, R. E., & McKersie, R. B. (1991). *A Behavioral Theory of Labor Negotiations* (2nd ed.). ILR Press.

Part III

Working with Unions and Collective Voice

6

Informing and Consulting—Practical Processes and Structures for Employee Voice

Abstract One of the philosophical foundations of collective employment relations is that engagement with employees and their representatives is vital for successful organisations. Therefore, building effective dialogue throughout the organisation, from senior leaders to local managers with union and employee representatives, is a business-critical issue. In this chapter we will review different approaches to the enactment and delivery of collective employee voice. These range from information sharing to more participative forms of consultation and co-determination. We advocate the development of joint strategies to facilitate voice and provide practical examples of how this can be achieved. Furthermore, we also discuss the importance of developing voice in a way that promotes inclusion, diversity and psychological safety.

Keywords Consultation · Information · Communication · Co-determination · Information sharing · Meetings

6.1 Introduction

In Chapter 2, we discussed the growing 'representation gap' (Addison & Teixeira, 2021; Towers, 1997) as a consequence of the progressive erosion of trade union organisation. Moreover this 'gap' has not been filled by alternative non-union channels of representation. This has arguably created a

---

The original version of the chapter has been revised. A correction to this chapter can be found at https://doi.org/10.1007/978-3-031-65471-8_13

crisis in collective employee voice which has three main components. First many organisations actively choose to minimise and constrain voice, seeing this as a barrier to change and flexibility. Even in countries where there is regulatory support for information, consultation, co-determination and collective bargaining, organisations sometimes choose to limit the participation of representatives in decision-making. Second, the marginalisation of employment relations means that many HR practitioners and organisational leaders do not have a good understanding of both the benefits of collective voice or the different processes and structures, through which this can be channelled. Third, even when an organisation has existing voice structures or develops new mechanisms, these are not utilised effectively and in a way which encourages meaningful and inclusive dialogue.

As we have argued earlier in this book, collective voice is critical in building trust, a sense of organisational justice and ultimately employee engagement (Purcell, 2014). It is perhaps most effective where there are channels of representative voice via trade unions, complemented by parallel mechanisms to give a voice to those employees who are not union members (Purcell & Hall, 2012). A leading union official that we interviewed for this book argues that a structured approach to collective union voice has real business benefits in helping the organisation to manage change.

> **A union view of collective voice**
>
> "Unions are skilled at assembling collective opinion. They can use this for collective bargaining and are able to agree changes to contracts. For this you need structure and process. Many employers seem to have forgotten that unions help to manage change. Without them, change management is handled very badly. The union provides an independent voice to the organisation, which is so much more powerful than a single employee voice. Collective employment relations is not going away. Even without unions, employees will use social media or other organising tools and adopt a collective approach, but it won't have the structure and process that unions are guided by with employers."

In this chapter, we examine how employee voice is enacted in practice. We explore the different structures and processes that can be used to inform, consult and negotiate and examine the benefits and challenges of developing and sustaining these approaches. However, the existence of structures does not guarantee that employee voices are heard. Therefore, we also discuss what happens within these processes and structures and what organisations can do to ensure that employee voices are not only heard but also shape organisational decision-making.

6.2 Employee Voice in Practice

Most organisations use a range of processes to engage with their workforces. At a basic level, organisations will communicate collectively—sharing information directly or through trade unions, employee representatives or forums such as listening groups. Where there is a need for greater employee involvement in decision-making, a consultation process may be used. Indeed, in many countries, consultation may be a legal requirement in respect of important issues such as redundancy or restructuring. In addition, where employees are represented by trade unions, issues relating to pay and working conditions may be subject to a process of negotiation or collective bargaining.

Defining employee voice

Communication is the exchange of information between the parties, which can be carried out directly or via email and other forms of written and electronic communication.

Consultation is a process whereby issues of mutual concern are jointly discussed and explored by management, and employees or their representatives jointly examine and discuss issues of mutual concern. Managers will ask for the views of employees, and/or their representatives and provide them with adequate relevant information. They will then listen to and consider these views before making a decision.

Co-determination is a process of joint decision-making involving employees. This is often concerned with key issues relating to the level of employment and the nature of working practices. It often operates alongside and complements other employment relations processes such as collective bargaining.

Collective bargaining is a process of negotiation through which management and trade unions will seek to reach agreement on issues related to pay, and terms and conditions of employment.

These definitions help to ensure that the parties are clear about the purpose of a particular meeting and also set the parameters for the specific discussion and the limits of managerial authority. It is important to note that these definitions may vary depending on the national context. For example, some matters which would be subject to consultation in an organisation in the UK, such as restructuring and redundancy, would be subject to co-determination within a German company with a Works Council.

> **Exercise 6.1: Employee voice in your organisation**
>
> Thinking about the organisation that you work in, or an organisation that you are familiar with, how would you categorise the main channels of employee voice based on the above definitions?
>
> How effective are these and are there any ways in which the approach to employee voice could be improved?

The way in which organisations use the voice mechanisms outlined above will vary widely depending on the legal and economic context, and also their strategic orientation (as discussed in Chapter 3). Some organisations will develop multi-layered structures involving consultation and collective bargaining with unions, information-sharing through employee fora and even representation at board level (Rees & Brione, 2023). Others may simply rely on much more basic structures of information and consultation. Whichever approach an organisation adopts, it is vital to ensure that employees can influence the key decisions that affect their working lives.

> **Tip**
>
> Enabling employee voice should never be a token exercise—it is vital that organisations do not simply listen but also act on the concerns of their employees.

6.3 Information and Communication

As set out in Chapter 2, the benefits of employee voice range from better productivity to reduced absence, and dignity and respect in the workplace. To achieve that there needs to be structured and effective communications. The exchange of information and ideas is critical to running any organisation. This means making sure there is a clear and effective mechanism to feed the views and concerns of employees to the most senior stakeholders. However, while many organisations have effective ways to share information from the top down they do not always provide a clear channel for feedback from the 'shopfloor'.

In the context of formal employee engagement, it is vital to know if the topic for discussion is one for information only. These conversations would tend to be about strategic issues which are important for everyone to understand but which are within the control of the senior leaders of the organisation. This could include organisational performance, budgets, market outlook, and major developments and plans. In essence, this provides the broad context which frames more detailed employment relations issues and challenges. Below is an example from an international charity based in the UK, whereby a staff council made up of union and non-union representatives is a forum through which information is shared. In this case, the organisation has separate structures and processes for consultation and negotiation. Therefore, it is important to clearly define the scope of each process.

Information-sharing in the third sector

The role of the Staff Council will be to contribute to the continuous improvement of the organisation and its working environment through the involvement of our people by:

- Sharing information with them about the organisation and our strategy.
- Seeking general views, ideas and 'hot topics' about the organisation through engagement with their representatives.
- Promoting open and timely communication.
- Encouraging a culture of trust.

The case study below provides an example of a more sophisticated approach to information and communication. The organisation based across Europe created an 'Involvement Group' alongside existing trade union structures for consultation and negotiation. This reflects a trend in many large organisations to use dual channels of engagement for union and non-union groups. This can be due to the nature or history of the organisation. But, in some cases it is driven by a decline in union membership and a democratic deficit whereby some groups have no representation or voice. While this case provides for extensive two-way communication and the potential for the organisation to use this in its decision-making, the organisation is not obliged to take these views into account (consultation) or to negotiate with representatives (collective bargaining).

Case study 6.1: Involvement and engagement

The Involvement Group meets monthly and has working groups dedicated to specific issues such as benefits. The organisation has a detailed set of expectations for elected non-union representatives, and the role has a substantial responsibility for communication.

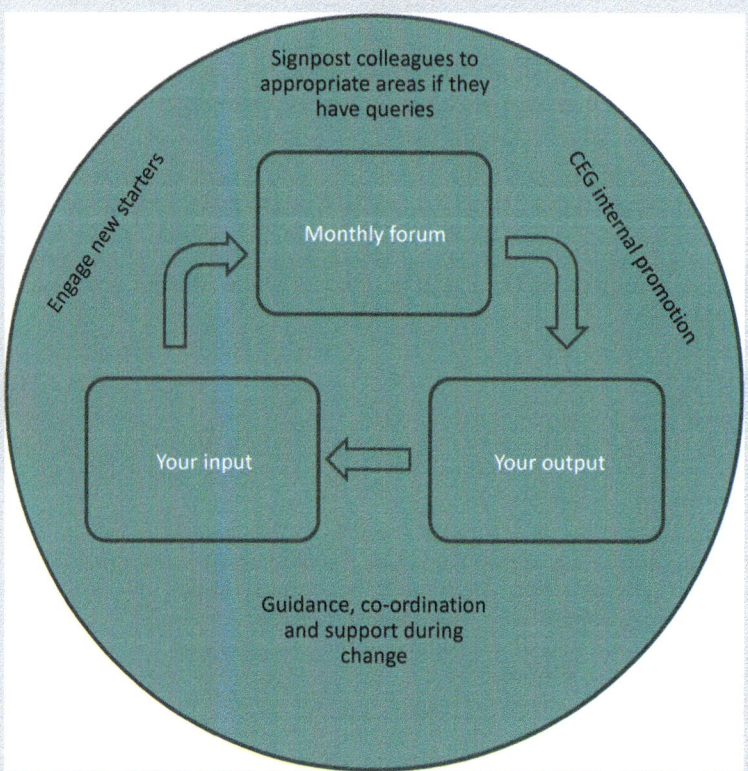

Figure 1 Case Study 6.1 A structure for communication and information sharing

The representatives are expected to meet with functional directors and senior management teams to share feedback and information as well as seek views and opinions from colleagues. They have responsibility for actions from the meetings as well as a formal role during change and signposting colleagues to support when they cannot help. They work closely with other representatives in the Involvement Group and the Human Resources (HR) team and proactively identify issues and ways to resolve them. There is a high level of expectation on the representatives to take actions, share feedback, involve the senior managers in their areas and propose initiatives.

The role of representatives is specified as follows:

- Input into the agenda of the forum and its meetings—challenging where you don't think things will add value and championing where you think they will.
- Seek opinions from colleagues in your business function at every possibility to help you represent their views and ideas in discussions at the meetings.

- Attend and contribute at the monthly forum meetings, plus any working groups you volunteer for and come prepared to give updates on your actions.
- Use the forum as a sounding board for ideas and feedback and encourage others to do so as you come across opportunities in your day-to-day work. Proactively share your best practice examples with the other reps.
- Take ownership of a fair share of actions coming out of the forum meetings or from talking to colleagues.
- Take on the role of meeting Chair and note-taker as allocated. If you can't make your turn, you'll take responsibility for swapping.
- Make sure that your business unit colleagues receive the post-meeting cascade communication within a week and that you follow up on your actions to colleagues.

Key questions

1. What are the benefits and challenges associated with the Involvement Group described in this case?
2. If you were thinking of developing a similar group in your organisation, what would you do to maximise its effectiveness?

The examples discussed so far in this chapter represent very different approaches to employee voice and therefore different structures. Sometimes, the options available to organisations will be limited by the existing arrangements in place, the history of consultation and negotiation in the workplace, and the strategic choices made by leaders. Irrespective of the model, it is important to provide a structure that facilitates a clear route through which issues can be 'laddered' to the top of the organisation and that ensures effective two-way communications. Furthermore, in our experience, where organisations have dual channels of voice, it is important to clarify the role of union consultative and negotiation structures, and non-union fora. Each may cover a different constituency and will bring a different perspective. The best organisations have an open dialogue about how these intersect and what they discuss. They should be complementary rather than competing against each other.

> **Tip**
>
> Non-union fora should not be used to undermine or marginalise trade union voice. If you have trade unions in your organisation but you want to develop a parallel voice channel, it would be beneficial to discuss this with your union representatives.

6.4 Consultation

In our experience many trade union representatives have negative experiences of consultation. They often argue that consultation is merely 'lip service', where the employer asks for their opinion but does what they were going to do in the first place. There is a danger that organisations confuse consultation with communication or simply go through the motions of asking for the views of workers and unions.

Therefore, many countries have specific rules about when consultation between an organisation and its employees must happen and how this should be conducted. In the US, employers are compelled to provide 60 days' notice if intending to close a site or make 'mass layoffs', under the WARN Act. However, there is no legal duty to consult with unions—instead this is left to the specific agreements, or contract, between unions in unionised organisations. In contrast in the UK, there is a legal obligation to consult with recognised trade unions or elected employee representatives if proposing to make 20 or more employees redundant—this should last for a minimum of 30 days or 45 days if 100 or more workers are involved. The scope and nature of these consultations are also specified in the legislation. However, while the consultations should be 'meaningful' there is no obligation to agree and management retains the ultimate decision-making authority.

In Germany, there are complex legal obligations when employers are intending to make collective redundancies. However, employers with Works Councils must seek to negotiate a 'reconciliation agreement' and a 'social plan'. If no agreement can be reached, the matter can be referred to arbitration. This demonstrates the variety of obligations imposed by different legal frameworks within which organisations must operate. It also demonstrates a progression from information to consultation and to negotiation—with each step workers and unions have greater influence on the eventual result and the authority of employers diminishes.

> **Exercise 6.2: A tale of three systems**
>
> Thinking about the different approaches to consultation in the US, UK and Germany, what do you think are the main factors which explain these differences? Which of the three approaches do you prefer and why?

Despite the specific requirements and the complexity of legal frameworks, most consultation deals with day-to-day workplace issues without specific legal implications. In many unionised organisations, the way consultation takes place is set out in collective agreements between the union(s) and the employer(s). Consultation typically takes place over issues including workplace policies, health and safety, working conditions, organisational change and restructuring. The example below is taken from a large public organisation in the UK with a strong union presence.

> **Example of consultation**
>
> For the purposes of this agreement, issues for consultation concerning the bargaining unit include policies on recruitment, diversity and inclusion, anti-bullying and harassment, health and safety, sickness and restructuring. 'Consultation' involves the joint examination and discussion of problems of concern to both management and affected employees, involving a search for mutually acceptable solutions through a genuine exchange of views and information.

The above example highlights that there are formal meetings which are established to discuss such issues. They sit in an overarching hierarchy which enables discussions at the right level within the organisation. In particular, managers and representatives play defined roles in any consultation process. Below is a comparison of the key elements of the roles of representatives and managers taken from a large change programme in the financial services sector.

> **Roles and responsibilities**
>
> **Role of leaders and managers**
>
> - To provide information that is clear, regular and in good time, which allows employees to ask questions to understand the proposals and reasons for change.

- To ensure consultation meetings have clear and relevant agendas and to prepare for the meeting in a professional and considered way. To chair the meeting effectively, follow-up on actions and next steps, and put in place arrangements for feeding back.
- To respond to requests for information in a timely way to allow the consultation to proceed effectively and to be open and helpful. Where a request for more information is refused, leaders and managers should explain why this is the case.
- To ensure consultation is early enough to allow employee representatives the opportunity to influence the outcome of the proposal before key decisions are taken. And if a proposal from representatives is not implemented, the reasons for the rejection should be explained.
- To provide employee representatives sufficient time and resources to collect the views of colleagues and provide a structured response.

Role of representatives

- To understand the organisational context, the industry it operates in and the future plans and where relevant procedures and agreements.
- To communicate openly, effectively and share information. Put in place mechanisms for two-way communication to hear and understand concerns of colleagues—represent views accurately and honestly.
- To be honest about problems, with both leaders and co-workers.
- To be professional in discussions and when feeding back to colleagues.
- To be reliable, clear and structured in your approach.

Implicit in the defined roles played by managers and representatives is the benefit of consultation to all parties. When it is done well, consultation provides a clear route to reaching a decision, a mechanism for proposals to be tested, changed and understood. It ensures a voice for those that the decision impacts. Managers don't have a monopoly on good ideas and well managed consultation ensures different perspectives are considered, different options are evaluated and ultimately decision-making is improved.

In 2020, the Covid-19 pandemic provided a unique challenge and a new lens through which to view consultation. A new external threat which needed a significant response at short notice created a number of dynamics which help to explore the themes above. The example below uses interviews with key personnel from a professional services organisation to explore how the employment relations team and union representatives approached these unique circumstances.

Case study 6.2: Consultation at a time of crisis

"At the start of the pandemic it was chaos. No-one guessed what was going to happen. One day it was business as usual and the next everyone was working from home. Things were moving so quickly; it was impossible to keep up. We had to massively increase the number of meetings we had and the level of communication with employee representatives. We had multiple meetings each week, sometimes more than once a day.

Once lockdowns started, we knew this was a medium-term issue. From that point we started sharing all our communications and FAQs with the union reps. This was vital given the public health and safety implications and we frequently tweaked the tone of the messages on the back of their feedback. The unions provided a very important source of information on how staff were feeling and behaving on the ground. There were some employees who had significant concerns about team members with Covid and what they should do, in particular, where people were clinically vulnerable. There were also breaches of rules such as colleagues who weren't following the guidance on the maximum number of people in the lift. We would target specific teams or managers and ensure the reps knew how we were approaching it. Working with the reps we increased communications overall; the feeling was that this was reassuring and the pace we worked at meant there was an acknowledgement we had done the right thing.

As we moved through the pandemic, the meetings we had in place became embedded and moved to a more proactive focus. One of the areas this worked really well was in relation to potential issues; we knew there was going to be a greater level of working in the office and assumed there would be a lack of consistency. When planning the return to physical workplaces, we created some high-level principles to guide employees, managers and leaders. With some basic data we were also able to look at any themes, address the underlying issues and escalate problems so they could be resolved informally but quickly. We didn't always agree. There were significant issues about providing home office equipment. However, we reached a compromise which meant there was a basic provision in place for everyone.

Keeping the unions up to date during Covid-19 meant they were able to answer questions from their members and explain the reasons for the approach which was being taken. They were able to prevent rumours from spreading. They also brought best practice from other employers and made some really positive suggestions. Realistically, some of our employees trusted the unions more and to hear them saying the same things as the organisation and sharing the same sources of information really increased the credibility of the messaging. No-one would choose to go through it again but it was an example of working together constructively and achieving a significant improvement for all our employees."

Key questions

1. How would you describe the employer's approach?
2. How would you describe the approach of the union representatives?
3. What would you have done during this period to ensure staff were consulted and informed?

> 4. How would the employer have got this feedback about employee sentiment without the trade unions?

The above example does not mention specific meeting structures or processes. There is no consideration of legal requirements and the risks and potential costs of failing to consult. There is open and constructive dialogue. Ultimately, whatever the formal structures and processes in place, the approach and the attitudes of the parties is a critical success factor. It is vital that senior managers share information in advance of meetings to facilitate meaningful consultation and discussion. However, they should also extend access to information to a wide range of issues such as "financial performance, strategic plans and HR policies" (Purcell & Hall, 2012: 10). Firms who 'actively consult' in this way provide the time, space, and opportunity for representatives to be included and have a meaningful chance to influence decisions.

> **Tip**
> Good consultation takes place before a final decision is made. It should be an open and honest exchange of views between management and union representatives. Although management has the right to make the final decision, this needs to be properly explained and well-reasoned.

6.5 Co-determination

An alternative model is Germany's dual system of employment regulation, supported by a detailed legal framework (Jacobi et al., 1998) balancing regulation and market forces (Hyman, 2001: 116). Under the Co-Determination Act 1976, organisations with five or more employees must establish a Works Council if requested by employees. Its size and function depends on the extent of the organisation. Although Works Councils do not collectively bargain pay and conditions, they have a wide range of rights to information, consultation and co-determination. Issues subject to co-determination include:

- Working hours and overtime and policies relating to holiday.
- Introduction and application of new technology.

- Application of wages structure and allocation of bonuses and performance-related benefits.
- Hiring, transfers and dismissals.
- Restructuring.

Matters subject to co-determination must be agreed and if no agreement is reached, they can be subject to arbitration. Works Councils have strong powers in relation to decisions over employment changes. For example, they must be consulted before each dismissal. In addition, if the employer is considering restructuring, they must reach agreement on the way in which this is to be implemented and what measures could be put in place to mitigate the impact on affected employees. In addition to Works Councils, German companies with more than 500 employees must have a Supervisory Board, with one-third of the members elected by employees (or 50%

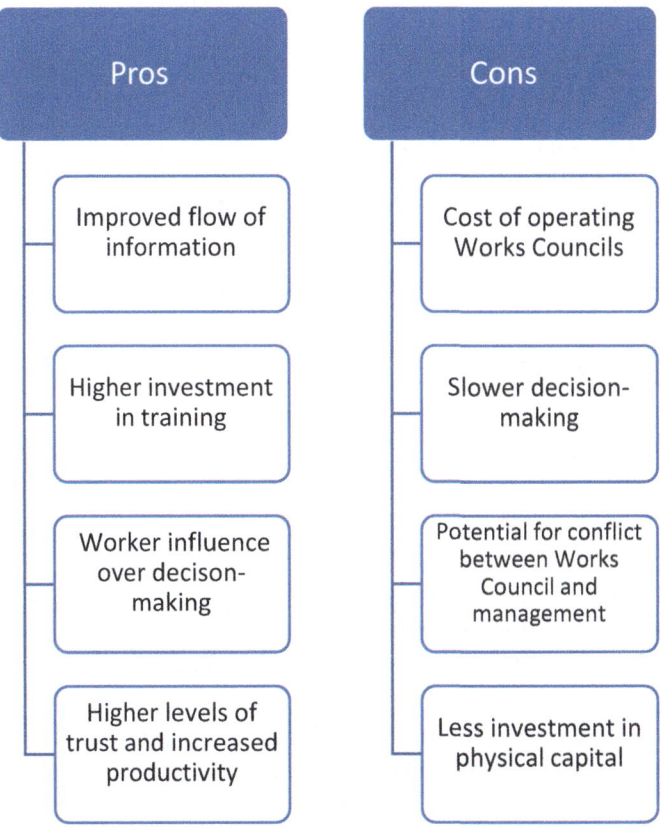

Fig. 6.1 Pros and cons of works councils (Based on: Hubler [2015])

for firms employing more than 2000 workers). The Supervisory Board is not responsible for the day-to-day running of the company; however, it supervises and monitors the work of the main management board and controls appointments and remuneration. The potential advantages and disadvantages of Works Councils are set out in Fig. 6.1.

A wide-ranging survey of the empirical evidence on the impacts of Works Councils in Germany (Mohrenweiser, 2022) suggests that they have positive impacts on productivity—potentially related to higher levels of firm-specific training, greater collaboration leading to incremental innovation and lower levels of staff turnover. However, the evidence in relation to profitability and employment growth is more mixed. It has also been argued that the German system of collective voice, together with sectoral collective bargaining, have contributed to relatively low levels of conflict (Jacobi et al, 1998). Despite the largely positive effects of Works Councils, their use has contracted and they covered just 10% of organisations in 2011 and 44% of workers in 2013 (IFO Institute, 2015), similar to comparable figures for the UK noted in Chapter 2.

> **Exercise 6.3: The German system**
>
> What are the main benefits of the German system of co-determination? If your organisation was to adopt a similar approach with a Works Council playing a substantial role, what challenges and problems would you envisage?

6.6 Managing Structures

So far in this chapter, we have outlined the different structures that are available to organisations. We now turn to how employee voice is enacted, with a particular focus on management-union interactions. As we noted above, HR practitioners often have a perception that these meetings are difficult and adversarial. However, it doesn't need to be this way—this section goes on to look at two very different ways to engage with workers and trade unions and listen to employee voice. Firstly, we take an example from the transport industry and then we look at how meetings are managed. Although we look at bargaining and negotiation in more depth in Chapter 7, it is useful to see how the two processes combine within an overall approach to collective voice.

Case study 6.3: Negotiation and consultation in a unionised transport company in the UK

As a result of high levels of unionisation and historical patterns of conflict there is a very structured and hierarchical framework of meetings. There are also separate bodies reflecting the needs of a number of distinct occupational groups.

Figure 1 Case Study 6.3 sets out the key levels where trade union consultation and negotiation take place. At the organisational level, consultation and negotiation takes place at the Joint Negotiating Committee (JNC), where representatives and officials from four different unions meet quarterly with senior management to negotiate company-wide issues such as pay, and any other issues escalated from a lower level. These meetings would also discuss the strategic direction of the organisation. This is a highly formal meeting where name places, detailed minutes and who can attend are important details.

Below this level there are seven occupational groups where issues relevant to those workers are discussed. There may be some limited collective bargaining over working conditions and practices, however most of the discussion takes the form of consultation. In the event of a dispute, issues can be escalated to a meeting at director level. If the issue is still not resolved, it can be referred to the JNC or to the Advisory Conciliation and Arbitration Service (Acas—a UK government agency, which mediates and conciliates industrial disputes). Whilst there is less formality than the JNC, there is still a large focus on minutes, attendees and the actions from each meeting.

Underneath this, consultation takes place at a local level discussing issues at specific offices, units and depots. There are generally good relationships at the local level and some scope to resolve issues and problems for staff working in that area. There is less formality, more regular engagement and the frequency of communications will depend on the strength of local management and the local representatives. The quality of these fora varies widely depending on the managers and representatives involved. In total in this organisation there are over 350 formal meetings a year.

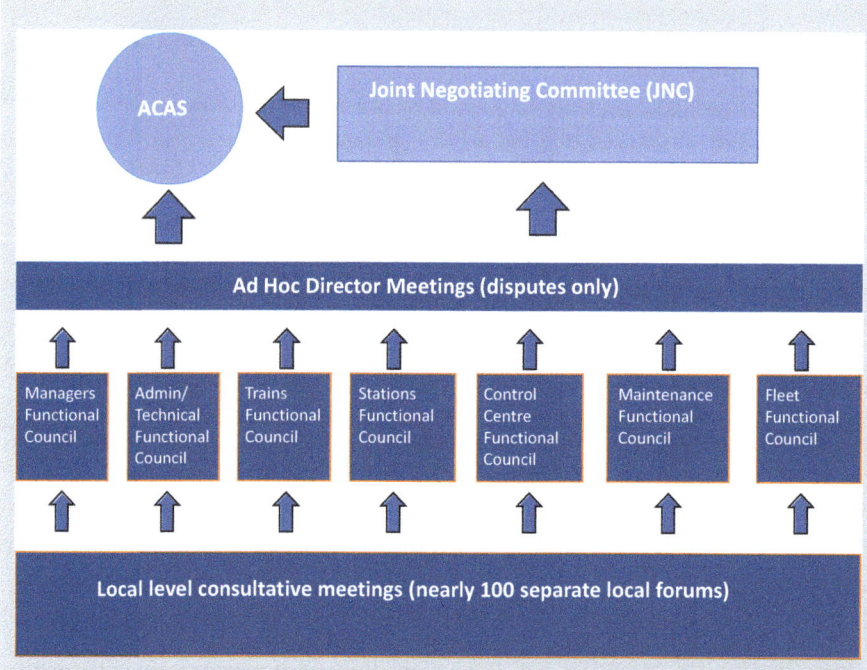

Figure 1 Case Study 6.3 Consultation and negotiation structure

Key questions

1. What are the main benefits of this type of approach to collective voice?
2. What are the main limitations of this approach?
3. What can this organisation do to maximise the effectiveness of this approach?

Case study 6.3 is an example of a traditional approach to consultation and negotiation in a unionised setting in the UK. However, in most organisations there will be large numbers of staff who are not members of a trade union and there is a danger that these 'voices' are not heard. Consequently, even in a unionised setting, there is a case for developing parallel channels of voice.

Exercise 6.4: Declining union membership and democratic deficit

You have just started in the role of an employment relations specialist in a large organisation which recognises trade unions for all employees. Over the last five years union density has declined to around 40% overall and in some areas you believe it is as low as 15%. You don't have any up to date membership figures. Evaluate the benefits of creating a channel for non-union voice.

> How could this be implemented without damaging relationships with your trade unions?

6.7 The Management of Meetings

Whilst the structures you have in place to inform and consult are important, what happens in them (and informally outside them) may be more critical in determining the success of the discussions. In Chapter 3, we explained the importance of taking an intentional and purposeful approach when developing employment relations strategy. The same purposeful approach applies to meetings whether they are for informing or consulting. Without thought and planning, they will be less effective. Senior leaders need to be clear about the purpose of the meetings and how they wish to engage their employees and their representatives in them.

The reality is that leaders, managers and unions can have very mixed experiences of meetings. We asked a number of HR professionals what words they would use to describe meetings which took place in their organisations with employee representatives. As can be seen in Fig. 6.2, many of the dominant adjectives used are negative—'emotive', 'heated', 'unpredictable' and 'challenging'. This environment will not create effective meetings where people feel listened to, or problems get solved.

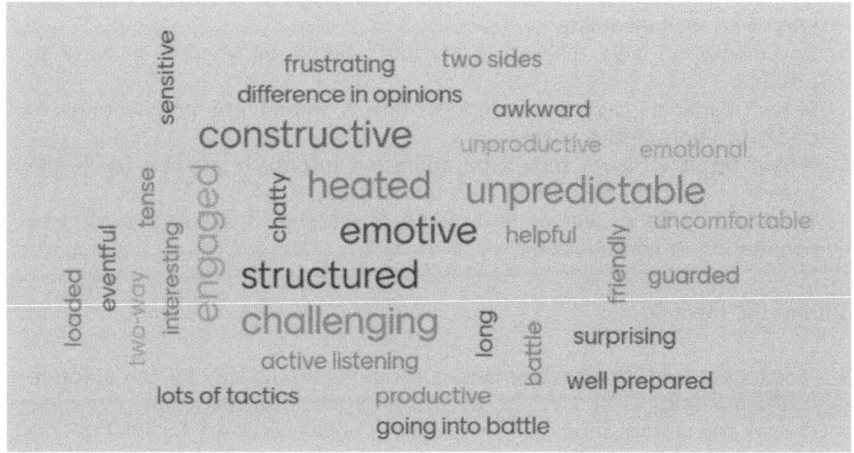

Fig. 6.2 What words would you use to describe management-union meetings?

On the positive side, meetings with representatives are also described as "constructive", "engaged" with "active listening". Treating them like any other business meeting is critical. They must have a clear purpose, promote behaviours which encourage listening, be accepting of differences of opinions, and a focus on actions which help the organisation, and its people move forward. The next case study describes the journey taken by one organisation to improve employment relations through more effective joint meetings.

Case study 6.4: More effective meetings, better employment relations

The background

This private sector employer was highly unionised and industrial action was a significant risk factor for the business. Following a review, low quality meetings were identified by both management and unions as having a significant negative impact on the employment relations climate. All parties provided examples of unhelpful meeting behaviours such as lateness, poor attendance and taking calls/working on laptops/texting in meetings. Disrespectful behaviour on both sides was also a common occurrence. Meetings were often cancelled or were not supported by proper documentation. It was agreed that improving meetings was an important first step in developing more effective employment relations. To that end, a group of union representatives and managers devised a set of meeting principles to guide all union-management meetings.

Before the meeting

- Clear objectives and agreed agenda items should be set with realistic timescales.
- Standing agenda items should be agreed.
- Only relevant parties should be invited, reducing the size of meetings and improving manageability.
- Documentation and relevant invitations should be shared as early as possible.
- Senior managers and union representatives should use pre-meetings to clarify positions and prepare.
- Where possible, issues should be addressed informally at local level—the agenda should not be packed with minor issues.
- There should be a clear understanding of whether issues were subject to negotiation or consultation.

During the meeting

- Meetings should start on time and participants should stay for the duration of the meeting.
- Phones and laptops should be switched off, unless necessary for the business of the meeting.
- Internal politics should not intrude on the conduct of meetings.

- There should be a clear commitment to work together to resolve issues, and honesty and integrity at all times.
- Any agreed actions and resolutions should have clear timescales.
- Where there is no clear resolution, consideration should be given to a problem-solving format outside the meeting.
- Participants should listen to other parties with respect—confrontational styles are not acceptable and will be challenged.
- All parties should feel free to contribute and participate—sharing of ideas and experiences should be encouraged.
- Confidential information should be respected, and all joint communications agreed.
- Meetings will finish on time—important topics should be disciplined to finish on time and prioritised, with unfinished business carried over.

After the meeting

- Agreed minutes will be produced within agreed reasonable timescales.
- Chair of the meeting should be alternated.

The benefits

These changes resulted in increased trust, respect and honesty when dealing with employment relations issues. Better decisions are made when all parties are well-informed, opinions are listened to, and all parties have their say in an effective meeting. This helps leaders and the unions to deliver change.

Key questions

1. To what extent are the principles outlined above followed in the meetings that you participate in?
2. How could the meetings in your organisation be improved?

If meetings between management and representatives are going to provide a genuine reflection of employee voice, it is crucial that they are inclusive and reflect the diversity of the workforce. Unfortunately, power structures and privilege can create an unhealthy dynamic. Meetings are often dominated by senior male colleagues whose views are prioritised, while women, people from minoritised groups and more junior representatives, are ignored and side-lined. One way to address these issues is to design and apply specific meeting principles.

> **Important**
>
> **Good practice for running effective meetings**
> - **Good preparation and management buy-in** are crucial.
> - **Clear structures and mechanisms for escalation** to ensure the focus is on the right challenges with the right people in the room, talking about the issues of concern to them.
> - **Effective agenda management.** Enable employee representatives to put forward agenda items in advance and encourage union representatives to explain why something is on the agenda.
> - **Avoid long lists of any other business** which can derail the agenda. Any other business (AOB) should be for exceptional circumstances only.
> - **Share information and documentation** in good time so that participants can contribute effectively.
> - **Ensure attendees are representative of all colleagues.** For example, are those in field/operational-based roles able to participate fully?
> - **Review the language and practices used** to make sure that everyone has a voice and that meetings are inclusive.
> - **Regularly review meeting effectiveness** to make sure it is meeting its objectives.

Meeting discipline which encourages contribution from all parties can be an effective way to increase participation and get a range of different views. The chair of the meeting should make sure that no one person or team dominates and that the stage is set for an inclusive and open meeting.

Thinking about different ways for participants to contribute is key. Large meetings can be intimidating (another reason to keep them small) and those with specific communication preferences may struggle to receive information.

> **Tip**
> - Confirm in advance the tone of the meeting. Come ready to share as well as listen.
> - Assign attendees a role to play in the meeting or a specific perspective to explore or articulate.
> - Establish that no one speaks twice until everyone has spoken once.
> - Agree that the most senior person at the meeting speaks last.
> - Get participants to write down their view before discussing.

In our experience, a combination of effective structures throughout the organisation, which capture the views of diverse groups, alongside respectful behaviours which promote listening and dignity, are vital in creating good employment relations.

6.8 Training, Facilities and Time to Participate

One of the key factors in effective collective voice is ensuring the resources are in place so it is done well. As set out above, the benefits are clear. However, line managers may consider time for training and consultation as absence from the day job. Training is critical—not only is it important to understand the topic under discussion (such as redundancy) but also to understand how the organisation works and to have the ability to understand and interpret financial information. To contribute and challenge, employee representatives will need training in these areas and the softer skills such as listening and questioning. This is particularly important for non-union representatives. Union representatives will normally receive a substantial amount of training from their own trade unions. For employee voice to be effective, it is essential that representatives have the skills and confidence to take part in discussions on equal terms with managers. They also need to be able to understand and analyse the information being provided to them. If representatives are not adequately trained, they are likely to play a passive role and meetings will be reduced to exercises in communication. While this may be comfortable for senior managers, it represents a missed opportunity for the organisation.

Figure 6.3 provides an example of a skills matrix developed by a large organisation which realised the need to train its non-union employee representatives ahead of a large change programme. However, training alone is not enough. To help put their skills into practice, time away from their day-to-day role is needed. Representatives will need to be released from their role for training but also to engage in meetings, to seek views before and to give feedback after meetings. It is important this is prioritised and the approach by the organisation and senior managers will signal the value that they place on employee voice.

Understanding who you are training, why you are training them and providing those representatives with adequate time sends a clear message that their role is important to the organisation—this recognition is also a key ingredient in building trust as we saw in Chapter 5. All organisations will find there is a tension between operational delivery and time off for employee and trade union representatives to attend meetings. This investment is crucial, as is getting the structures right, making the meetings inclusive and productive, and having clear outcomes. These will all help to demonstrate the tangible (and intangible) benefits.

Finally, employee representatives will need resources and tools to help them to establish themselves and work with their colleagues. Physical issues need to be considered such as meeting space and technology (e.g. phones or laptops).

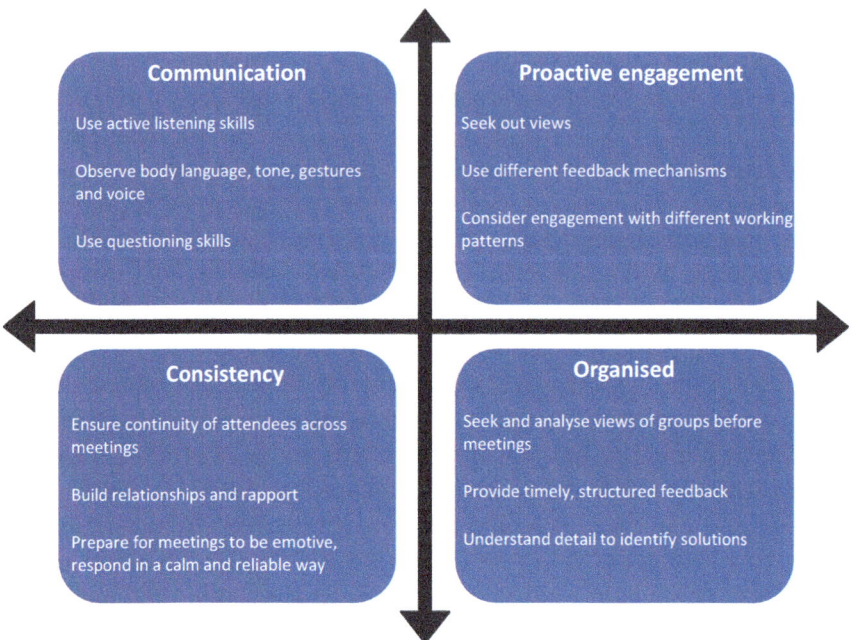

Fig. 6.3 Skills needed by employee representatives

Increasingly, considerations such as data protection, confidentiality and access to information need to be fully considered. It is unlikely representatives will be locking paperwork in drawers or cupboards and online storage options may need to be considered.

6.9 Conclusion

The distance between the theory (and benefits) and practice of employee voice seems to be increasing annually. Conflict over the cost-of-living highlights a very emotive example of the gap between perceived and actual representation. This growing representation gap also reflects a 'philosophy gap' when it comes to employee voice. Employees and their representatives want more involvement and participation in decision-making, but employers are reluctant to share power and surrender authority and control. However, this approach is self-defeating—it undermines trust, which in turn has a negative impact on employee engagement and ultimately performance. Where unions are in decline, employers are increasingly looking at other ways to listen to employee voice including online tools such as Viva Engage. Where you have meetings they should be effective and represent a clear choice by leaders. This chapter has not only explored the benefits of collective employee voice but has also explained why some organisations have the structures they do, what can be done to improve them and how information-sharing and consultation takes place. However, the most carefully defined structures and systems will fail if the practice of conducting effective meetings is ignored or taken for granted.

> **Questions**
> 1. What are the main organisational benefits of creating effective structures for collective voice?
> 2. Discuss the main differences between the German and UK approaches to collective employee voice—what are the main lessons for policy and practice that you draw from this comparison?
> 3. How can negative behaviours undermine management-union meetings? What are the main principles that you would advise an organisation to adopt to ensure more effective meetings?

References

Addison, J. T., & Teixeira, P. (2021). What Do Workers Want? The Representation Gap at the EU Establishment as Perceived by their Workplace Representatives. In S. W. Polachek, K. Tatsiramos, G. Russo, & G. van Houten (Eds.). *Workplace Productivity and Management Practices (Research in Labor Economics, Vol. 49)*. Emerald Publishing Limited.

Hübler, O. (2015). Do Works Councils Raise or Lower Firm Productivity? IZA World of Labor. 137 [Online]. https://wol.iza.org/articles/do-works-councils-raise-or-lower-firm-productivity/long [Accessed 21/11/2023].

Hyman, R. (2001). *Understanding European Trade Unionism: Between Market, Class and Society*. Sage.

IFO Institute. (2015). *Workplace Representation in Europe: Works Councils and their Economic Effects on Firms*. [Online]. https://www.ifo.de/DocDL/dice-report-2015-4-oesingmann-december.pdf [Accessed 2/12/2023].

Jacobi, O., Keller, B., & Muller-Jentsch, W. (1998). Germany: Facing New Challenges. In A. Ferner & R. Hyman (Eds.), *Changing Industrial Relations in Europe*. Blackwell.

Mohrenweiser, J. (2022). Works Councils. *GLO Discussion Paper, No. 1103*. Global Labor Organization (GLO).

Purcell, J. (2014). Employee Voice and Engagement. In C. Truss, R. Delbridge, K. Alfes, A. Shantz, & E. Soanne (Eds.), *Employee Engagement in Theory and Practice*. Routledge.

Purcell, J., & Hall, M. (2012). *Voice and Participation in the Modern Workplace: Challenges and Prospects (Acas Future of Workplace Relations Discussion Paper Series)*. Acas.

Rees, C., & Brione, P. (2023). Employee Voice at Board Level: Responses to the Revised UK Corporate Governance Code and the Prospects for Workplace Democracy. *Economic and Industrial Democracy, Advance Online Publication.* https://doi.org/10.1177/0143831X231195692

Towers, B. (1997). *The Representation Gap: Change and Reform in the British and American Workplace*. Oxford Academic. https://doi.org/10.1093/acprof:oso/9780198289463.001.0001

7

Negotiation in Collective Employment Relations

Abstract Negotiation is a critical process in collective employment relations and can lead to agreements on a range of issues of importance to employers and their workforce. Fraught negotiation is often a stereotype of collective employment relations, especially where unions are recognised. This has been evident in many high-profile and difficult negotiations held between employers and unions in many countries since the global pandemic. This chapter aims to take the reader through a series of steps to ensure negotiation is constructive and helps the parties to move towards an acceptable solution where possible. It focuses on practical issues such as planning, team selection, the main stages of a negotiation and the final agreement. It provides examples of how negotiation works in different industries. The chapter also helps practitioners and students reflect on their own style and the style of others. The chapter ends with a discussion on the difference between negotiating approaches which focus on win–win rather than win-lose.

Keywords Planning · Conflict style · Negotiation · Distributive bargaining · Integrative bargaining · Collective bargaining

7.1 Introduction

In Chapter 6, we explored the ways in which organisations can use different approaches to communicate and consult with their employees and their representatives. We argued that involving workers in shaping the decisions that affect their working lives is crucial in building trust, engagement and organisational justice. Moreover, collective channels of representation are vital in negotiating and maintaining the employment relationship. In most organisations, it is neither practical nor efficient for managers to negotiate change with individual workers, however representatives can articulate the concerns and interests of workers and seek to reach agreement through a process of collective bargaining. Some of the classic stereotypes of management-union negotiations revolve around images of middle-aged men in smoky rooms arguing. However, most interactions between trade unions and employers are nothing like this. Nonetheless these images also reflect negative perceptions of collective bargaining which developed as the scale and scope of collective bargaining declined. At the same time, we have seen a fundamental erosion in the capacity of organisations to negotiate effectively and in a way which minimises conflict and maintains high-trust employment relations. Therefore, in this chapter, we will introduce the core concepts that underpin collective bargaining and take a close look at how these can be applied in a contemporary setting. We will explore the roles which the main parties play in bargaining processes and examine how a greater understanding of our own styles (and understanding those of others) can help reach an agreement. Furthermore, we will identify different bargaining approaches and discuss how organisations can develop more constructive and integrative approaches to negotiating change.

7.2 The Third Core Process—Negotiation

In the previous chapter, we discussed the importance of structures for collective voice in information-sharing and consultation. These structures can facilitate and encourage discussions at a practical level and provide a forum for bargaining and negotiation to take place. However, high inflation, tight labour markets and increasing dissatisfaction with work has led to workers looking towards union organisation and demanding improvements in their pay and conditions. This has been particularly challenging for Human Resource (HR) practitioners and managers who had become used to dealing with largely passive workforces and unions denuded of power. Consequently, they often do not have the experience of having to engage in detailed and emotive negotiations on issues such as pay. This has meant having to rediscover the core processes of employment relations.

As we suggested in Chapter 6, it is critical to be very clear about which of the three key processes—information sharing, consultation or negotiation—you are engaging in. There are legal differences between sharing information, consulting and negotiating, which vary from country to country. There will also be specific points in union recognition agreements and processes which need to be followed. Entering a discussion with a very clear view of which you are engaging in and what outcome you want or need (and why), is extremely important and we will look at each of these in turn. However, your approach will need to align with the legal environment, your organisational structures, your strategic approach and the behaviours and values which you prioritise as an organisation. There is a huge range of material written about negotiation and bargaining, and for practitioners developing their skills in this area it can seem daunting. Negotiation tends to be associated with conflict as Fig. 7.1 illustrates. This word cloud is based on an activity we conducted with the delegates on our Employment Relations Development Programme, when we asked them to tell us the words they associate with negotiation.

It is notable that almost all of these words are negative and suggest an adversarial, competitive and confrontational process. For managers and practitioners educated and trained within a unitarist frame of reference, which dominates contemporary Human Resource Management (HRM), the very idea of negotiation feels very alien. However, at its core, negotiation is simply a process of communication with a defined structure and a target outcome. Moreover, the language and acronyms which have emerged around this field can make it seem very inaccessible. Some of these concepts over-complicate negotiation processes and do not help identify the strategy or approach which should be adopted. They often focus too much on tactics and winning. It is more important to have a clear idea of what you want (or need) to achieve, and to understand how it contributes to your overall strategy and what the

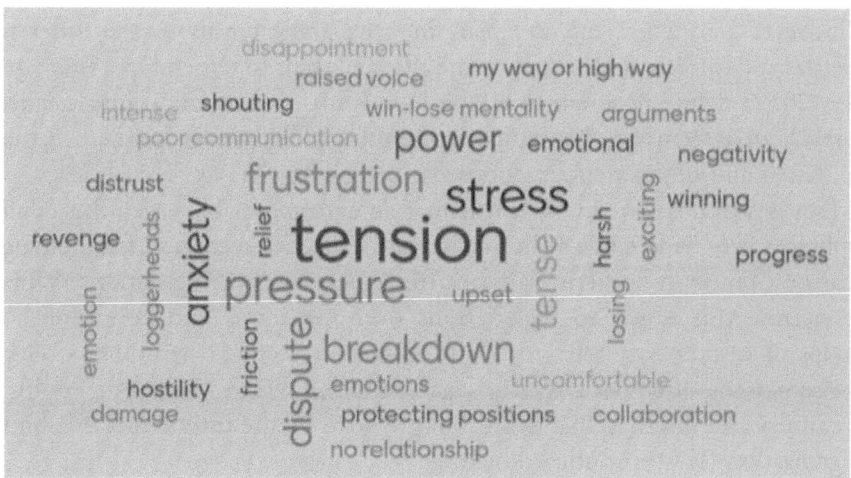

Fig. 7.1 What words do you associate with negotiation?

boundaries for that are. Three of the most widely used concepts in negotiation are explained below. These definitions set out some of the common language with a practical basis.

> **Common negotiation terminology**
>
> **BATNA** (best alternative to a negotiated agreement)—this is the price/cost of the alternatives available to you. This is easier to calculate in a straightforward commercial negotiation. In an employment relations context, the alternatives such as public relations damage, low morale and strike action can be hard to quantify. If you want to buy a car, and you know that there are many available to you from a range of car dealers—you will have a wide range of alternatives—the lowest price you can find will be your best alternative.
>
> **ZOPA** (zone of potential agreement)—this is the range where an agreement may be possible. Again, this is easier to do in a financial/commercial scenario. There may be competing priorities and subjective issues which arise from the discussions. In the scenario where an organisation is closing a facility, there may be a very limited ZOPA.
>
> **BAFO** (best and final offer)—during any negotiation, the point beyond which either party cannot go will be reached and they will need to make their best and final offer. It is more often the employer who makes this statement. The most common mistake is that people claim that they have made their BAFO, only to increase it later or after stakeholders have changed the parameters. If you are going to use this language, you must not increase your offer again or you will risk losing credibility.

One of the key things to remember with the tools and terminology around negotiation is that the underlying logic and preparation are crucial. Whichever acronyms you use, planning and thinking about the different agendas and interests in the process are the vital skills to remember. Fisher and Ury (2012) define negotiation as "back-and-forth communication designed to reach an agreement when you and the other side have some interests that are shared and others that are opposed".

This is a discussion aimed at reaching an agreement. However, this could apply to a very wide range of individual and collective scenarios, from buying a car or a house to brokering a peace treaty between warring nations. When we narrow this down to negotiations over the terms and conditions of groups of workers, we refer to this process as collective bargaining. Collective bargaining often has a specific legal definition which varies from country to country. An international definition provided by the International Labour Organisation (ILO) is outlined below.

The ILO defines collective bargaining as:

"all negotiations which take place between an employer, a group of employers or one or more employers' organisations, on the one hand, and one or more workers' organisations, on the other, for:

(a) determining working conditions and terms of employment; and/or
(b) regulating relations between employers and workers; and/or
(c) regulating relations between employers or their organisations and a workers' organisation or workers' organisations". (Convention 154, Article 2)

The issues which are subject to collective bargaining (the scope) are described in very broad terms in the ILO definition. However, these will be set out in much more detail in recognition agreements between employers and trade unions, which set out the bargaining procedure and process. In contexts where trade unions have significant power, the scope of collective bargaining tends to be relatively wide but where they have less influence, employers will often try to limit collective bargaining to core issues such as pay and working hours. This is illustrated in the following two examples drawn from the transport and housing sectors.

The Scope of Collective Bargaining

Transport

The following collective bargaining issues for negotiation are within the purpose and remit of this agreement. For the purposes of this agreement, negotiation is defined as a discussion set up or intended to produce a settlement or agreement between the Company and trade union representatives:

- Pay awards—i.e. basic pay/ salary as defined in the individual's employment contract
- Terms and conditions of employment as outlined in an individual's employment contract, namely:
    o Contractual hours of work
    o Holiday entitlement
    o Collective agreements
- Collective grievances raised by the unions on behalf of their members in respect of the above issues can only be discussed by the Company Negotiating Council.

> **Housing**
>
> Collective bargaining will only take place on the issues of pay, hours, holiday, pensions and other contractual terms and conditions. This will happen with a subset of the recognised union representatives drawn from the Joint Council.

7.3 Pay Negotiation—A Worked Example

In this section, we will explore the key steps to take when undertaking a pay negotiation in a unionised environment. This is rooted in the experience of collective bargaining in a voluntarist model but the specific steps can be deployed in any workplace negotiation.

We use the Hollywood Writers Guild as a template to assess the different stages of the negotiation process and what aspects you need to consider. The contract negotiation between the Writers Guild of America (WGA) and the Alliance of Motion Picture and Television Producers (AMPTP) started in November 2022 with the announcement of the team who would represent the writers.

The 2023 negotiation was set to be a contentious one, as the online streaming model had led to discontent among writers who were concerned about how they are paid by streaming services for these projects, as well as small writers' rooms that work during the development process, before official writers' rooms convene. The contract was due to expire on 1 May 2023. While this case study is specific to contract negotiations in the USA, which have different basic procedures, we have drawn out the key practical considerations which are applicable in most unionised contexts.

7.3.1 Planning a Negotiation

While the focus of many observers is on the "cut and thrust" and outcome of negotiation, most of the foundations are laid during the preparation before the bargaining begins. Before invites for meetings are even sent, a significant amount of work must go into the planning and preparation for the discussions. The first step is to establish the parameters of the negotiation—for example in a pay negotiation, the employer's negotiating team needs to know how much money is available and what the key issues are. Therefore, they will need to liaise with key stakeholders who can provide information and advice so the negotiation strategy can begin to be framed. The HR director

7 Negotiation in Collective Employment Relations

or employment relations lead will usually be responsible for managing this process and making sure all internal stakeholders are engaged.

> **Tip**
> It is important the negotiating team is aware of the resource implications for potential negotiating outcomes, so that any eventual agreement can be fully implemented.

For a pay negotiation in large organisations, this process will normally include writing a board paper, including the organisational context and how this fits with the wider strategy. It will also include what the projected budget is to finalise the negotiation, the wider economic environment and what competitors are doing. It will outline other non-financial elements which may be part of the discussions and the timelines and approach for the discussions. Once discussions start, it may be necessary to revisit the mandate with the board and a mechanism to do this should be agreed in advance.

Sometimes the "horse-trading" required within the management team can be harder than the negotiation with the unions. This may mean navigating the organisation's politics and ensuring that stakeholder management is a strong focus of your approach. Notwithstanding the internal processes and governance, having a clear narrative for what you want to achieve, and why, is critical.

> **Negotiation planning template**
>
> Table 7.1 provides an example of a template that can be used in planning pay negotiations with unions. While the specific issues outlined in the template will vary depending on the scope of the negotiation and the context, many will be relevant to the majority of pay negotiations with unions such as an analysis of the external environment, the employee groups covered, the mandate, the team and meeting dates.

Table 7.1 Example: negotiating planning template

Bargaining unit/staff group	Drivers, warehouse operatives
Reason for mandate	Pay negotiations
Scope of mandate	Base pay, non-consolidated lump sum, non-pay items (e.g. flexible shift work)
Current budget	% of total and £
Mandate sought	% increase and £
Risk of industrial action	Low/medium/high
Impact of industrial action	Low/medium/high
Financial considerations	Financial performance and future cost pressures (e.g. fuel prices)
Benchmarks	Internal and external pay awards
Inflation forecast	History of pay agreements vs inflation
Negotiation items (employer)	List of employer priorities with £ value, feasibility and red lines
Negotiation items (union)	List of assumed/confirmed union priorities with £ value, feasibility and red lines
Negotiation team	Roles, responsibilities, RACI, union rep availability
Meeting schedule	Insert dates – are all dates communicated or some held as placeholders as contingency
Implementation process	Operational impact, payroll timelines, communications, union ballot process

In highly unionised sectors such negotiations will be captured on the corporate risk register. The appetite for risk and potential industrial action will inform the approach and the flexibility required to reach an agreement. Understanding the bargaining power of both parties is critical to a successful negotiation and also to managing expectations of stakeholders such as the board.

> **Tip**
> As well as considering who needs to be in the negotiating team, also consider who needs to be kept informed or consulted as the negotiations progress.

> **Exercise 7.1: Assessing bargaining power**
> You are an employment relations specialist working in the US for a large vehicle manufacturer, which operates across 10 countries in the US, UK, Europe and South America. Between 2020 and 2022, inflation increased from 1 to 6%, but has now fallen to 4% and is expected to fall further next year. The cost of living, including energy prices and housing costs, have increased sharply in the last two years. Since the pandemic, recruitment and retention has been

7   Negotiation in Collective Employment Relations   139

> challenging and absenteeism has increased. Trade union organisation is high at the plants for which you are responsible, although in recent years there has been no major strike action and your relationship with the trade unions is generally good. The union has submitted a claim asking for a 10% pay rise for the current year.
> What is your assessment of the bargaining power of the employer and unions in this scenario and the potential risk of industrial action? What further information would help you to make a more accurate assessment?

The employer needs to try to assess the ability and likelihood that the trade union could take effective industrial action—this will be based on the strength of union organisation, membership levels, and levels of dissatisfaction and anger within the workforce. Employer bargaining power revolves around the nature of the product or service and whether industrial action can cause significant disruption and unrecoverable losses. For example, companies that provide passenger transport are vulnerable to strike action because cancelled journeys cause immediate and irretrievable costs. Other issues will include the health of the organisation and wider economic and labour markets conditions. The balance of bargaining power will therefore need to be reflected in the planning, approach, budget and in contingency plans. A key element of this is your alternative to a negotiated agreement or BATNA. What is the outcome which is most likely if you don't agree? To bring this to life, we return to the negotiation in the US which resulted in 188 days of strike action.

> **Case study 7.1: The Writers' Strike—Preparation**
> The 2023 'writers' strike' started on 2 May 2023 and ended 148 days later on 27 September. The Writers Guild of America (WGA), representing 11,500 screenwriters, took strike action as a result of its ongoing dispute with the Alliance of Motion Picture and Television Producers (AMPTP). On 8 April 2023, 97.85% of members of the WGA voted to go on strike if they did not reach an agreement with AMPTP. The key issues in the negotiation were:
>
> - the reduction in financial payments to those involved in making film and TV shows (viewer payments) where they are shown as cable reruns, syndication, DVD release, or licensing to streaming media;
> - the fact that some streaming services (such as Apple TV) were not covered by the agreement which set a minimum wage and other conditions for film and television writers. This left writers to negotiate individually with Apple TV;

- the risk that artificial intelligence (e.g. ChatGPT) would replace writers. The WGA proposed that it may only be used as a tool that can help with research or facilitate script ideas.

It was estimated that the total value of the WGA's proposals was $429m pa. The value of the proposals by the AMPTP were estimated to be $86m pa. The cost of strike action was estimated to be $150m per week.

Key questions

1. Taking the role of AMPTP, what would be your priorities in addressing the issues highlighted above?
2. What would your approach to the negotiations be?
3. What factors did you consider in formulating this approach?

7.3.2 Selecting the Team

Both unions and organisations will need to decide on the make-up of their respective negotiating teams. The employer-side in pay negotiations at an organisational level will normally be a mix of senior HR and operational leaders from the most unionised parts of the organisation. The union side will normally include local representatives plus more senior full-time officials. The team should not be too large but needs to contain the correct balance of expertise and experience. Interpersonal relationships can make a big difference to how a negotiation proceeds. Is there mutual respect between the individuals and do they have the ability to communicate effectively? Ensuring that you have the right individuals with the skills and emotional intelligence can make a huge difference. In addition, ensuring that there are clear responsibilities within the group means that miscommunication will be minimised. If there is a high risk of industrial action these elements take on even more importance.

For example, the chair should be a senior leader with authority to make decisions and credibility with the unions. Very successful leaders in this role have a deep understanding of the role of unions and a respect for what they do. They will generally lead the discussion, answer questions and bring in others to contribute or buy time to think. One member of the team may act as a summariser, keeping track of the discussions and providing focus on the goal of the negotiation when discussions may be going off topic. They may ask questions to test understanding and highlight areas of agreement. By probing aspects of the other party's needs, they may get helpful information and create time to reflect on the response. Finally, one of the group may be an observer. They will watch and listen intently to pick up insight into the motivations or priorities of the other party to help shape the approach and identify areas where progress may be possible.

> **Tip**
> Make sure that all team members have a specific role to play—if your negotiating team is too unwieldy it will be difficult to deliver a coherent message. Understand who you are negotiating with, their priorities and approach.

7.3.3 Starting the Negotiation

At the first formal meeting there will normally be a presentation from the organisation with a 'state of the nation' update from the CEO or a senior leader. This will set the context for a discussion of the key issues with the aim of establishing areas of discussion from both parties. However, this will depend on the nature of the negotiations—if they have been triggered by a written pay claim for example. The trade union would normally present their claim to start the negotiation. As the negotiations progress, some organisations don't share any detail with employees, some confirm discussions have started and some share the detail of the discussions on a rolling basis. This will be informed by the wider strategy and the levels of trust that the detail of negotiations can be kept confidential.

> **Tip**
> Start the negotiations in the right way—make sure that you have a prepared and structured opening statement. Try to set a constructive tone from the outset—avoid grandstanding and demonstrate that you understand and respect the position of the other side even if you disagree with it.

Planning and agreeing what you will discuss over three or four meetings gives everyone visibility of the route to a potential agreement and helps both parties manage their separate stakeholders. To complement this, it is useful to think about the way the meetings are set up, the venue and how breaks will be taken, which are all important parts of the process. Ensuring one person is responsible for managing the invitations, the plan for the room layout, when breaks and refreshments will be taken and how the meetings will be sequenced, can help ensure that the overall process runs smoothly.

7.3.4 Offer and Counter-Offer

Following the start of the negotiation the organisation and the union engage in a series of meetings to explore their priorities, propose solutions and attempt to seek agreement on the issues at hand. This is most usually done through meetings but there may also be informal discussions outside the formal negotiation to help identify the boundaries of each party and the zone of potential agreement (ZOPA).

> **Tip**
>
> Where you are making a new offer or proposal you can position it in a way which increases the likelihood it will be received in the spirit in which it was intended. For example, to try to prevent the other team from simply asking for more, an increase in one element can be positioned hypothetically and with a corresponding request. For example, "if you were to increase the level of revenue which goes to writers, we will be flexible on the use of AI in the writers' room".

This part of the process can be incredibly delicate. It is important to ensure that you have documented the progress which has been made, highlighted the areas where further discussion is required and narrowed down the areas where you need to make a revised, or amended offer. Where possible, if you can reach agreement on a number of the easier elements (which may be cheaper or straightforward to achieve) this can provide a foundation to move the negotiation forward. On the basis that nothing is agreed until everything is agreed, there is a risk that the gains are lost. Psychologically, many people will experience some level of 'loss aversion' which may help them to find flexibility to reach agreement on the other outstanding areas.

One important aspect of this is how the offer or counter-offer is framed and how you communicate it. Your approach and personal style may be the difference between a positive response and a breakdown.

> **Tip**
>
> To help the process of offer and counter-offer it can be useful to focus on common ground. This can be done through interpersonal interactions (shared

interests or common friends) or substantive issues (a policy area such as well-being or a shared frustration such as customer complaints). Finding common ground can be easier in informal environments, such as over lunch or outside the meeting room.

7.3.5 Understanding Your Style

It is also important that participants reflect on their own approaches to communication, problem-solving and negotiation. A key part of this is understanding your own preferences for communications and approach to dealing with conflict. A useful tool is the Rahim inventory of conflict management styles (Rahim, 1983), which assesses the way in which managers approach problems and conflict at work and provides a score across five different dimensions (see below). This type of measure allows those involved in negotiation and the resolution of conflict to consider their style and identify areas to develop in the future. Five categories help them reflect on their approach to negotiations and how to respond to others' approach.

> **Case study 7.2 Measuring conflict management styles**
>
> In 2023, nearly 1000 managers took part in a programme to develop their conflict management skills. As part of that, they completed a questionnaire to help them assess their styles. The five main types which were assessed in the work are summarised below:
>
> **Integrating/problem solving**—this means working with others to develop joint solutions, taking the interests of all the parties into account, including those of the manager and the organisation. This style is generally more likely to create viable and lasting outcomes.
>
> **Compromising**—refers to trying to solve problems by negotiation. Although negotiating is an important part of conflict management, some compromises can merely 'split the difference' between the parties rather than reaching sustainable and effective solutions.
>
> **Obliging**—this style is often found in highly pressured environments where managers try to keep their team happy, often by 'accommodating' their demands. In addition, empathic managers who are concerned about the well-being of their staff often adopt this style. Unfortunately, 'accommodating' conflict often produces solutions that don't address the root cause of a problem and therefore often don't last. It can also undermine the credibility of the manager.

> **Dominating**—refers to managers imposing a solution on others without taking their views into account. This is problematic because we know that involving staff in decision-making can increase engagement. However, 'competing' can also reflect decisiveness, which is an important part of managing conflict effectively.
>
> **Avoiding**—conflict avoidance is very common among managers and tends to reflect low levels of confidence and support. Nonetheless, we know from research that if issues are not addressed, they can escalate and be much more difficult to resolve. Therefore, a low avoiding score tends to be consistent with good conflict management.
>
> The research created one of the largest data sets of managerial approaches to managing conflict. It found that while most managers had dominant collaborative styles, they also had a relatively high score for avoidance.
>
> **Key questions**
>
> 1. Given the five dimensions above, what do you think your dominant style is and what areas do you need to work on in future?
> 2. How would you characterise the conflict management style of the managers, HR practitioners and/or union representatives that you know or work with?
> 3. How could you develop and encourage more collaborative approaches to negotiation and conflict management?

There is no single best style or approach, and the key is to be able to recognise your natural style and be flexible, depending on the situation. Even where the parties adopt a constructive approach to employment relations, there will be times when an issue escalates, or a dispute moves towards industrial action. One common cause of this can be the egos of those leading the discussions. This can create a negative perception between the parties and a siege mentality. One party can begin to break this down by highlighting the common ground, testing underlying assumptions of the stated positions, remaining calm and not rising to the bait.

Similarly, poor communication or non-engagement in the process by one party can create a difficult bargaining environment. This can be addressed through significant leadership commitment to the discussions, respect and stability in the tone and approach, and the use of a third party to change the communication dynamics. This isn't easy to address and may take time and effort, but a structured and proactive approach can begin to build a path to an agreement.

Finally, through difficult or protracted discussions, positions can become entrenched or frozen. In these situations, there may be a focus on personalities rather than issues, a lack of detail and repetitive issues arising. Picking some specific areas where there is some agreement or common ground, or review through a subgroup and agreeing priorities and next steps, may help to unfreeze some issues and build trust to address larger or more emotive issues.

7.3.6 The Agreement

Hopefully the negotiations will lead to an agreement—in most cases this will involve a compromise on both sides. It is crucial that the terms of the agreement are clear and set out in writing. It is also important that both sides can deliver the agreement. Employers need to be sure that they are able to resource any commitments and that the agreement has the support of the senior leaders of the organisation. Unions must be able to 'sell' the deal to their members and will sometimes ballot their members on an offer before formalising an agreement.

However, in certain situations, negotiations will break down as the gap between the aspirations of the two sides is too great to bridge. This raises the prospect of industrial action, which we examine in more detail in Chapter 9. However, industrial action is in some ways a stage in the bargaining process as it is a source of leverage. This can work two ways—if the action is well supported and is damaging to the organisation, the union may well be able to force the employer into making significant concessions. However, if industrial action is poorly supported and/or has limited impact, the bargaining power of the union may be undermined. We now return to the negotiations involving the WGA and the AMPTP which resulted in a drawn out and costly strike.

> **Case study 7.3: The Writers' Strike—the outcome**
>
> At the end of the strike action on 27 September 2023 the parties reached an agreement. The consensus was that the WGA had achieved a significant victory. Table 1 Case Study 7.3 provides a summary of some of the issues and the outcomes from the negotiation.

Table 1 Case Study 7.3 The Writers' Strike—issues and outcomes

Issue	WGA proposal	AMPTP proposal	Agreement
Increase financial payments to those involved in making film and TV shows	Establish an additional viewership-based payment to reward programs with more viewers. This requires transparency regarding program views.	Rejected WGA proposal with no alternatives.	Viewership-based streaming bonus: High budget subscription video on demand series and movies viewed by 20%+ of service's domestic subscribers in first 90 days of release get bonus equal to 50% of the fixed domestic and foreign payment. Streaming data transparency: Companies agree to provide the WGA total number of hours streamed of self-produced high budget streaming programs
Some streaming services were not covered by the agreement which set a minimum wage and other conditions	Extend television agreement terms to high budget shows made for subscription video on demand	Agreement only applies to high budget Comedy/Variety programs made for subscription video on demand. Budget limit is $700,000 for 30-minute show, $1.15 million for 60-minute show. No guarantees would apply, and writers can be employed on a daily-rate basis.	Agreement terms apply to high budget comedy-variety and other non-dramatic shows made for subscription video on demand for compensation purposes. Budget limits are $600,000 for once/week 30-minute show, $1.15 million for once/week 60-minute show. Projects with four episodes per week have lower levels. For high budget daytime serials that move to subscription video on demand, the company must give notice and negotiate with WGA for all terms and conditions.
Writers were concerned about the risks that artificial intelligence (e.g. ChatGPT) would replace the role of writers.	Regulate use of artificial intelligence on relevant projects: AI can't write or rewrite literary material; can't be used as source material; and material from shows covered by the agreement can't be used to train AI.	Offered annual meetings to discuss advancements in technology.	Regulate use of artificial intelligence on covered projects: AI-generated written material is not considered literary material, source material or assigned material and AI is not a writer under the agreement. A writer can elect to use AI when performing writing services, if the Company consents and provided the writer follows applicable company policies. Company cannot require writer to use AI software when performing writing services. Company must disclose to writer if any material given to writer has been generated by AI or incorporates AI-generated material. The WGA reserves right to assert that exploitation of writers' material to train AI is prohibited.

Based on: Sharp (2023)

Key questions

1. How would you assess the outcome of the strike?
2. To what extent did the WGA achieve its main objectives?
3. What do you consider to be the key learning points from the negotiation, based on the information available?

Commentators criticised the approach of the employers in the dispute and argued that this not only caused the strike action but undermined the employers' own bargaining position. First, they suggested that studio executives were out of touch with the wider sentiment in the US. Workers' priorities had changed post-pandemic and, with a tight labour market and a cost of living crisis, they misjudged the motivation and solidarity of the WGA negotiating team. Second, the employers had shown little respect to the WGA—there was a lack of meaningful engagement, there were public attacks by CEOs and attempts to undermine workers with threats they would lose their homes. This only hardened positions and made a negotiated outcome less likely. Finally, the employers' negotiating team took an 'old school' approach. They used stalling tactics, made small and meaningless concessions, and generally did not engage in good faith.

7.4 What is 'Good' Negotiation?

The approach followed in the WGA dispute could be described as a classic example of distributive bargaining. This is the traditional approach to bargaining and is based on dividing up a set amount of resources—the bargaining process therefore is based on how these resources are divided, with the outcome fundamentally based on bargaining power.

> **Definition**
> 'The joint-decision process for resolving conflicts of interest is distributive bargaining. The term itself refers to the activity of dividing limited resources. It occurs in situation in which one party wins what the other party loses'.

Consequently, these types of negotiation often have a winner and a loser, or at least one party who comes out with the best end of the deal. The problem with distributive bargaining is that it tends to be adversarial and confrontational. It also involves using a range of tactics and sleight of hand to get 'a bigger slice of the pie'. This means there is a high chance that it ends in conflict and also that it undermines trust—even if an agreement is reached, one of the parties will feel aggrieved.

A review of collective bargaining conducted for the government of the Republic of Ireland defined some useful benchmarks for what 'good faith engagement' between enterprises and trade unions looks like (Doherty,

2022). The key points are set out below and focus on the procedural aspects of negotiation and collective bargaining:

> **Important**
>
> **Key factors for constructive engagement**
> - Attending, and participating in, any meeting within a reasonable timeframe;
> - Giving genuine consideration to representations made by the other party;
> - Providing any relevant information (other than confidential or commercially sensitive information) in a timely manner;
> - Giving a clear, considered, and reasoned written response to representations made by the other party following a good faith meeting within an agreed timeframe;
> - The parties should be responsive, and must not do anything likely to mislead or deceive each other;
> - The size, composition and representative nature of the trade union and employer representatives should be reasonable and balanced between the parties;
> - Refraining from capricious or unfair conduct (this could include, for example, refusing to meet, or discuss, with properly nominated representatives of the other party; penalisation of an employee due to trade union activity; interfering with the process of the parties' nomination of their independent representatives; unduly hurrying the engagement to prevent proper consideration; taking extreme positions with the intention of shutting down the engagement).
> - Each party should be responsible for making its own record of discussions held.

The above guidance complements the points made in multiple chapters within this book. Clarity on expectations, structures and behaviour are all key and ensures that any debate and disagreement are limited to the substantive issues such as pay rather than the procedure itself.

7.5 Collaboration and Integration—A Different Approach?

At the beginning of the chapter we looked at HR professionals' perceptions of negotiation and the largely negative associations that they hold. However, if we ask the same group to think about negotiation from the perspective of collaboration, the change in the language used is stark. Our delegates used much more positive language about both the process and potential outcomes. In reality, dealing with the inherent differences between employees and employers is difficult as there is conflict at the heart of the employment

Fig. 7.2 What words do you associate with negotiation from a perspective of collaboration?

relationship. But it doesn't have to characterise the process leading to the negative language we saw earlier in the chapter (see Fig. 7.2).

One way to move towards a more collaborative approach is defined by Walton and McKersie (1991) as integrative bargaining. This is a strategy which aims to increase or create value for both parties. Rather than arguing over the distribution of the pie, the aim is to increase its size. The approach is the opposite of distributive or win-lose negotiation strategies. In Chapter 5 we looked at the importance of focussing on shared interests rather than divergent positions when trying to manage conflict. This concept lies at the heart of integrative bargaining. Some of the key benefits of such an approach are set out below.

Integrative bargaining improves the quality of the agreements reached. By exploring the underlying interests and needs of both parties, integrative bargaining can generate more creative solutions that address the core concerns of both sides. Rather than focussing exclusively on salary increases, discussing other factors such as flexibility, working hours or career development may highlight other areas for agreement, with both parties achieving a positive outcome.

Integrative bargaining improves relationships. If it is done well, integrative bargaining can build a collaborative, problem-focussed environment. Over time the participants treat each other as partners not opponents. Through open

> communication, listening, and respect for the other's position, the parties can increase trust levels. In particular, in an employment relations context, integrative bargaining can help employers and representatives to build long-term, future-focussed relationships.
>
> **Integrative bargaining reduces the likelihood of conflict.** When it is positioned in this way and structured well, this negotiation strategy can avoid (and neutralise) a competitive approach to maximise one party's approach at the expense of the other—very common in employment relations contexts. With an approach which places the focus on common goals, the natural tension within competing priorities can be reduced. It also helps to identify new avenues of discussion and novel opportunities, increasing the creativity in the discussions. This increases the chances of reaching an agreement and avoiding dispute or industrial action.
>
> In very practical terms, this means recognising that there are different interests in a negotiation, and that we must look behind the public positions and focus on where shared interests and needs overlap.

7.6 Conclusion

This chapter has set out the key concepts and stages when negotiating. The process of collective bargaining has been at the heart of employment relations for over 100 years and will continue to be fundamental to any collective relationship within organisations. To get the most from the collective relationships with trade unions, there needs to be a greater focus on relationships and integrative bargaining rather than a binary focus on telling, asking and winning. The increase in collective conflict across the world after the Covid-19 pandemic, in response to high inflation, exposed that many organisations had forgotten how to negotiate when the power balance had swung in their favour of their employees. Not only did this highlight the lack of capability within the HR profession, but it also underlined that attitudes towards engagement with staff in many organisations reflected an assumption of managerial prerogative and authority.

The process described above and the structures which facilitate them, are crucial to creating an environment where difficulties can be addressed and resolved. Negotiation is often a source of conflict. Even more so in ambiguous and volatile economic and political environments. However, as we have already argued earlier in this book, collective bargaining can have positive organisational and societal effects. It is particularly important in navigating fundamental change as illustrated by the Writers Guild dispute. However, where collective bargaining takes a distributive approach, there is a danger that it can erode trust and trigger conflict. More integrative and interest-based approaches to negotiation and bargaining offer a different way forward. This approach focusses on shared goals and interests. The next chapter will look specifically at how problem solving can be used in employment relations for the benefit of organisations and its workers.

> **Questions**
> 1. Why is planning and preparing for negotiations so important? If you were preparing to negotiate the annual pay claim in your organisation, what are the key steps you would take?
> 2. How has the changing context of employment relations in the wake of the Covid-19 pandemic shaped the relative bargaining power of employers and trade unions?
> 3. In what circumstances might it be appropriate to make a last and final offer? How would you do this and what are the risks?
> 4. What are the advantages and disadvantages of taking an integrative approach to collective bargaining?

References

Doherty, M. (2022). Progress Updates and Final Report from the Labour Employer Economic Forum (LEEF) High Level Group on Collective Bargaining. [Online] An Roinn Fiontar, Trádála agus Fostaíochta Department of Enterprise, Trade and Employment. https://enterprise.gov.ie/en/publications/leef-high-level-group-on-collective-bargaining.html. [Accessed 20/11/2023].

Fisher, R., & Ury, W. (2012). *Getting to Yes: Negotiating an Agreement without Giving in*. Random House.

Rahim, M. A. (1983). A Measure of Styles of Handling Interpersonal Conflict. *Academy of Management Journal., 26*, 368–376.

Sharp, K. (2023) *What Have We Learned from the Hollywood writers' strike?* [Online] The Guardian. https://www.theguardian.com/commentisfree/2023/oct/04/what-have-we-learned-from-the-hollywood-writers-strike?CMP=Share_iOSApp_Other [Accessed 21/11/2023].

Walton, R. E., & McKersie, R. B. (1991). *A Behavioural Theory of Labor Negotiations—2nd edition*. ILR Press.

8

Problem-Solving with Trade Unions

Abstract Joint problem-solving is a powerful tool for leaders, managers and union representatives to use, bringing pragmatic and practical solutions to real workplace problems. It does not bypass consultation or negotiation but can be used alongside these if the environment is conducive and some core conditions are in place. Problem-solving requires trust, a structured approach and different skills and behaviours from traditional win-lose negotiation. It can be used to resolve specific operational, and people challenges, or to signify a new way of working after conflict. The use of practical examples in the chapter demonstrate how problem-solving can help resolve differences of opinion, moving people on from entrenched positions. If it becomes a natural way of working, problem-solving can positively impact organisational and employment relations culture, giving employee representatives a genuine voice at work. It can lead to sustainable change which is better understood and accepted as both parties have shaped the solution. There can be obstacles, and this practical chapter discusses how these can be overcome.

Keywords Problem-solving · Problem statement · Trust · Tools · Action log · Activity plan

8.1 Introduction

In Chapter 7, we discussed the potential benefits of integrative and interest-based approaches to collective bargaining. In essence these are based on the principles of joint problem-solving. In this practical chapter we define problem-solving in the context of collective employment relations and the conditions required to enable effective problem-solving between managers and union representatives. We share approaches we have developed in organisations and describe practical considerations, tools and techniques. We discuss the skills required and argue that problem-solving has far reaching benefits such as the design of practical, sustainable solutions and building critical skills. If successful, it gives parties confidence to adopt the approach again, thereby potentially positively impacting the employment relations culture of an organisation.

8.2 Benefits of Problem-Solving

A problem-solving approach has a number of significant benefits. The organisations described in the case studies in the chapter all reported real business benefits including: keeping work in-house due to more stability in collective employment relations; new agreements to facilitate change and modernise the business; progress on previously unresolvable issues such as new policies to help attraction and retention; and ongoing commitment to joint approaches to ways of working. European research has also shown that companies that make a real effort to solve problems with their employee representatives "had higher than average productivity and experienced increases in productivity" (Cox et al., 2011). Examples from the US also show that joint problem-solving teams "can improve the operations of your company and give workers a more direct voice in their work" (Bahat et al., 2023).

As well as solving a critical problem and helping the business move forward, all parties learn and practise valuable, transferable skills. They practise listening to other views, learn how to undertake small surveys or interviewing, how to build a case for presentation and practise presentation skills. They also demonstrate to the wider business the power of joint problem-solving, thereby reducing the resistance to this style of working. There is potential for cultural change across the organisation if there is a commitment to sustaining this as a way of working. In our view, this should be the goal as it can lead to transformational change in employment relations.

By involving representatives and employees, the organisation gets a different view of the issue involving those who do the job, face the problem, try to work around the problem or have lost faith that it could ever be solved. Often the person doing the job is the one who can see the solution. Our experience has shown that both parties often see things differently after problem-solving. The "facts" were different from their initial views when they looked at the problem solely with their own group. They also had a much higher level of understanding of the problem, which can make a return to a win-lose approach less likely.

8.3 What is Problem-Solving?

There is a lot written about problem-solving due to its wide range of uses. In its simplest form, it involves the following key steps:

- Defining a problem
- Determining its cause
- Identifying, prioritising and selecting alternatives for a solution
- Implementing a solution.

It involves gathering objective facts, understanding root causes and encourages multiple views of the problem to be considered. It has been described as "creating a culture of inquiry rather than advocacy" (Grant, cited in Nawaz, 2017), where problems are tackled by a pool of people with diverse views and knowledge of the issue. In conventional approaches to employment relations, we often see advocacy, which involves parties having pre-defined positions on potential solutions which they argue and lobby for, often without consideration of other perspectives.

Problem-solving is a technique used in multiple situations in organisations and can be very effective in the employee relations environment, where "the effort is not devoted to determining who is right and who is wrong. Nor is it devoted to yielding something to gain something. Rather, a genuine effort is made to discover a creative resolution of fundamental points of difference" (Blake et al., 1964: 12).

It differs from more traditional employment relations processes in two fundamental ways. Firstly, the groups that initially look at the problem together are a mixed group of union representatives and managers. Once the problem is defined, they collect facts, research solutions and test ideas as a group. They often bring their recommended solution back to a joint steering group who sign off the solution to be implemented.

> **Important**
>
> Unlike conventional bargaining, managers and union representatives don't work up their own solutions separately with a tactical plan of how to persuade each other that their view is right, and the other is wrong. Problem-solving requires a different mindset, the right conditions and commitment.

A second fundamental difference from more traditional employment relations processes, particularly integrative bargaining, is that "the alternative solutions which emerge may not be ones held by either of the contending groups at the onset" (Blake et al., 1964: 87). In effect, the parties are very likely to come up with a better solution, more suited to the organisation and the people doing that job. Problem-solving requires different skills to a conventional win-lose negotiation. It isn't about power or being determined to win at all costs. It requires a sharing of information to define the problem and provide the facts behind it. It involves really listening to each other's perspectives and thinking of creative solutions that could work. It can involve data collection, analysis and presentation of data with recommendations. It requires a "more positive mentality" where "understanding, confidence, trust and respect are the bases for achieving agreement and integrating group efforts. The effect is to unify interdependent groups, rather than to cast them further apart" (Blake et al, 1964: 87).

8.4 Problem-Solving and Employment Relations

The opportunities for using problem-solving to deal with a range of workplace challenges are vast and this is shown in our case studies in this chapter. We see the following situations as particularly suitable for a problem-solving approach:

- When both parties agree that there is a need to address a specific problem but there is a lack of clarity or agreement on how this should be approached
- Where there is an innovative approach to a problem which needs to be explored, problem-solving can be used to resolve some of the main issues and provide a foundation for more detailed negotiation

Table 8.1 Suitable topics for using problem-solving

Topic
Making meetings more effective and inclusive
A review of approaches to collective voice to ensure all employees are involved
Policy changes
Identifying "good employment relations" in the organisation
Building employment relations training for new managers and representatives
A range of operational issues

- When traditional processes have reached an impasse and there is no real agreement about the nature of the problem
- If your relationship with your unions is increasingly conflictual and there is a need to reboot the relationship and commit to a new way of working.

In Table 8.1 we suggest some topics which are well-suited to a problem-solving methodology and especially suitable for organisations which want to experiment with a new approach on some less contentious issues.

Case study 8.1 is a positive example of the impact of adopting a problem-solving approach in the engineering division of a global organisation. Agreements had become very hard to make and negotiating change was increasingly difficult.

> **Case study 8.1: A new, single modern agreement**
>
> **Background**
>
> The engineering division of this company was struggling financially due to newer technology reducing the need for maintenance tasks and poor overall performance. The employment relations climate was seen as a contributor to the decline in performance.
>
> **The current climate**
>
> Key characteristics of the employment relations climate at that time were:
>
> - A lack of trust in each other's motives amongst union representatives and managers.
> - Managers felt that union representatives did not understand the business or care about its future and were unwilling to embrace change.
> - Unions felt managers bypassed consultation with the unions and did not understand agreements.
> - Low level issues were escalated to senior managers and officials rather than being solved at local level. This slowed change and frustrated local teams.
> - There was an inability to agree changes to agreements which were necessary for business survival and growth.

Commitment to change

Senior leaders and union officials committed to a programme to improve the working relationship. More than 100 managers and union representatives took part in a series of facilitated sessions to review and improve how they worked together in the business. There was a strong desire from the participants to move towards a problem-solving approach rather than one of conflict and stalemate. The sessions had a significant impact on the working relationships and the future of the business.

Evaluation of impact

When this programme was evaluated five years later, both parties gave an example of how they had approached a recurring and difficult problem differently after the sessions described above. The parties had been trying to draw up a new agreement for seven years. Previously managers had drafted an agreement and the union had rejected it as they had not been involved and did not trust the management intent. This time they saw it as a problem to solve together. A new agreement was drawn up in two months using problem-solving tools and working in small groups. This agreement brought in more flexibility, new shift patterns and revised facility time for union representatives.

Improved relationships contributed to a turnaround in the state of the business. Over a five-year period, output doubled and costs nearly halved. As a result of this change, the company decided to invest in engineering rather than sell it off or outsource it—the business began to bring in work from other companies and built a strong apprenticeship scheme.

Critical pre-conditions for sustaining change

A number of factors were identified as being crucial in sustaining the positive elements of the programme over a longer period:

- A newly appointed senior leader believed in collaboration and partnership working and the unions fully engaged in the process.
- The early success demonstrated by the collaboration and implementation of the new agreement gave impetus to the programme and enabled some who were more sceptical to support the new ways of working.
- In the year after the sessions, a key union representative and manager who had bought into the idea that collaborative working was beneficial, had moved into the top two senior roles and were now in a position to influence others and make the case for sharing common goals of job security and business success.
- The company continued to invest in the skills and behaviours of its leaders and union representatives.

Key questions

1. What are the main benefits of using a problem-solving approach in a case like this, compared to a more conventional negotiation?
2. What are the challenges and limitations of problem-solving in this context?

Suggesting a problem-solving approach can be seen as brave—taking on the deep-rooted conventions and traditions of employment relations. It can also be seen as naïve, proposed by someone who does not fully understand the dynamics of employment relations. Some managers and union representatives will be resistant to trying something new and therefore work will need to be done to build trust and get buy-in from all parties.

> **Tip**
>
> Managers and union representatives may feel comfortable with traditional approaches to collective bargaining even if these are not working. In winning support for a new way of working, it is important to acknowledge the reasons for resistance and focus on the interests of the parties to build a case for change.

8.5 Conditions for Effective Problem-Solving

We have identified a number of conditions which must be in place to enable effective problem-solving with union representatives and managers.

8.5.1 Organisational Culture and Employment Relations Strategy

The first condition is the culture of the organisation and the current employment relations strategy. Problem-solving will not work in a competitive employment relations environment and will feel very alien and be undermined from the outset. All parties need to value the views of the others and see them as legitimate stakeholders in the process. They also need to share information and work as a team. This will be difficult if information is withheld, people are misled and regularly undermined. Therefore, culture and strategy are critical.

8.5.2 Trust Between the Parties

The second condition is one of trust between the parties. Lack of trust is a critical obstacle to union representatives adopting new ways of working. In low-trust environments, unions may well see a suggestion of problem-solving as a tactic to undermine their traditional bargaining role (Kelly & Kelly, 1991). Studies of union and management co-operation have shown that trust is increased when managers are more willing to share business information. This can lead to changes in patterns, frequency and scope of communication, quicker responsiveness by both parties and discussions about a wider range of subjects (Ospina & Yoroni, 2003).

> **Tip**
>
> A good way to build trust is to be as open and transparent as possible—this includes sharing information and demonstrating that you trust the other party to keep sensitive issues confidential.

In most successful cases, work is usually undertaken before problem-solving to rebuild trust between the parties (see Case study 8.1 and 8.3). This can be done through externally facilitated discussions where both parties are able to describe what it feels like to work together, what they want the other party to change and what they are prepared to do differently. They must believe that the other is prepared to move from the ways of the past into a different future. These can be very enlightening discussions if well facilitated and can "change the perceptions (perhaps, more accurately, misperceptions) that the two groups have of each other" (Cummings & Worley, 2009: 282).

8.5.3 Recognise There is a Problem to Solve and Commit to Solving it

The third condition is a recognition that there is a problem which both parties want to solve. If one party is happy with the status quo, there is little incentive to try something different. At this stage, both parties may be in the situation described by Blake et al. as "motivation may be no more than a faith or, at least a hypothesis… that both groups have the potential to achieve a better solution through collaboration" (1964: 86). In the case studies in this chapter, it is clear these were shared problems, felt by both parties. For example, in one organisation, the shared problem was how to secure the future viability of the business (Case study 8.1). In another, it was a shared problem to improve industrial relations due to ongoing conflict (Case study 8.3).

Research has shown a number of other pre-conditions for successful problem-solving which include:

- participants must volunteer for this type of activity;
- the approach must be backed by leaders;
- there must be a common goal which both parties can align with;
- union representatives should be able to play a role as a full partner in the design of the programme (Kochan et al., 1985).

Case study 8.2 highlights how identifying a shared problem from the outset changed the dynamic with benefits to the organisation and the people who work in it. A common problem in many organisations is where there is a need to consult and sometimes negotiate on changes to employment policy. Many HR teams find it hard to agree policy changes with union representatives and our experience has shown that this is often due to the process that is followed. Starting from the position of identifying a shared problem and defining the problem jointly enabled a much more successful outcome than a traditional negotiation process in the following case study.

Case study 8.2: Modernising employment policies

Background

In the organisation's People Strategy, there was an objective to modernise a range of outdated employment policies to enable the company to retain and attract employees. Changes to employment policy had to be negotiated with the trade unions. To do this, the HR team would draft a new policy and take it to the unions in a special meeting. This is likely to have been the first time the unions saw the policy and they did not always have sight of the rationale for change. Changing policies had become very difficult, with long negotiations ending in stalemate. The HR team and business leaders felt that it was just too difficult to change anything.

A new approach

A company-wide review of existing joint structures found there was little regular formal dialogue between union representatives and the HR team. The head of employee relations suggested the establishment of a formal Policy Forum made up of union representatives from each of the three unions and members of the HR team—the head of reward and head of HR operations—to discuss the strategic people agenda. This would now be the place for policies to be developed, revised, simplified and/or terminated as appropriate. The two parties agreed the terms of reference, relevant attendees, frequency of meetings and the standard agenda items.

The process

The HR team decided to try a problem-solving approach to modernise policy. The company and the unions had begun to rebuild some trust in the previous year which was an important pre-condition for this type of approach. The trade unions agreed to try problem-solving as they also recognised the need to improve a range of policies. First, both parties set out what policies they would like to change in the next 12 months, and explained their rationale. Areas of common ground were identified—these were prioritised and a one-year plan was agreed. To trial the process and build momentum, the group agreed to look at three new policies in the first year.

Everyone had a short training session on the problem-solving approach. For each policy under review, an HR representative and a union representative took the lead. They specifically defined the problem with the existing policy and agreed how to gather further information. They then invited other interested parties to join them to discuss the issue and develop a new draft. These were piloted, refined and brought back to the Policy Forum for discussion. There was a time limit for the process of 12 weeks.

Results

In two years, the joint Policy Forum modernised more key people policies than had been achieved in the previous decade, when a more traditional negotiation approach had been used. This involved policies such as absence, discipline, grievance, performance management and some new policies around agile working. The approach also built trust and constructive relationships between the trade unions and the HR team, which helped in all other areas where the parties worked together. According to the Head of Reward in the organisation:

> the policy forum really transformed the process for policy change, not only by creating a simple structure based on joint objectives, but also through a focussed and realistic plan on priority areas that were important to the business. This approach removed the paralysis that seemed to manifest when previously reaching agreement seemed too hard or too big. With focus, momentum and common ground with the trade unions, we were able to work efficiently to create the change that the business and our people needed.

Key questions

1. Why do you think the previous approach using conventional negotiation was so unsuccessful?
2. What were the key success factors in the new approach and the development of the policy forum?
3. Could this approach be used in your organisation?

8.6 Problem-Solving Needs Structure

Our case studies suggest that problem-solving can be used in a variety of situations. One organisation used problem-solving to tackle specific operational issues, another focussed on policy modernisation, and the other used it extensively as part of a wider bottom-up industrial relations change programme, supported by other company-wide changes. While the circumstances may differ, once the parties were committed to the process, they all took a structured approach to problem-solving to increase the opportunities for a successful outcome and minimise the chance of it being undermined. Although problem-solving may appear to be a slightly less formal and more discursive approach than traditional negotiation and bargaining, it is, in fact, very structured. Moreover, putting a clear structure and process into place is vital (Blake et al., 1964: 136; Schein, 1999: 153).

In the following sections, we set out some of the most important structural elements to consider if embarking on problem-solving in employment relations and these are summarised in Table 8.2.

> **Important**
>
> Blake et al. (1964) suggest a simple but clear process for union management problem-solving.
>
> 1. Joint subgroups establish the facts behind the problems.
> 2. They feed back to the full bargaining team of unions and managers.
> 3. The groups search for solutions.
> 4. The group evaluates the solutions.

Another example is one where problem-solving involves the wider workforce in problem identification and resolution, alongside union representatives and managers (Blake et al., 1964: 141). Given the scale of the event, this approach would require detailed planning, preparation and structure. In this example, the exercise revealed a number of problems which the organisation had been unaware of, enabling them to be addressed and resolved. The involvement of team leaders and employees also built trust and increased day-to-day collaboration on problem identification and solution. Team leaders

Table 8.2 Effective structures for problem-solving

Step one	Define the problem
Step two	Define the group size, ensuring an equal number of union representatives and managers
Step three	Define membership criteria – what skills and experience must the group have
Step four	Choose a facilitator
Step five	Define the lifespan of the group
Step six	Plan a kick-off meeting
Step seven	Establish ground rules for the group
Step eight	Plan meetings and activities to be undertaken
Step nine	Use tools to keep meetings on track
Step ten	Finalise recommendations and sign off

felt involved rather than watching from the sidelines and having centralised agreements made from "above".

> **Tip**
>
> Many issues and changes will be better resolved and implemented if employees have a voice in shaping the solution. Find opportunities to work jointly with union and employee representatives where possible, as much as possible. Tap into their knowledge and enable their contribution.

8.7 Practical Considerations When Setting up Problem-Solving Groups

From our experience, we have identified several practical issues to be considered when setting up problem-solving groups.

8.7.1 Defining the Problem

The groups must have a well-defined issue or problem which is tangible, work-based and practical. This can be worked up into a problem statement before starting the work. However, this can be difficult—some problems are too big while others may simply not be solvable by the group. Therefore, it is crucial that the problem is not only clearly defined but that finding a solution is realistic and achievable. The problem-solving team should be set up to achieve a clear, deliverable aim. Any "permission" required should be gained prior to the start and the decision-makers should be part of the broader process to ensure the team is not blocked. Where the team agrees a project objective that impacts on other departments or groups of staff, a member of the team should accept responsibility for discussing this with the relevant people in other teams or departments. They should agree a solution and come back to the team and facilitator.

Some groups use tools such as "five whys" or the "fishbone" (ASQ, 2023) to help identify the problem at this stage and these can be very effective in helping teams at the start of the problem-solving process. The "five whys" process starts with an initial statement of the problem—the group then asks why this problem occurred until there is an actionable statement or lesson that can be learned. An example of this, which relates to an organisation's grievance policy, is outlined in Table 8.3:

Table 8.3 Example of five whys

Initial statement	Staff bringing grievances are increasingly likely to take long-term absences from work
Why?	They are suffering from poor mental health
Why?	The stress of the process
Why?	They do not feel they are being listened to
Why?	The average time for an investigation is three months
Why?	Because investigating managers are under too much pressure
Actionable statement	Managers do not have sufficient time and space to conduct grievance investigations promptly

8.7.2 Group Size and Composition

The group should be small (up to six people). It can be smaller or larger, but membership should not be so large that the group becomes a committee where problem-solving is not achievable. There must be an equal number of union representatives and managers with an interest in and knowledge of the topic to be analysed. It is important that those taking part in the team are prepared to contribute and have a commitment to the process and output.

Expectations of a member of a problem-solving group

- Knowledge or interest in the subject or problem.
- Open-minded and willing to listen to others.
- Commitment to regular attendance and contribution.
- Willingness to consult on proposals and gather information.
- Ability to draft reports.
- Action-oriented.
- Good communication skills.
- Keep others informed of what the group is doing and any problems/progress.

8.7.3 Facilitation

Problem-solving teams often have a facilitator. Their role is critical, and the person should be chosen very carefully. They must be independent of the members of the problem-solving team and of the subject but trusted by both parties. For example, it is unlikely to be successful if you choose, as facilitator, a manager who has a strong view on the issue and is the manager of some team members. It would be better to look for a manager from a different function or location who is considered impartial. It may also not be appropriate to have a member of HR if it is not a trusted team. The facilitator role is to keep the participants focussed, to stick to timescales and processes, to follow up actions, to deal with differences between members and to guide the process. The team must accept the independence of the facilitator if the process is to work.

> **Tip**
> Given the importance of facilitation, it is a good idea to ensure that problem-solving teams are supported by well trained and experienced facilitators.

The facilitator sets the scene for the team to achieve the objective. They need to create an open environment which promotes interaction, encourages participation, promotes respect for others' views and holds members accountable. They must be prepared to challenge ideas and ask questions that get the group to focus on core issues. The facilitator must be able to seek common ground, manage conflict and build consensus amongst team members. It is vital that the facilitator sets behaviour standards by their own actions. For example, the facilitator should complete their own actions on time, start and finish meetings on time. They are also responsible for energising the group to achieve their objective.

8.7.4 Lifespan of the Group

Groups have a limited lifespan, coming together for a defined period. In our experience, this has been for around 12 weeks, although it may be much shorter if groups are taken away from their normal roles to focus on this full-time rather than be given some time off alongside their roles. They are not "talking shops" or committees; they tackle one issue and disband when finished or if they are failing.

8.8 Key Steps in the Problem-Solving Process

In our experience there are a number of key steps to follow which help to guide the team from initial meeting through to sign-off and implementation.

8.8.1 Plan a "Kick-Off" Meeting

Once a project has been identified and team members chosen, the facilitator runs a "kick-off" meeting which, in our experience, could take half a day. The team members discuss their project theme unchallenged, helping them to identify any concerns, obstacles and common ground. It ensures that everyone is clear on the project and what it is trying to achieve. Doing this will enable the team to move towards identifying its objective and identifying the key steps that need to be taken to reach that objective, which can be recorded in a simple spreadsheet or activity plan.

8.8.2 Establishing Ground Rules

At the first meeting the team members should establish ground rules for how they are going to work together. These should be drawn up by the group so that everyone is in agreement. They will cover issues such as dealing with non-attendance, an agreement that meetings start on time, how the team will work, how to contribute constructively and sharing of workload.

8.8.3 Planning Meetings

Subsequent meetings should be put in diaries and last no more than two hours. These sessions should focus on decisions and problem-solving. The group meets regularly enough to manage its task. It is normally weekly at the onset but could move to once every two weeks or even monthly when it is clear who is doing what and by when. The criteria for the frequency of meetings should be discussed and finalised once the team has specified a clear objective and established the tasks to be completed.

8.8.4 Keeping on Track

To keep the problem-solving group focussed there are a number of processes which are useful to follow. Documenting the objectives, deliverables and scope of the group is important. An example of this type of document - a Project Initiation Document- is set out below. We have also used activity plans and action logs. All three documents are now explained in more detail.

A Project Initiation Document is a simple way to lay out the objectives of the team, the scope of the project, identify overall steps, allocate responsibilities and assess any risks. To start any project the team needs to set down some words that explain to itself and others what the team is doing and what it is aiming to achieve. Creating the PID ensures that the team asks itself what exactly it is doing and how, who is doing it and when. It can also clarify success criteria and deliverables. The PID should be written after the initial meetings of the group. After that, it is likely only to be used to ensure that the team is on course to meet its objectives.

We share an example of a PID below, which was drawn up by a problem-solving group whose task was to identify the key components of good employment relations in a global organisation. This group was one of a number running at the same time with an overall goal of improving employment relations. This group specifically wished to identify good practice so that this could be shared and built across the global company. The deliverables are clearly defined.

Example: Project Initiation Document (PID)

Objectives

- To identify the principles, processes and behaviours of good practice in industrial relations that are common to areas of good practice within XYZ company.
- To identify the areas of the company where these elements of good practice are demonstrated and to understand the reasons behind them.
- To contrast good practice and poor practice and establish their different impacts on the business and the people.

Deliverables

- A self-assessment checklist for any area to use.
- The design of a facilitated session for areas wishing to use the checklist.
- A self-assessment diagnostic tool to be used, anonymously, by individuals prior to their involvement in the facilitated session.
- A report and a presentation explaining our research, analysis of findings and recommendations.

Scope of work

- Specific focus will be given to those areas identified as particularly good or particularly poor.

Approach

- To share information about areas of good and bad practice between members of the problem-solving team.
- To seek information about good and bad practice from other problem-solving team members.
- To interview managers and trade union representatives involved in the areas identified.
- To consult the industrial relations department.

Responsibilities

- Problem-solving team members and facilitator

Timescales

- Early April at the latest

The PID can be supplemented by an activity plan which charts the key steps needed to achieve the stated objectives. It sets out steps against dates, allowing progress to be monitored and it becomes the reference point for the group to ensure that it stays on course. An action log can then be used to track the specific actions needed, ensuring they are completed on time. It is a basis for managing progress towards the overall objective and an indicator of next steps. At each meeting, the facilitator can go through the log from the previous meeting to ensure that members have done what is expected of them. Using the activity plan as the overall guide, new actions will then be allocated and recorded. Actions should be cleared at each meeting, as a rule, although there may be times when this is not possible.

8.8.5 Sign-Off and Implementation

After the allotted time, the team will draw up its recommendations in a report or a presentation. The recommendations will need to be signed off by the appropriate leaders or a steering group made up of leaders and union representatives. The governance arrangements for a wide change programme with problem-solving as a key component are described in Case study 8.3. In this example, all the proposals from the problem-solving teams were signed off by the joint steering group. The proposals then move into the implementation phase. In some circumstances another team can be established to support the implementation of the proposal.

Tip

It is important that those taking part in problem-solving teams are given recognition within the company and their union for their contribution.

Case study 8.3: Problem-solving at the heart of a wide change programme

The context

In this case a problem-solving approach was central to a wider change programme in a large organisation. An initial analysis of what was not working in employment relations, involving both parties, showed there was a desire to work together as problem-solvers. The aim was to capitalise on the experience and knowledge of both parties to resolve some of the problems within their own areas of the business.

The benefits of this approach

While organisational and union leaders had agreed to the approach, they needed to persuade their "constituencies" to also adopt this and to take part. They set out the benefits of a problem-solving approach rather than a "top-down" change programme.

- It allows both "sides" to collaborate on a particular project of importance to the business and to them.
- It allows both "sides" to develop skills which can be used in other aspects of their work.
- It allows everyone to see the benefits and opportunities which are demonstrated during joint working.
- It allows a wider number of people to get involved.
- It is participative and consultative and not "top-down."
- It is the beginning of a better way of working.
- It is an opportunity for all parties to show that they are committed to change.
- It allows all parties to be involved in tackling some of the essential issues facing the company.

The rationale

While in the short-term, particular problems were being tackled and solutions proposed, in the long-term, the overriding objective was to slowly change the relationships between managers and union representatives. All parties would develop new skills while seeing the benefits of working collaboratively rather than in an adversarial way. It was seen as a "stepping stone" approach where the longer-term benefits would come from the success of the projects in the short-term.

The governance of the change programme

The new approach was led by a joint steering group made up of senior union representatives and senior leaders and it was supported by the CEO and union officials.

Outputs from the problem-solving groups

The groups proposed changes to how joint meetings were run, they helped to design and run a training programme for all people managers and union representatives on consultation, negotiation and problem-solving, helped develop a new intranet and designed a process for structured industrial relations support for managers as their career developed.

The impact of the change programme

The perception of key managers and union representatives was that the employment relations climate improved over the five-year period of the new approach. Fewer issues escalated to formal bodies as they were resolved more effectively at a local level. This enabled the formal bodies to focus on more strategic issues. Meeting principles enabled more constructive meetings and more joint solutions. Two areas of the business regularly used problem-solving teams to resolve operational issues. Line managers gained more clarity over their role in employment relations and where to go for support. Managers were no longer recruited into employment relations-sensitive roles without experience or a clear development plan. Union representatives and managers had a shared understanding of each other's roles through the joint training.

Key questions

1. What are the long-term and short-term aims of this change programme?
2. Identify the main elements of the approach which ensured its success?
3. What lessons can you take from this case for your own practice?

8.8.6 Overcoming Obstacles

There are likely to be some obstacles which can be related to problem-solving itself and others that are related to the employment relations angle of the process or dynamics in the group. Hurdles to creative problem-solving can include vague problem statements or too many intertwined problems, not having the resources needed, unclear responsibilities and not being sure of how to measure success (Cloke & Goldsmith, 2000). Most of these can be overcome by having a well-facilitated kick-off meeting where the problem is further discussed and defined. Using the tools we describe above will also help to untangle problems and give the team more clarity. A robust governance process which is supportive of the goals of problem-solving should also ensure the team has the resources it needs to follow the process with confidence.

> **Exercise 8.1: What's wrong with this approach?**
>
> This highly unionised organisation had a series of operational issues it needed to solve. The problem-solving approach with unions was something it wanted to try as it recognised that getting employee input to the solution would be beneficial. Historically there was very little trust between the managers and the union representatives. The organisation set up some management teams to define the problem statements. They also worked up their proposed solution. It then talked to the unions about the problem-solving approach and how it would work. The unions were very sceptical and insisted they wanted all their full-time officials and union representatives involved, which made the groups too big. They didn't trust the company-appointed facilitators who they didn't feel would be independent. The initiative failed before it got started.
>
> What do you think went wrong from the outset? What would you do to get this back on course?

To build confidence in the process, our case study companies all started with smaller and less complex problems. Seeing success helped them to build momentum and gain impetus, enabling those who were more sceptical to slowly support new ways of working.

Typical problem-solving obstacles

- Members don't turn up.
- Members don't do the work asked of them.
- Timescales slip.
- The team faces obstacles within the business.
- Conflict between members.

It is essential that the facilitator confronts these issues and reinforces the problem-solving principles and purpose and revisits the ground rules agreed by the group. The facilitator, in consultation with the team, will have to decide how best to resolve the problem but they should be wary of disbanding a team—although this should remain an option—as this can undermine the process in the long run.

8.9 Conclusion

Problem-solving is a way of working which offers huge benefits in the employment relations field, enabling union representatives and managers to become regular problem-solvers. It can be used alongside consultation and negotiation on specific, defined issues. It can be used to signify a change of direction and unblock a change which has failed to be resolved via negotiation. If it becomes more commonly used in organisations, either party can suggest using a problem-solving approach at the outset of some joint discussions or if issues get bogged down in one of the other processes.

There is a role for the employment relations practitioner to influence others to take an opportunity to do something different. If the environment is conducive and both parties commit to the process, there is a real opportunity to use the minds, knowledge and experience of union representatives, employees and managers to solve a range of workplace problems. The environment may require an intervention prior to problem-solving to address the current relationship and firmly establish a desire by both parties to change. All these interventions do require an understanding of the current relationships, culture and strategy. They require an assessment of both party's appetite for a new approach. It may require external support to independently facilitate as the groups build confidence and trust, and enable the relationships between the groups to change first.

This is not a process which pits one party against the other and there is no need for either party to feel it has lost its identity or sold out. Problem-solving can widen the influence of employee voice—solving real problems of great relevance to people at work. "If intergroup problem-solving can be achieved then each group is in a position to retain its autonomy. At the same time, each is able to make its full contribution to the goals they share in common" (Blake et al., 1964: 100).

> **Questions**
>
> 1. Consider how you could build a business case for bringing problem-solving into your organisation.
> 2. What specific issues do you think are suitable for problem-solving with unions in your organisation?
> 3. What are the key differences between the approach to policy modernisation described in this chapter and the approach that you have taken with your unions?
> 4. Evaluate whether this approach could work in your organisation. Which factors would work in your favour, and which would work against you? What could you do to minimise the factors working against you?

References

ASQ. (2023). *Fishbone Diagram.* [Online]. https://asq.org/quality-resources/fishbone [Accessed 13/9/2023].

Bahat, R, E., Kochan, T, A., & Rubenstein, L, W. (2023). The Labor-Savy Leader. *Harvard Business Review*, July—August 2023.

Blake, R. R., Shepard, H. A., & Mouton, J. S. (1964). *Managing Intergroup Conflict in Industry.* Gulf Publishing Company.

Cloke, K., & Goldsmith, J. (2000). *Resolving Conflicts at Work—A Complete Guide for Everyone on the Job.* Jossey-Bass.

Cox., Higgins, T., & Speckesser, S. (2011). *Management Practices and Sustainable Organisational Performance: An Analysis of the European Company Survey 2009.* Dublin: European Foundation for the Improvement of Living and Working Conditions.

Cummings, T. C., & Worley, C. G. (2008). *Organization Development and Change.* 9th Ed. South-Western Cengage Learning.

Kelly, J., & Kelly, C. (1991). Them and Us: Social Psychology and the New Industrial Relations. *British Journal of Industrial Relations, 29*(1), 25–48.

Kochan, T. A., Katz, H. C., & Mower, N. R. (1985). Worker Participation and American Unions. In Kochan, T.A. (ed.), *Challenges and Choices Facing American Labor.* MIT Press.

Nawaz, S. (2017). The Problem with Saying "Don't Bring Me Problems, Bring Me Solutions". [Online] *Harvard Business Review.* 1/9/2017. https://hbr.org/2017/09/the-problem-with-saying-dont-bring-me-problems-bring-me-solutions. [Accessed 8/12/2023].

Ospina, S., & Yaroni, A. (2003). Understanding Cooperative Behaviour in Labour Management Cooperation: A Theory Building Exercise. *Public Administration Review., 63*, 455–471.

Schein, E. H. (1999). *Process Consultation Revisited: Building the Helping Relationship.* Addison-Wesley Publishing Company.

Part IV

Managing Conflict

9

Managing Industrial Action

Abstract Collective conflict can take many forms from disorganised resistance to full-blown strike action. Any type of action can be costly and damaging to employers and workers. Therefore, this chapter aims to help students and practitioners understand how issues or changes in the workplace can lead to collective conflict and in particular strike action. The chapter will outline the different roles parties play during a strike, how a strike develops and some of the practical steps which can be taken during a period of industrial conflict. There is first-hand information from workers who have gone on strike, practical hints and tips from mediators who help to address conflict and a detailed case study to draw out the important points to consider. Overall, the chapter will help readers to understand the dynamics of industrial conflict, so they can represent the interests of their organisations, identify opportunities to resolve issues and maintain relationships with employees and unions.

Keywords Dispute · Conflict · Industrial action · Strikes · Collective conflict

9.1 Introduction

Workplace conflict comes in many forms however it reflects the 'structural antagonism' that lies at the heart of the employment relationship which in turn revolves around the "the basic conflicts of interest which exist between employer and employee" (Blyton & Turnbull, 2004: 349). Where unions are not present, conflict tends to be expressed through individual and organised expressions of discontent. This can range from disengagement, grievances, litigation, 'cyberloafing', 'pilfering' and even sabotage (Ackroyd & Thomson, 2016). In some cases, non-unionised workers can act collectively. For example, Deliveroo drivers have staged unauthorised walkouts by collectively not logging in for their shifts (Vandeale, 2018). In unionised workplaces resistance is much more likely to be expressed in a more organised collective form. This can take the form of refusing to work overtime, not undertaking specific tasks or refusing to undertake key activities. For example, university lecturers may refuse to mark student assignments. However, strike action is the epitome of workplace conflict. Strikes themselves range from a 'discontinuous' (or indefinite) strike to strikes on specific days, shifts or times. Although strikes are relatively rare, they can have significant impacts on those involved, the organisations affected and the wider societies that they take place within. For this reason, in this chapter we look at how strikes develop and the ways in which practitioners can respond and facilitate effective resolutions. The chapter brings this to life through a series of examples from unionised organisations in the UK. While the legal and social environment will differ across countries, the principles and strategies discussed in the chapter can be used in any environment.

> **Definition**
> A strike can be defined as a "temporary stoppage of work by a group of employees in order to express a grievance or enforce a demand" (Hyman, 1972: 17).

9.2 The Cost of Strike Action

In Chapter 2 we noted an increase in collective conflict in some countries in the wake of the Covid-19 pandemic and pressures on the cost of living. This suggests that the basic reason for strikes has always revolved around economic issues and job security. This followed a general decline in strikes and other industrial action in most developed economies in the previous three decades. This mirrored declining union density, the erosion of union organisation and increasingly hostile employer attitudes. However, the apparent lack of conflict arguably gave employers a false sense of security, creating a lack of investment in the capacity and capability to handle the threat of strikes and industrial action. This is particularly important given the potential of strikes and industrial action to impose severe financial and economic costs on organisations.

The total costs of a potential dispute by courier company UPS in the US in 2023 were identified by economic research organisation, the Anderson Economic Group. If it had not been averted, the dispute would have been the costliest strike in the US at the time. The Anderson Economic Group estimated the cost to the US economy of a 10-day strike at $7.1 billion and included lost wages to workers, lost earnings to the company, lost goods, services and worker wages in other industries, and direct losses to consumers.

Strikes in the UK rail industry in 2022 were estimated to have cost the UK economy more than £1 billion. They also cost the UK rail industry £25 million on a weekday and £15 million per day on a weekend (Topham, 2023). The cost of these disputes spilled over into the hospitality industry during the festive period of December 2022, and this was estimated at £1.5 billion and £2 billion for night-time industries (CEBR, 2023).

In addition to these direct costs, it is also important to consider the indirect impacts of strike and industrial action. These can include reductions in share prices, profitability and dividends. Strike action can also undermine brand reputation, which could have a knock-on impact on sales and make it more difficult to attract and recruit new staff. Furthermore, industrial action can reduce morale and staff engagement which, in the longer-term, can erode organisational performance. Therefore, understanding the wider costs of collective conflict helps organisations to get a more complete picture and provides the foundation of a business case for investing time, resources and effort in good employment relations.

> **Exercise 9.1: Estimating losses from an industrial dispute.**
> 1. Consider an industrial dispute that you are aware of and think of all the direct and indirect costs.
> 2. What impact do you think it would have on employers and unions if the full costs of disputes were calculated? Do you think it would change their actions? If so, how?

9.3 Strike Action—Roles and Responsibilities

No one wants to go on strike. It is an emotive situation where people will feel they are letting down patients, customers, or the travelling public. One trade union General Secretary we interviewed for this book explained that "people don't come to work to have a fight every day. They want to earn to sustain themselves, progress if they can and have employment security to plan their futures". Those taking strike action lose pay and it can damage workplace relationships for decades. In this chapter we look at the factors that drive collective conflict and mobilise workers. Collective conflict generally plays out in an eco-system of rules, procedures and agreements. There are multiple people involved and the subject matter is often a fundamental part of an individual's life (pay for example). Therefore, when there are disagreements, it is unsurprising that they escalate. Sometimes a resolution is extremely difficult to find. However, some disputes and strikes are avoidable, and some arise accidentally. To help demystify collective conflict and strikes, it is important to first explore the key roles and responsibilities of those involved.

Whilst economic issues are the reason for many strikes, all strikes are unique and caused by a complex set of contextual, institutional and personal factors. The roles and considerations in a strike vary considerably and may be influenced by a wide range of factors. Ego, personality, philosophical and political beliefs, and the quality of relationships within the organisation, combine to create different incentives between the key parties, which in turn can influence the dispute and strike process. Perhaps most importantly, the actions of those involved will have a profound impact on affected employees within the organisation. The tone of communications and the overarching relationship will be determined by the CEO and leadership team. Managers may want to balance resolution of the strike with additional costs, depending on the nature of the product or market they operate in. Equally they may have triggered the dispute through changes to what they thought were innocuous items such as break times. They may also have sympathy with striking workers and conflicting feelings about the strike.

> **Important**
>
> This book does not provide guidance on the legal aspects of industrial action. This varies from country to country and each jurisdiction will have specific rules on issues such as balloting, the right to strike as well as norms on picketing and protesting. For the employment relations practitioner, legal routes can create additional procedural problems as part of a dispute rather than providing solutions to the issues which have brought employees to withdraw their labour.

Local union representatives will need to deal with the pressure from their members. They will be asking themselves what can be done to resolve the issues? Are there issues of trust between the management team, Human Resources (HR)/employment relations and/or the full-time union official? How do we keep morale and motivation for the strike high? How much money will members lose and what happens when this is over? Senior union officials will help the local representatives in the planning and execution of the strike and bring experience and perspective from other employers. Employees themselves can be overlooked but experience a strike in a very visceral way. The interview below describes the experience of one frontline employee during a strike and the key considerations from their point of view.

Case Study 9.1: Strike action—voices from the frontline

"We were the biggest and best supported housing provider in the sector. We were going through a merger with a smaller organisation, but rather than us absorbing them and bringing their staff and services up to our standards, it was more like they were taking us over. Their managers were creaming off the senior roles, and their inferior terms and conditions, policies and procedures were to be imposed on us. Having prided ourselves, for decades, on the unparalleled quality of our services and staff, we were suddenly in a race to the bottom.

When it came to the strike ballot, I didn't vote. Going on strike just wasn't something I ever saw myself doing. I wasn't political. I'd never been to a demonstration. I rarely even voted in general elections.

I went to my first ever union meeting the night before the strike, looking for reasons not to have to do it: I couldn't afford the loss of wages. I thought I'd be marked a troublemaker and passed over for promotion, our vulnerable service users would suffer, the public would turn against us, there was no guarantee we'd win. It was standing room only – everyone from admin assistants to senior managers and, by the end of the meeting, I knew that, contrary to what the new CEO was telling us, cheap labour, downgraded roles, staff working to minimum standards was no way to 'secure the future' for anyone. We couldn't just sit back and watch the soul being ripped out of our organisation.

On the first strike day I got ready as if I was going to work. I don't know why. Then the time I would have to leave to make my shift passed, and then my shift start time passed, and I was still sitting on my sofa. It felt strange yet exhilarating – as if I was doing something wrong.

I didn't know what a picket line was but on the second day, I joined one. It wasn't mounted police and violence. It was passers-by bringing us coffees and donuts, and people signed our petition, bus drivers honking their horns and giving us thumbs up, and the police officers that did show up just said they wished they could do what we were doing. It was as if we were all in it together – not just us, but ordinary members of the public, doing the right thing.

> And we won. Eventually, the new management saw sense, and, rather than diminishing everything, they improved their terms and standards to match ours.
>
> Before the strike, the strike was the only thing I could think about – fretting endlessly about the consequences, how I'd pay the rent, whether it was the right thing. After the strike, the strike was the only thing I could think about – the camaraderie, doing the brave thing, being part of something and knowing that if you fight you won't always win, but if you don't fight you will always lose."
>
> **Key questions**
>
> 1. Based on the case study, what do you think the key differences are between the perceptions of senior managers and employees towards strike actions?
> 2. How would you feel if you were in the position described by this employee?

This case shows that the different interests and positions during a dispute create a complex internal dynamic which must be recognised and carefully managed if it is to be resolved and long-term relationships protected. For this reason, operational HR teams and the union representatives are often the key to finding a way forward because of their depth of local knowledge and day-to-day experience.

> **Tip**
>
> Tap into the local knowledge of union representatives, managers and HR practitioners—they often have a much better feel for what is really going on than senior leaders and union officials.

However, local knowledge is often ignored, and wider organisational and union politics, status and self-interest can mean that conflict escalates, and positions become increasingly entrenched. Almost every strike is resolved sooner or later. The process for getting there may mean more pain for one or both parties. In the next section we will look at how we arrive in a position where strike action is a last resort.

9.4 How Do You End Up with a Strike?

Whatever the root cause of conflict, there are multiple points in the collective bargaining process at which an agreement can be reached to avoid industrial action. However, at times conflict is required to provide closure. An issue is raised. It isn't dealt with. It is escalated. Eventually the union decides it is time to use the last resort of a strike. However, this is never a decision taken lightly and there will often be a range of procedures or legal processes which unions need to navigate before action can be taken. The case study below outlines the steps and considerations from the perspective of a trade union in the UK, where industrial action is tightly controlled by legislation.

> **Case Study 9.2: Strike action—jumping through hoops**
>
> As well as the ongoing discussions about the dispute, there may be a lot of activity going on behind the scenes from a union perspective. This case sets out some of the key issues which union representatives and full-time officials will need to consider in a ballot for industrial action to meet the legal requirements in the UK to hold a strike.
>
> **Step 1—What is the problem?**
>
> Identify the issue at the heart of the dispute and make sure it meets the legal definition of a trade dispute. Only industrial action relating to a trade dispute with an employer is protected by law. This includes pay, working conditions and employment. However, it is unlawful for unions to take strike action in connection with a political issue or the actions of another employer. This is a key legal step, although most issues will fall within one of the categories. There may be an opportunity to refer the issue for conciliation—in the UK this is through the Advisory Conciliation and Arbitration Service (Acas).
>
> **Step 2—Testing the water**
>
> In the UK, industrial action has to be supported by a secret postal ballot of all members who may be called on to take strike action. However, before moving to a formal ballot, some unions consult their members via a survey or informal vote called a consultative ballot. This has no legal status and can be as simple as an online survey or a show of hands in a meeting. This helps to establish the strength of feeling about an issue and identify what type of action members will favour. This may be an indefinite strike, one-day strike or other industrial action such as an overtime ban. This can also be used as a bargaining tactic as a 'yes' vote will give the union significant leverage in discussions with the employer.
>
> **Step 3—The ballot**
>
> Having established the issues, the appetite for strike action and the preferred approach, UK unions must follow specific legal steps before they can call on their members to take strike action. They must give the employer seven days'

written notice of the intention to ballot members. This needs to include details of the specific group of members to be balloted, the dates the ballot will open and close, and a copy of the ballot paper. This gives an employer an opportunity to plan its response but also to scrutinise and challenge the legality of the process. The ballot has to be conducted by an independent organisation.

Step 4—The result

In the UK at the time of writing, when the union receives the results, it must inform the employer of the number of ballot papers returned, the number voting yes, the number voting no and the number of spoilt papers. The union then needs to decide what action to take. The union can only call industrial action if a majority of those voting vote yes. In addition, there must be an overall turnout of at least 50% for the vote to be valid. There are even more stringent requirements for specific 'important public services'. Here, at least 40% of the total electorate must vote in favour.

Step 5—The strike notification

Once a positive vote has been received, the union must decide what to do. It has 28 days to take industrial action and there are several further legal requirements to be met. Unions must give the employer 14 days' notice of industrial action, summarise the dispute, confirm the type of action which will be taken and who is taking it (including numbers, work groups and workplaces). The action must take place within six months, after which a new ballot will be required. This provides a window of opportunity to resolve the dispute—if there is a strong vote in favour, it is more likely that the action will go ahead but it also gives the union more bargaining power to push the employer to make concessions. However, if there is weak support, the bargaining position of the employer may harden and the union may feel that taking action could be ineffective.

Step 6—Taking Action and Picketing

Assuming all of the above steps have been met, there will be a lot of communication about what will happen during the industrial action. Information on what to do on the day is particularly important and the union and employer will usually both communicate what employees and members should do. Picketing or demonstrating may form a large part of the activity on the day of the strike and the union will play a large role in organising and supporting this. There will be different rules on this in different countries.

Key questions

1. What do you think are the impacts of the balloting requirements explained above on the bargaining power of the two parties?
2. These requirements are designed to control union action, but are there any benefits for trade unions?
3. If a union does not follow these requirements, should the employer always mount a legal challenge? What are the risks in doing this?

Although views will vary on whether regulating industrial action in this way is necessary or desirable, the consequent process provides natural windows within which a dispute can be resolved and useful information which can help to break the deadlock. However, taking strike action is not easy and not undertaken lightly. Finding a way to avoid it means there needs to be maturity and resolve to address the issues.

> **Tip**
> Think carefully before trying to restrict industrial action through litigation. Even if the union has breached a regulation or law, challenging this could harden attitudes of union members in support of a strike.

9.5 The Employer's Perspective

How an organisation perceives and plans for industrial action will be influenced by its attitude to risk. There may be an entry in the corporate risk register covering the impact of, and contingency plans for, any industrial action. From an employer's perspective, the core process involved in the early stages of a dispute is arguably more structured that the way a union will run a dispute or campaign. It is largely bound by the terms of its recognition agreements and the dispute avoidance procedure. Figure 9.1 summarises the key stages many organisations use to resolve a dispute and avoid industrial action.

Once the employer is facing the prospect of a strike, its focus shifts to contingency planning and developing a strategy to resolve the dispute. The strategy adopted will depend on the wider approach to employment relations, the impact of strike and the relative bargaining power of the two parties. Some organisations will take a hard stance to bargaining, refusing to make concessions. This is more likely where an organisation perceives the union to be weak or where there is no room for bargaining. However, in some situations, the employer will want to 'win' the strike in order to undermine or challenge union influence. While this is not uncommon, it can have negative impacts in the longer-term on staff morale, turnover and organisational performance.

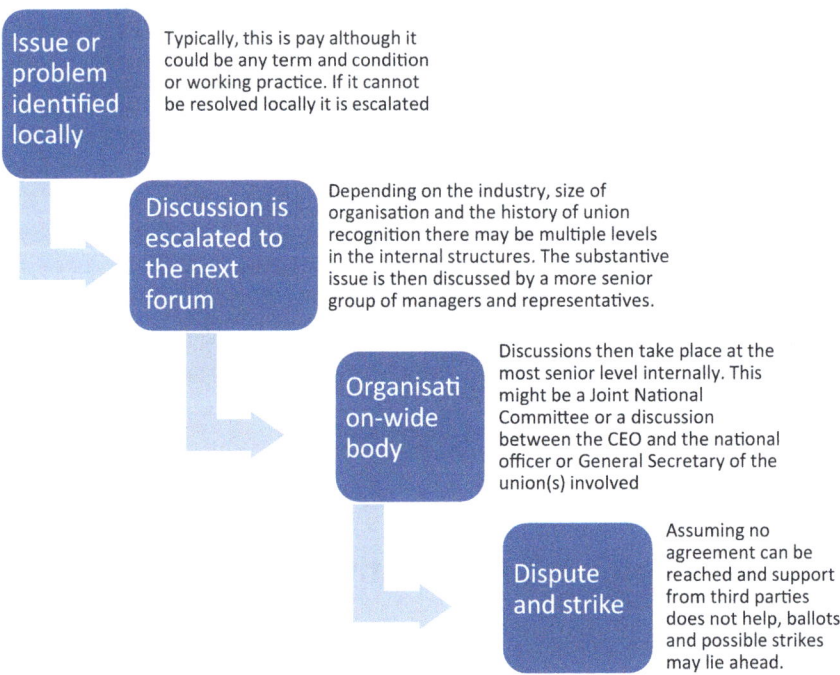

Fig. 9.1 Collective disputes procedure

Tip

Remember that 'beating' the union also means defeating your employees—this can have adverse impacts on morale, engagement and performance in the long-term.

In other cases, employers try to adopt a much more consensual approach in resolving industrial action—they recognise that the action itself shows the depth of feeling within the workforce and therefore try to find a collaborative solution. Although this may mean making concessions, there are real long-term benefits, and it is much easier to get back to normality relatively quickly.

9.6 Conflict in Action

To illustrate how conflict plays out we will take an actual dispute from the UK between an employer and a trade union. This will allow us to examine the issues involved at each stage and analyse what could be done differently and why.

In the winter of 2021 and spring of 2022, a union organised a wave of industrial action amongst refuse workers. Skills shortages, a period of inflation after years of pay stagnation and a track record of winning pay rises in other local organisations created an environment where refuse workers and the union were able to leverage their bargaining power. Some employers dealt with this better than others. This case study looks at one employer and how it handled the dispute with a union (Union A) that it didn't recognise for collective bargaining.

Case Study 9.3: Trouble brewing

The first public news that trouble was brewing came from a Union A press release on 9 January 2022, which sets the scene for the dispute and strike action.

"This ballot has come about after disillusioned and angry HGV drivers and loaders contacted [Union A] seeking support in taking their pay claim and grievances against the council forward. The issues which include Pay Levels, Terms and Conditions being below not only current market rates but are in comparison less than their council workforce colleagues just a few miles down the road carrying out the same public service work. There is a long list of issues which if [the employer has] any sense, they will seek to resolve directly with the union on behalf of our members at the earliest opportunity possible, and not choose to entrench themselves behind a belief that archaic welfare treatment of their environmental services staff and in work poverty pay scales are going to be acceptable any longer."

On 19 January, Union A confirmed it would be balloting for strike action and bemoaned the lack of engagement by the employer. The lead local Union A representative stated in a press release that:

"Strike notice has been issued and given the employer refuses to meet us formally and negotiate a settlement…residents' rubbish goes uncollected and the town centres and communal streets uncleaned. Even though both [the Chief Executive] and [Director for Digital, Sustainability & Resources] seem to want to bury their heads in the sand, we're issuing a stark warning that they have three weeks to speak to us or it'll be rubbish that they'll be buried in."

By 24 February BBC news reported the two perspectives on the dispute as below:

"Union A said more than 60 of its members working in domestic refuse and recycling will strike from 14 March. Union A officials have given [the employer] three weeks to table a suitable pay offer. The spokesman for [the employer] said: "[Union A] has refused to explain to us what the issues of its members are, so we are still unclear as to why the strike has been called and how it can be avoided."

On 9 March an [employer] spokesperson stated that frontline teams were being given a "decent" pay rise adding that:

"We would urge those staff who have voted to take strike action to rethink. In the context of the current economic situation, with all public sector organisations facing considerable restraints on budgets, this review has managed to fund salary rises considerably above what many others in the community will be getting."

Key questions

1. What is the dispute about?
2. What are the key issues that both sides need to consider based on the information available?
3. If you were the employer, what would you do next?

Ideally, the parties to any collective conflict should try to resolve the issue(s) at this point, before positions start to harden and defensive attitudes become entrenched. However, this means putting some of the adversarial rhetoric to one side and trying to adopt a constructive approach. Unfortunately, in many cases, the parties adopt more reactive and adversarial stances which lead to an escalation.

Case Study 9.4: Escalation

After the council set out its position on 9 March, there was an escalation in communications, mostly in the public domain. The council started to set out the work it had already done with another trade union, Union B, in a press release.

"In October last year (2021) [we] commenced an internal review into the pay of 109 members of staff in its refuse, recycling and cleansing department. This was significantly ahead of the [union] contacting the Councils in December last year. [Union B] is the recognised union not [Union A] and has been involved in the review process. Although we have approached [Union A] for details of their demands, the union has refused to respond, leaving the authorities unclear of the reasons for strike action."

Two days later another press release went further, highlighting that [Union B] had negotiated and agreed a deal:

"It might seem that the strike action is about [Union A] trying to push [Union B] out of the service – not about getting a good deal for its members –and we hope that common sense can still prevail."

The response by [Union A] to this was unequivocal. The headline on its press release read: "[Management] officers can make deals with whoever they wish, but any agreement to halt industrial action by [Union A] members would have to be made with [Union A]."

"We are, as always, happy to end this formal dispute, but this would have to be through formal negotiations and a formal agreement, as a chat won't cut it. We have patiently waited for the call that means real negotiations can commence... we've headlined our demands to the council in the hope that we might start formal talks and yet have received nothing in return... From Monday, [Union A] will be even easier to get hold of as we'll be on the picket line with our members."

With these two opposing approaches yielding little result, the strike action took place from Monday 14 March 2022. However, despite the start of industrial action the tone of communications did not change. On 15 March the employer published further information about the pay deal, claiming to show that its pay rates were higher than in comparable organisations. The accompanying press release claimed there were "serious questions about why [Union A] has taken strike action", and that such an "aggressive approach hardly bodes well for future dealings with [Union A]". The following day this was followed with another press release adding that it wanted to correct misinformation and highlight the role played by [Union B] as the recognised union. It ended with a quote from a spokesperson that: *"We were concerned from the very first communications that we received from [Union A] that they were going to be difficult to deal with threats of strike before we had even understood who they were, how many they represented and even what they wanted."*

Over the next two weeks there were three press releases in three days by the council outlining meetings, refusals to meet, refusals to pause the strike action and on 30 March an invitation by [Union A] for the Chief Executive to come to the picket line to address striking workers. The war of words continued ("unfair on residents and businesses") and took an unusual turn when the employer sent a press release confirming that [Union B] had made an official complaint about [Union A].

The strike action continued further into March with no sign of resolution.

Key questions

1. What does the communication from the union and the employer tell us?
2. How would you describe the tone of the communications?
3. What would you do next?

This shows how a conflict can escalate and become difficult to unwind. It is important to remember that most strikes and industrial disputes are settled in one way or another. However, this will need either or both parties to back down. This is often difficult because the longer a dispute goes on, the more both the employer and workers have invested in terms of time, emotion and lost revenue or wages. This is when the intervention of a third party to act as a mediator can be crucial.

> **Case Study 9.5: Towards an agreement?**
>
> The strike action continued and on 31 March, Acas hosted a meeting of the employer and the two unions. There was hope of a constructive forum for dialogue and that things were finally beginning to move forward.
>
> The employer issued a press release outlining the "positive and productive" discussions. The outcome—to draft a recognition agreement and begin discussions on pay—suggested hope for the end of the strike. However, by 2 April this hope was dashed after [Union A] highlighted comments on social media by management claiming that it had said that *"Goodwill and patience will suffer if [Union A] continue to hold [the employer] and our residents to ransom"* that this was *"Unnecessary and provocative industrial action"* and ultimately that *"Residents suffering might have to be paid for by cuts to service or perhaps increases in [taxes]"*.
>
> The response from [Union A] was clear; the strike continued. Union A then tweeted to the employer that "your inflammatory comments online and to the public may be putting your own staff at risk of attack".
>
> By the end of the first week in April, [Union A] was continuing to highlight what it called "game playing" and "mistruths and misdirection". Despite signing a recognition agreement, [Union A] issues a statement saying *"We unfortunately have little belief in the [employer's] ability to do anything other than use smoke and mirrors to avoid reporting matters accurately...Needless to say, it's being made so much harder than it need be."*
>
> Following further discussions, industrial action was paused on 12 April to allow for "substantive talks" to take place on pay and conditions and a "catch-up payment" was agreed to facilitate the additional work to clear up refuse. A joint statement was released and press releases on both sides had a more considered tone.
>
> On 21 April an agreement was announced. The employer outlined that new pay grades would be established for some workers, there would be improved weekend and bank holiday pay for cleansing crews and an increased specialist skills payment for HGV drivers, in addition to the agreement reached by Union A earlier in the year. The council press release hailed it as "Talks a success as [Union A] ends bin strike". [Union A] had a slightly different description. "The pay deal will mean an increase of 8.2% for refuse loaders on the pay award previously offered and accepted by members of another union. Cleansing drivers will see their pay rise by 10.4% above the previous offer, with some HGV drivers set to emerge with 20.7% more".
>
> However, it was not immediately clear that the dispute was definitely over. [Union A] outlined that while the strike would be called off with immediate effect, it reserved the right to bring its members back out on strike until November, should any of these commitments not be honoured within the agreed time period. The press release ended with, "This once again shows the value of being in a union, and the message is clear: anyone else looking to improve their pay should give [Union A] a call".

> **Key questions**
>
> 1. What does the final outcome tell you?
> 2. Could this have been dealt with differently?
> 3. Could this have been avoided?
> 4. What do you think happened next?

9.7 Mediating Collective Conflict

As the above case study highlights, collective conflict is not always avoidable. However, when it does happen there are ways to prevent it escalating into industrial action. Independent mediators such as Acas in the UK and the FCMS in the US can play a key role. We discussed the experience of collective conciliation with one of Acas's most experienced mediators.

> **The role of Acas—the independent perspective**
>
> Strikes can be emotive and a key part of the conciliator's role is reducing the level of emotion and tension in the room. The conciliators often don't feel the stress of the strike per se, but the role does come with significant challenges, not least because you have to establish trust and rapport with parties, and in an extremely short period of time gain an understanding of the issues in dispute, the nature of the industry and all the associated jargon. When dealing with multi-union disputes with large numbers in joint meetings this can be daunting. The engagement with parties prior to the joint meeting is essential to help everyone feel more confident in the process and with sharing information with the conciliator.
>
> For the participants, HR/employment relations practitioners, managers, and trade union representatives and their full-time officials, the process can be tense and tempers might fray. For that reason, Acas provides separate rooms for unions and management. In multi-union disputes, you may have different unions sitting in different rooms due to differences between them. But it may also be difficult within each camp. The local representatives may not agree with the full-time official. The employment relations/HR representatives may be at odds with the CEO or senior operational managers. Sometimes, the best thing a conciliator can do is to step out of the room to allow parties time to resolve those internal issues. But the process provides the ability to remove

some of the emotion referred to above and help parties concentrate on the substantive issues.

Having clear processes and procedures for dealing with conflict is fundamental. They can provide much-needed structure to what can be complex and messy disputes. They can also contain guidance and a common understanding on key concepts and terminology as well as helping everyone understand where they are in the process and who needs to be involved. But, they are not the "be all and end all". If a process is used as a tick box exercise, without meaningful engagement, or those engaged in the process outside of the employment relations role don't have a proper understanding of what it means to have an industrial relationship, this will undermine negotiations because there will be no trust. Equally, attempts to personalise attacks on either side, via social media or the press, can take the focus away from attempts to have a constructive dialogue. Where there are long-term, established industrial relations, the impact may damage the overall relationship, but in sectors where these relationships are less established the impact can be more personally damaging, and there are cases Acas has dealt with where senior leaders have stepped down post-dispute because of their experiences.

In terms of trends, Acas is seeing issues consistent with the impact of interest rates, inflation and the wider cost of living crisis. This is feeding through to pay deals, often with an expectation of inflation by employees, particularly where this has been the case historically. This is particularly prevalent in the private sector but less so in the public and voluntary sectors where pay restraint and impact on funding have been a significant feature. Combined with a greater propensity by employees to take strike action, it means there have been many difficult discussions.

Employers are also struggling to communicate the impact on their businesses of increased costs brought about by energy prices, raw materials and fuel costs. In this context, presenting the latest financial results or explaining the reason why the reserves/surplus is a specific number is very difficult. The words used are important to provide a common framework to explore issues and the more emotional the words, the less engagement there is with the issues. The language we see in these situations is highly emotive. 'We don't trust you'. 'I don't know how you sleep at night'. 'This is all smoke and mirrors'. An employer may clearly lay out the financial evidence for its position but if trust is not there, unions will repeatedly question the veracity of the figures provided.

Top tips

Despite challenges in the wider economy, organisations are reaching agreements and building positive relationships. Below are some of the key elements that can support more constructive relationships.

- At a general level, make sure there are strong relationships between unions and the organisation at all levels—not just in the HR or employment relations teams. Leaders and managers need to understand the role of union representatives (it can be a really difficult job). Understanding how the union works, its democratic processes and the process it needs to follow to initiate industrial action, are critical to finding a path through a dispute.

- Ensure you have a process in place for collective conflict and are clear on concepts like consultation and negotiation. Everyone should understand the basis for these conversations. Sharing information to enable such discussions is critical and helps build trust and demonstrate there is transparency.
- Organisations need to have the right people in the room when there is a dispute. And once you are there, listen. Having key decision-makers present (on both sides) means there is a greater awareness of the issues and why they are important. This is particularly true of difficult people who may seek to derail the agreement outside of the room. Delays in decision-making can also be fatal to a deal.
- Minimise media. No one ever reached an agreement through the press. When statements are made in the public arena it can harden positions, close potential routes to a deal and raise the temperature.
- Finally, Acas would always recommend a post-dispute review. Acknowledge the mistakes made and find ways to avoid them in future. There may be underlying issues which contributed to the dispute and addressing those will help the overall relationship moving forward.

9.8 Planning and Communication

On paper, conflict resolution may seem like an easy, logical and rational process. There are theories to explain it and processes to follow. However, emotion, ego and self-interest may create interpersonal barriers to compromise or even to listening. But as our case study shows, despite this optimism, strike action can escalate and take place quickly. Therefore, it is crucial that employment relations professionals, managers and leaders understand what to do in these circumstances. Given the impact on the organisation and people, taking a structured approach to how you deal with the arising conflict may help you save the relationship with employees and unions in the future. After all, when the conflict is over, you will all be working together again. Whilst contingency planning may be seen as part of the bargaining process (the ability to manage during periods of industrial action may influence the employer's approach to a negotiation), it should be considered as a core activity independent of the dispute process.

9.8.1 The Role of Operational Managers and HR

Everyone will be nervous; it is completely natural and one way to manage the situation is to provide as much guidance as possible and plenty of opportunities to ask questions. Briefings for managers can help to prepare them and give them confidence to speak to their teams. Some managers will want to know absolutes. Can I make people come in? Can I engage agency workers? Can I make them tell me if they are going to be on strike? Some of these questions are easy to answer, but the approach and tone are crucial. The guidance needs to be as even-handed and neutral as possible. Clear and fair processes are key. HR specialists locally will be in a difficult position, they might need some guidance and support on how to handle the strike period and engage with representatives.

The day(s) of strike action will be challenging—there may be picket lines, loud demonstrations, bands playing, barbecues and we have even seen a large inflatable rat. Of course, there will be safety considerations and the organisation has a duty of care to those employees not taking part in the action. However, it is important that managers and HR practitioners accept displays of emotion as part of the process and do not react in a negative way. Management may well be on the receiving end of over-personalised comments and communications from strikers and union representatives. Being prepared for this and understanding it will quickly pass may help to keep emotions in check and avenues of dialogue open. When the strike is over and people are back at work, managers and HR practitioners need to have a plan and be receptive to those returning to the workplace. It will be an emotive period and they will need to reintegrate everyone. We look at this in more detail in Chapter 10.

> **Tip**
> Operational managers and HR practitioners often take the brunt of the anger and frustration of workers and union representatives during industrial action. Make sure they are supported and that you check in with them regularly.

9.8.2 The Employee Perspective

Strike action can be a difficult experience for employees as illustrated in Case Study 9.1 at the start of this chapter. They may not know what to do and may be torn between their team, commitment to the organisation and their bond with striking colleagues. Crossing picket lines can be particularly daunting and can create conflict between colleagues which can have long-lasting effects. The way that the organisation communicates with its employees needs to reflect the uncertainty they feel and take into account the on-going relationship with the trade unions. Some employers instinctively try to persuade workers not to support the strike and often this takes the form of criticising the trade unions and urging staff to work as normal. However, we believe that employees can see this type of approach as divisive and even threatening. It can harden attitudes and be counter-productive—even if some employees feel pressured to break the strike, they are unlikely to feel positive towards the employer. Nonetheless, employees will want clarity on issues like leave, absence and reporting. How will a day's pay be calculated if it is being deducted? The communications teams need to be prepared to take an even-handed tone and not be too management oriented or too eager to 'win' the strike. In our experience, you rarely win the media war during the strike and it may alienate non-striking workers.

> **Tip**
>
> Keep communications with employees even-handed and information-based—taking a critical and adversarial line is likely to be counterproductive, increasing support for industrial action and damaging relationships.

The tone of communications is critical. Looking at the language used in the case studies above, mis-timed or ill-judged communications are flammable. Employees who are concerned about whether they will participate in strike action are not interested in point scoring and most customers will not read your communications. Make sure it is balanced, factual and that there is nothing you would not repeat in a room full of employees.

9.8.3 Developing a Communications Strategy

Although the way the employer communicates with its employees and stakeholders about industrial action is crucial, it is often overlooked and badly managed. You cannot control the communications issued by the trade unions. It is important to keep channels of communication open and not react negatively. Careful planning and execution of all communications is a core activity during industrial action. To help outline some of the areas to consider and factors to take into account an example communications plan is outlined in Table 9.1.

Table 9.1 Communications and industrial action

Goal - to ensure regular, honest and informative communications for all stakeholders					
Audience	Key messages	Channels	Timing	Products	Feedback
Employees	Reasons for dispute and negotiation updates Balloting information Sources of support Consequences for taking strike action	Email, intranet site, team meetings, online forums.	Weekly, after ballot sent to members, after ballot results, day before strike action, day after strike action.	FAQs	Via dedicated email address and team meetings.
Customers/service users	Impact on products or services and contingency plans Reasons for dispute	External website and social media.	On specific dates linked to strike action.	Page on external website	External website and existing mechanisms
Managers	Understanding of reasons for dispute and timeline of negotiations. Where to find information and support for staff Contingency plans	Email, online briefings, in-person briefings at specific sites	Weekly information linked to employee communications with specific messages when ballot announced, the day of the strike and the day/week after the strike	Key messages, team briefings	Through management teams into the senior leadership team
Leadership team	Expectations for a strike.	Briefings and one-to-ones for leaders with impacted teams.	Early engagement and preparation Weekly updates	Briefings	In-person and individual feedback
Union	Clarity on what and how you communicate	In-person meetings and formal correspondence	At beginning of dispute and key points in process	Letter/email, (in)formal meetings	In-person, correspondence.
Press	Reasons for dispute, contingency plans and negotiation updates Key dates for strike action and impact on customers and service users	Email, briefings	At beginning of dispute and key points in process Ad hoc communication may be necessary to correct inaccuracies	Email. Media training for key leaders	Email

9.9 Conclusion

Strikes represent one of the most common and recognisable forms of conflict in the workplace and can be dramatic, difficult and damaging for employers, employees and workers. The fact that levels of strike action may be historically low does not equate to an absence of dissatisfaction. This chapter set out a series of practical considerations for those dealing with the emotion, dislocation and disruption which strikes can cause. It concluded with some real-life examples, practical resources and wider considerations. As the workplace continues to change and workers think of new ways to express resistance, employment professionals will continue to need to deal with conflict and understand the fundamental processes for resolving problems and disagreements.

> **Questions**
> 1. What are the main factors that determine the incidence of strike and industrial action?
> 2. To what extent do you think that strike action is a legitimate expression of discontent? Thinking about your answer to this, what can employers do to prevent and contain strike action?
> 3. What are the most important issues to consider in attempting to resolve a dispute which appears to be escalating towards strike action?
> 4. From the perspective of an HR practitioner facing union threats of strike action, what would be your key considerations in developing a communications strategy to respond to this challenge?

References

Ackroyd, S., & Thompson, P. (2016). Unruly Subjects: Misbehaviour in the Workplace In S. Edgell, H. Gottfried, & E. Granter (Eds.), *The SAGE Handbook of the Sociology of Work and Employment*. Sage.

Anderson Economic Group. (2023). *Potential UPS Strike Could Be Costliest in a Century*. [Online]. Available at https://www.andersoneconomicgroup.com/potential-ups-strike-could-be-costliest-in-a-century/. Accessed 23 Sept 2023.

Blyton, P., & Turnbull, P. (2004). *The Dynamics of Employee Relations*. Palgrave Macmillan.

CEBR. (2023). *Industrial Action Cost the UK Economy £243m in Q1 Due to Lost Working Days, but Indirect Costs Will Drive Bigger Overall Impacts*. [Online]. CEBR. 12/5/2023. Accessed 28 Oct 2023.

Hyman, R. (1972). *Strikes*. Fontana/Collins.

Topham, G. (2023) Rail strikes cost UK £1bn and settling would have been cheaper, minister admits. *The Guardian*. [Online]. https://www.theguardian.com/uk-news/2023/jan/18/rail-strikes-cost-uk-1bn-and-settling-would-have-been-cheaper-minister-admits#. Accessed 4 September 2024.

Vandaele, K. (2018). *Will Trade Unions Survive in the Platform Economy? Emerging Patterns of Platform Workers' Collective Voice and Representation in Europe* (ETUI Research Paper—Working Paper 2018.05). https://doi.org/10.2139/ssrn.3198546

10

Rebuilding Employment Relationships

Abstract After industrial action, conflict or redundancies, relationships between unions and employers can break down with negative implications for the organisation and its employees. Relationships can also often be strained without any industrial action taking place. Without intervention—an analysis of the problem, a joint mediation-style process, a commitment to change and/or a long-term joint change programme—the relationships are likely to continue to deteriorate, increasing the chance of a recurrence of conflict. It is important to understand the root cause of any conflict or deterioration in relationships and identify what needs to change to create a more positive employment relations environment. In this chapter we explore, via a series of case studies, what actions can be taken to rebuild relationships, the critical factors which must be in place, the barriers and obstacles and the potential impact of these approaches.

Keywords Conflict · Breakdown · Rebuilding · Relationships · Mediation

10.1 Introduction

As we have said throughout this book, conflict is an inescapable part of the employment relationship. Although good employment relations provide the basis for the prevention, containment and resolution of conflict, industrial disputes can, and do, occur. Inevitably these situations have the potential to undermine relationships between unions and organisational leaders. They can also damage employee engagement and staff retention and destroy the credibility of unions and their representatives. If leaders and unions work together, they can reconstruct trust and minimise the negative impacts on workers and the organisation. In this chapter we briefly explore the long-term impact of collective conflict before looking at how relationships between unions and leaders can be rebuilt. We provide a series of case studies focussing on different elements of, and approaches to, rebuilding after conflict. Firstly, we look at an organisation that intervened early, recognising the signs of a deteriorating relationship. In another case study we analyse the steps taken by an organisation after difficult pay negotiations, which were a sign of a reduction in trust. In our final case study, we explore the key stages in a large-scale employment relations change programme which was initiated after an unexpected high-profile dispute.

10.2 The Long-Term Impact of Collective Conflict on Relationships

Understanding the costs of collective conflict can help to inform employment relations strategy and build the business case for investing in positive employment relations. In some ways, it is relatively straightforward to estimate the economic losses due to strike action. For example, a rail strike will mean cancelled services and lost revenue. There will also be knock-on impacts as productivity is lost by people unable to get to work in the normal way.

While much of our attention and the media tend to focus on the disruption while industrial action is taking place, the longer-term impacts revolve around the damage caused to employment relationships. These negative effects can be minimised by the way in which employers behave in and around industrial action, however they cannot be avoided. The nature of the dispute will shape the specific longer-term impacts but may also influence the way in which organisations react after the industrial action is over.

As we have said throughout this book, good employment relations depend on trust. In most cases, this will have been damaged as a consequence of industrial action. To some extent this will turn on the strength of the original relationship and the work done by both sides to maintain dialogue during times of conflict. However, even where this occurs, union representatives and their management counterparts will have had to take on positions and adopt behaviours which will put relationships under strain. For example, critical statements may have been made by both parties in the media in an attempt to state or restate a position. There may have been difficult meetings during the dispute and the workforce may end up divided over the rights and wrongs of decisions and actions taken by the organisation and the union.

Most organisations will never have a public dispute, but collective relationships can slowly deteriorate for a number of reasons, as we have previously discussed. This deterioration impacts individuals and their morale, the organisation and its effectiveness, customer service and brand. With this type of underlying conflict, an intervention to understand what is causing this deterioration is a worthwhile investment, especially if this leads to a joint commitment and clear actions to address the issues raised.

> **Tip**
>
> Continuing to talk and communicate, often off the record, can help the parties to understand each other and the positions taken during a strike or other industrial action.

10.3 Rebuilding Relationships—Key Principles

It is important not to underestimate the damage that collective conflict can do to interpersonal and intergroup relationships. The longer a dispute is allowed to continue, the more damage there will be. However, even in the worst cases, there are steps organisations can take to rebuild relationships and restore trust. In some cases, industrial action is a trigger for a much-needed overhaul of employment relations. Therefore, the post-conflict period should not be seen as something to 'get through' with minimum fuss or a chance to undermine union organisation and influence or push through unpopular change—instead it should be viewed as an opportunity for renewal. It is a chance to look systematically at the organisational culture—how managers listen and engage, how both parties behave, what issues are discussed, whether employees are empowered to speak up and how employment relations is managed at all levels of the organisation.

> **Important**
>
> "As much as a five-year span may be needed before the root system that produced the original animosities can be replaced by a new and healthier root system – one that can cause the relationship to flourish" (Blake et al., 1964: 194).

Unfortunately, many organisations that face this problem don't know where to start to rebuild relationships and lack the capacity and skills needed to identify the problem and then to begin to repair the damage. We believe that adopting a systematic process that gives the parties an opportunity to voice their concerns is crucial. Listening to the views of all stakeholders is an essential starting point, however difficult this may be.

> **Tip**
> Be realistic about the scale and pace of change—relationships can't be repaired overnight. This will take time, commitment and patience.

Rebuilding after a dispute requires effort, planning, honesty, listening and a genuine desire to change on the part of leaders of both the organisation and the unions. Both parties must want to learn from what has happened and want to do things differently, understand the root causes of the dispute or breakdown in a relationship and work on these issues. If not, they are likely to be back in the same place again very soon. In our work in this area, we have identified that the following principles have helped organisations and unions to start to rebuild relationships. In some organisations, all of these steps have been required and work has taken many years. In others, the focus has been on some specific interventions only, such as a structured 'team mediation' style session.

> **Key principles in rebuilding relationships**
> - **Establish a motivation to change and support for change**: there must be a mutual motivation to wish to explore the reasons for the conflict or deterioration in relationships, plus a desire to invest in a new way of working and build bridges. Senior leaders of both the organisation and the unions must jointly agree that the relationship needs to change, and they are prepared to work together to establish common ground for moving forward. It is critical that this genuine commitment to change comes from the most senior leaders of both parties. All parties must volunteer to take part willingly in any process of rebuilding.
> - **Take steps to understand the problem and give people a voice**: undertaking an analysis is important so that all parties have an agreement on what is getting in the way of good employment relations. Gathering data is critical, usually through interviews or focus groups with an external facilitator. This helps understand the nature of the conflict, the underlying causes, the issues and pressures, and the willingness of the parties to work together to resolve it.

- **Use a facilitator who is trusted by both parties**: they must be neutral or unbiased. They may need skills in how to shape and conduct the initial diagnosis, be able to build relationships with both unions and leaders and be confident and experienced in facilitating groups in conflict. They should be "be highly sensitive to their own feelings and to those of others. They must recognise that some tension and conflict are inevitable and that although there can be an optimum amount and degree of conflict, too much conflict can be dysfunctional for both the people involved and the larger organisation" (Cummings & Worley, 2008: 261).
- **Listen to each other in a structured session**: at some point, both parties need to listen to the perspectives of the other party. The facilitator should design a process which allows productive dialogue between the parties so they can examine their differences, move on from entrenched positions and ultimately change their perceptions and behaviours to start to build joint solutions.
- **Design a way forward**: this may involve many discussions on what is achievable, with all stakeholders involved in the planning and preparation of the next steps. The aim is to reach a joint commitment to rebuild and establish common ground for moving forward. At this stage, parties may be able to set out some high-level principles or a future roadmap, describing what a new approach to employment relations will look like.
- **Identify areas for joint working**: joint design and problem-solving enables both parties to co-create solutions. This could include joint work on areas such as capability building in employment relations or improving structures for collective voice. This may involve discussions on what support is required, what approach will be taken, who needs to be involved and how to communicate to the wider community and workforce.
- **Follow up and keep momentum**: once the parties have agreed to move forward, a decision should be made as to how any work agreed will be managed and how to keep momentum with the changes agreed. Without this, both parties are likely to move on to other pressing issues and lose focus. Ensure there is a joint governing body or steering group to keep the work on track and keep momentum.

Tip

After a serious conflict, it is helpful if any analysis is conducted by a third party who is seen as impartial. It is important that if someone is hired from outside the organisation, both parties trust them to take an independent view.

10.4 Mediation and Positive Relationships

When reading literature on conflict and mediation processes, particularly in the field of psychology and organisation development, and reflecting on our own experiences, it is clear that joint, highly structured sessions are a fundamental part of the process when rebuilding relationships.

> **Important**
>
> "It has been shown time and again, in diverse situations, that in a relatively short time period (say, a day), these structured intergroup activities can result in improved intergroup relations" (French & Bell, 1984: 159).

From the case studies in this chapter, we can see that joint sessions can be used in various scenarios. For example, they can be helpful if there are signs that employment relationships are deteriorating, change is becoming more difficult and meetings are less constructive. They can and perhaps, should, be used more frequently to keep the relationships healthy and constructive before a more formal dispute surfaces.

However, Blake et al. (1964: 194) also emphasise that these interventions do not take place in a vacuum and "one should not expect that a single confrontation…will repeal all present positions, past practices, previous agreements etc."

> **Important**
>
> "Where the greatest impact will become evident, is when new issues and different problems arise. Here, the parties are able to apply themselves in a problem-solving manner. In other words, the background of conflict does not recede. Rather, it remains to colour and influence old issues born in that era. However, new issues, that do not have a past anchorage, do not have the same tug in the directions of old norms and past practices. Members in both groups are not bound by old expectations. Instead, they are free to explore jointly for new solutions under the collaborative conditions produced by the intergroup therapy sequence" (1964: 194).

10.5 Key Steps in a Facilitated Joint Session

With that context in mind, we now look at the key steps we have taken in designing and facilitating mediation-type joint sessions with organisational leaders and union representatives. This is essentially a process where an experienced facilitator helps the parties to resolve a disagreement or problem. We have assumed that crucial pre-conditions are in place—both parties have volunteered to attend, are committed to learn from the past and are prepared to build something new. While this process is based on the work undertaken by Blake, Shepard and Mouton (1964), we have adapted it for groups of union representatives and managers. We provide three case studies later in this chapter, which demonstrate how this works in practice.

1. The facilitator talks independently to key people from both parties prior to a joint session. This enables everyone to input their views, express their opinions with an independent person and also enables the facilitator to get a better understanding of how both parties see the current issue or situation. An overall analysis of these interviews may be presented back to both parties at a face-to-face meeting. This data often, helpfully, uncovers a lot of common ground, similar frustrations and creative thoughts on what could be done differently. This diagnosis also helps both parties to identify what needs to change and could include skills gaps, outdated structures and a focus on behaviours. It also starts the process of reflection and helps to overcome any doubts.
2. At the joint session, the facilitator may present back the broad views of both groups, identifying the common ground. Both parties will also be given uninterrupted time to explain their concerns and express their views. This is a very important and powerful part of any process of mediation. It forces people to listen and reflect rather than try to rebut and argue a particular point. It also allows all parties to feel heard—a key element of organisational justice.
3. Both parties listen to each other about what needs to change. The perceptions of all parties are important, and it may become clear in the session that this may be the first time they have looked at issues from the other's perspective. For many participants, these sessions can be very helpful in understanding some misconceptions that they held about each other. Often, they learn that their perceptions of each other are based on inaccurate stereotypes and that they hold some common opinions and beliefs.

4. Our experience has shown that when parties reflect on the feedback they receive and see the other party reflecting on feedback they have been given, at some point in the session they both begin to look to the future and what needs to change. Schein describes this as "a joint exploration… of how to manage future relations in such a way as to minimize a recurrence of the conflict" (Schein, 1988: 178). Both parties are able to identify behaviours they would like the other party to demonstrate more of and less of, and behaviours they are prepared to demonstrate more and less of to make their relationship more constructive.
5. Both parties make some specific commitments as a team with agreed timescales, to end the session in a very practical way. It is helpful if this session leads to a set of agreed actions so that parties can see that key issues are going to be worked on and resolved. It is likely to still feel like 'early days' but they may feel they can communicate more widely about the actions to which they have committed. This may be a jointly agreed approach to a new way of working with each other or a series of further steps or sessions.

> **Joint Session Based on the Work of Blake, Shepard and Mouton**
>
> An example of the types of activities undertaken in a structured process is outlined below, based on the work of Blake et al. (1964). It is considered widely applicable in situations where relations between groups are strained or hostile (French & Bell, 1984: 156) and aims to move both sides from adversarial positions to one where they are able to identify shared interests and make commitments to change (Table 10.1).

In our first case study, we focus on a short intervention undertaken by an organisation and its union and the positive changes that can be made during a one-day event. This organisation undertook a joint session with its union as both parties had expressed frustration that their relationship was deteriorating. It was therefore a pre-emptive approach to avoid further deterioration and formal conflict.

> **Case Study 10.1: From disagreement to constructive debate**
>
> The leadership team and union representatives requested external help as their relationship was increasingly tense and they were less able to hold constructive meetings without issues becoming personal. Reaching agreements and moving forward on organisational change were also becoming more difficult. They

Table 10.1 Structured joint process

Step one	Clarify the willingness of both parties to take part in the joint process. If both parties are able to accept that the relationships can be better and they are prepared to work on this, the following steps take place. It is important that the focus of the discussion is on the relationships between the groups rather than personalities or specific bargaining problems or grievances.
Step two	In the first part of the session, the parties are in separate rooms and are asked to build two lists. In the first, they identify their perceptions and feelings of the other party. The second list is made up of adjectives that they would use to describe themselves in relation to the other party.
Step three	The groups then come together and read their lists to each other in a structured way, with no discussion of the items, although questions for clarification are allowed. The aim is to build understanding in a controlled way.
Step four	The groups then work separately again, discussing what they have learned about themselves and the other group. According to French and Bell, "it typically happens that many areas of disagreement and friction are discovered to rest on misperceptions and miscommunication; these are readily resolved through the information-sharing of the lists" (p. 157).
Step five	In the second part of the session, the parties continue to work separately to make a list of the priority issues that need to be resolved between the groups.
Step six	These lists are then shared in a joint session and the aim is to make one combined list of the issues that need to be resolved, in order of priority. Together the groups generate actions and assign responsibilities for each action. This underlines the importance of actions and outcomes.

needed to 'clear the air' and make some agreed changes to ways of working before the relationship deteriorated further. They agreed to take part in a one-day joint mediated session.

Both parties spoke to the facilitator on their own before the joint session. This enabled them to be clear about the process and ask any questions. It also gave them the opportunity to state how they saw the current relationship and issues, and allowed the facilitator to begin to understand both parties' perspectives.

The next step was to bring the parties together and give them an opportunity to tell the other about what employment relations felt like from their perspective, using uninterrupted speaking time. Both parties were able to then ask for clarification before reflecting in their groups on the feedback they had been given.

They then worked separately on creating a list of tangible improvement ideas, specifically focused on improving the preparation of meetings, the behaviours in the meetings and how actions were captured and resolved.

Below is a list of the actions that both parties presented to the other about what they wanted to do differently in the future. Both were quick to notice the areas of overlap and agreement in what they wanted to change. These two lists were then combined by the groups into one joint list of agreed changes. The Human Resources (HR) leader agreed to continue working with all the key stakeholders to implement these changes in future meetings.

Leadership team 'improvement' ideas

- Bring issues to the meetings earlier and in a less cut-and-dried form to enable more open discussion and less presentation of pre-formed solutions.
- Link discussions back to the clarity of a shared goal about the success of the company.
- Don't personalise or attack other people's integrity or presume other people's motives.
- Listen actively and be willing to change position.
- Be flexible in accepting when circumstances and priorities change.
- Focus on making progress in discussions, not repeating known positions.
- Be willing to accept that we won't always agree, but when we don't agree, be willing to draw a line under it and move on.
- Where we agree to disagree, be willing to use the dispute process as a way of testing employee opinion.
- When an explanation is given, but the other party doesn't understand it, agree what type of information would help clarify.
- When an explanation is given, but the other party doesn't believe it, ask what is the alternative proposal?
- We both need to be able to trust the confidentiality of discussions.

Union 'improvement' ideas

- Be clear about a meeting's purpose—seeking assent or collaboration.
- Ensure meetings are a space for unions to meaningfully contribute to proposals.
- Implement a joint 'secretariat' to allocate time to agenda items and check the sense of their significance.
- Review who chairs the meetings and consider rotation of the chair.
- Avoid personalisation or making assumptions.
- Ensure all parties understand problems/proposals.
- Use joint 'problem-solving' groups to take items out of the Joint Negotiating Committee for working on (rather than continue to debate without conclusion), if appropriate.
- State, at the time, if you feel uncomfortable in meetings and feel issues have become personalised.

Key questions

1. Where are the areas of overlap in the two lists from managers and union representatives?
2. Can you categorise the improvement ideas under some key headings?
3. Can you identify the underlying causes of the issues raised?
4. Now the list of improvement ideas has been generated, what would you do next?
5. How could you ensure that these ideas were put into practice?

The two lists of areas for improvement have two purposes. First, they develop an agenda for discussion by identifying the areas of overlap. Second, they demonstrate that the unions and management have mutual interests.

In this case, the mutual interest was how to move from "disagreement to constructive debate".

10.6 Addressing the Root Causes of Conflict

In our second case study (10.2 below), we explore the work undertaken by an organisation and its unions who had come very close to a dispute over pay. It is a more complex example than our earlier case study as the conflict was more embedded, there were more parties involved and the organisation was more complicated. We explain the diagnostic phase, a joint session and the joint commitment to a new way of working and what this entailed over a three-year period. It shows that increasing understanding of each other and how the parties view the situation, and then identifying common ground, were key first steps in rebuilding relationships. Then, working together on the steps that will lead to a new way of working enabled trust to be rebuilt and ensured that perspectives were better understood while disagreement reduced over time.

> **Case Study 10.2: Rebuilding after a near miss**
>
> An HR director wanted to understand what had led to difficult pay negotiations and the involvement of the UK's Advisory Conciliation and Arbitration Service (Acas) and she wanted a plan for a consistent improvement in the employment relations climate. Trade union density was very high across the organisation. The union had strong bargaining power due to a global shortage of specialist personnel who also took years to train and qualify. She brought in a new head of employment relations to lead a change in the employment relations climate.
>
> Interviews with the executive, leadership team, managers and union representatives showed that the relationship had been struggling in key operational areas prior to the pay negotiations. It was this deterioration in relationships and the lack of trust that had led to the difficult set of pay negotiations. The interviews uncovered that meetings between senior leaders and senior union representatives had little strategic agenda, behaviours in meetings were unhelpful and both frequency and attendance were erratic. Issues escalated to the top of the organisation and therefore less time was spent on strategic issues. There was a feeling that conflict "festered". There was very little dialogue between managers and union representatives to solve operational problems or for representatives to understand strategic direction or challenges. Most interviewees had lost faith in their ability to work together for the benefit of employees and the organisation.
>
> **Joint sessions for key leaders and union representatives**

After the initial diagnosis, a series of joint sessions were run with senior leaders and senior union officials to enable parties to see the issues from each other's perspectives. During a highly structured session with a facilitator, both parties listened to each other's views on the current employment relations climate and what they were prepared to do differently and what they would like the other party to do differently. At the end of the session, both parties agreed to develop a new joint employment relations strategy as a first step, along with some very tangible "quick wins".

New employment relations strategy signed off

Both the CEO and union officials wanted to improve the working relationships. Over the next few months, a new employment relations strategy was jointly agreed and signalled the intent to build an employment relations climate which was robust and could withstand disagreement. The strategy said, we aim to:

- Build a partnership based on mutual trust and respect.
- Give leaders, union representatives and employees clarity on our employment relations style and approach.
- Equip leaders and representatives with the skills and capability to consult well, formally and informally, solve problems together and negotiate effectively.
- Run clear and focussed forums that discuss local issues, business unit issues and company-wide issues and give union representatives a voice.
- Encourage timely and regular review of the relationships and encourage a culture of continuous improvement created by both parties.

Setting out the forward plan

A three-year plan was agreed, identifying key areas which needed to be worked on to bring the strategy to life. Each area was worked on jointly with a set timescale and signed off by both parties.

The key areas of focus over three years were:

- Defining the employment relations behaviours that would help build the partnership of mutual trust and respect.
- Building capability of managers and union representatives.
- Refreshing structures and meetings to enable effective employee voice at executive, business unit and local level.
- Investing in conflict resolution as a core skill across the organisation.
- Joint working on policy modernisation.

Organisational impact

Over the following three years, the new structures were implemented across the business with clear terms of reference and attendees. A new strategic forum helped union representatives to understand the direction of the organisation while new operational forums worked effectively to inform and consult on operational change. A capability building programme was jointly designed and delivered, upskilling key managers and union representatives.

This included training a team of conflict facilitators who intervened when requested. An annual audit of the employment relations climate, focused on the demonstration of defined behaviours, showed a year-on-year improvement in the perceptions of both parties. Pay negotiations were conducted swiftly and change was effectively managed with no disruption to the business.

Key questions

1. What were the key success factors that kick-started this change programme?
2. What are the most important elements of the forward plan and how will these contribute to improved employment relations in the future?

10.7 Sustaining Change

Our final case study (10.3, below) looks at a company-wide programme designed to change the industrial relations climate in a global organisation. It summarises the key events that took place over a five-year period to rebuild relationships between leaders and the recognised unions. After a high-profile dispute and two company-wide failures to agree, this company and its unions undertook a diagnosis of the current state of industrial relations, to understand what had led to a deterioration in the employment relations climate across the company.

In this case, it was the unions that initiated this review but both parties gave their full commitment to work towards something better. This case study explains the process of diagnosis, followed by the joint design of a change programme using problem-solving groups. This enabled trust to be built as the parties worked together to design solutions to the problems identified in the diagnostic phase. Later in the programme, joint mediated sessions, along the lines of the structure explained above, were used extensively in one part of the business that requested further assistance to improve the relationship between union representatives and managers.

This case shows the importance of undertaking an initial analysis of the problem. This not only provides the basis for change but also helps to build confidence in the process. It is also important to note that in this case a problem-solving approach was at the heart of the change programme rather than a mediation process. Problem-solving and mediation share the same roots. They are interest-based processes that facilitate collaborative working. Both focus on rebuilding trust and personal relationships. By analysing and solving problems together, both parties begin to trust each other more and see the benefits of listening to each other to resolve problems effectively.

Case Study 10.3: Large scale employment relations change programme after a strike

Diagnosis of the underlying problems

The unions had declared industrial relations in this company 'bankrupt' and requested external support to review the current situation. This was not to focus on the dispute in detail but on the underlying problems with the way industrial relations was conducted. The CEO and his leadership team agreed to the diagnosis and recognised the value of the union in initiating this review.

A diagnosis was undertaken which involved sending an individual questionnaire to all parties—the leadership team, trade union representatives and managers—plus group discussions were held with union representatives and one-to-one interviews with directors. This enabled both qualitative and quantitative data to be collected on employment relations strategy and vision, negotiation, consultation and communication. Parties were also asked to state what they'd like future industrial relations to be like and three practical changes they would make. The data was formally presented to the leadership teams of both the unions and the company, including the CEO, and cascaded to key union representatives and managers in the business.

Designing the change programme

As a result of the diagnosis, all parties agreed to undertake an employment relations change programme with backing from the CEO and full-time union officials. This involved joint workshops to define the objectives and approach. In this example, a bottom-up approach to change was favoured, where joint problem-solving teams addressed the main issues from the diagnosis in order of priority. There were various phases to the programme.

Phase one

- Established a joint steering group with a clear role, membership and governance. Defined the objectives of the change programme to ensure there was a clear goal and this was used to inform wider stakeholders of the programme and persuade local managers and local union representatives to take part.
- Identified the first areas to 'problem solve' based on the diagnosis.
- Defined the role of the teams, identified members, agreed problem statements, provided training for teams and facilitators.
- Allocated time and provided a deadline for problem-solving teams.
- Problem-solving teams made their presentations to the steering group. All recommendations were accepted.
- Joint teams were set up to oversee the implementation of recommendations.

Phase two

- A second round of problem-solving teams were set up, focussing on the next issues raised in the diagnosis.

- Presentations were made by the second round of teams and an implementation team was set up.
- All people managers and union representatives attended a day's training on the change programme, aims and outputs. The training was designed and delivered by the trade unions and operational and industrial relations leaders.
- Evaluation of impact to date.

Phase three

- Consolidation and embedding of changes across the business. Major changes had been made to management selection and training, leadership development, meeting behaviours, role profiles and communication.
- Design and delivery of facilitated joint sessions to improve industrial relations in two specific business units.

Impact

The company had a recognisable settled period of industrial relations for the five-year period of the change programme. However, changes in leadership in the company, the unions, key operational leaders and within the industrial relations team had an impact on the sustainability of the improvements over a longer period.

Key questions

1. What are the main success factors in this case?
2. How does the approach taken compare with the other cases in this chapter?
3. What are the advantages and risks of this approach?
4. How would you ensure that the changes that are made to collective employment relations are sustained over a longer period of time and can withstand changes in key personnel?

10.8 Challenges and Barriers to Successful Rebuilding

Rebuilding relationships after conflict is necessary to repair trust and begin to build a more effective employment relations strategy for the future. However, it is important to recognise that this comes with significant barriers and challenges. Perhaps the most important of these is getting the two parties to commit to the process after a period of conflict. In some situations, it may be necessary to allow a little breathing space after a dispute—a period of cooling off. It is useful to do some analysis of the situation in order to build a case to invest in a more intense change process. Furthermore, if specific relationships have been particularly damaged, there may be a need to restore these before a wider process is entered into.

The parties may have different reasons to be sceptical of a rebuilding programme. For the organisation, work will need to be done to persuade senior leaders of the rationale for investing in this work—it will take significant time and often means hiring external mediators or consultants. It will generally be the job of HR and employment relations practitioners to develop a business case for mediation and change. In addition, senior leaders must be prepared to commit to implementing whatever actions flow from the process. As this is a joint process, leaders will have to be prepared to give up some control.

From a union perspective, a suggestion from HR of team mediation can be viewed with suspicion –as a management ruse to blunt the power and influence of the union. Building confidence in the process is therefore essential but may be quite challenging. This is where using independent facilitators and consultants can be quite helpful. However, the most important step is to involve the union in the design and commissioning of the process itself—ideally it should not be seen as a management initiative.

> **Tip**
> There is no point in forcing people to take part in a structured, facilitated session. It may be necessary to persuade them to take part, but it is essential that they are prepared to engage constructively with the process.

Here are some ways to overcome the challenges and barriers associated with this type of rebuilding initiative.

- Spend time getting ready. It is critical that the senior leaders of both parties are comfortable with starting this work and have the buy-in of their own communities before you start. Time spent at this stage is a good investment.
- Work with all the key stakeholders, however difficult. It is important to identify who needs to be involved early on. Even if they are considered 'awkward' or 'unlikely to change', key people need to be included from the outset.
- Joint approaches and bottom-up change are more risky but can be longer lasting. It may be tempting for HR to lead and run the programme but it is likely to be more sustainable if the underlying methodology is one of enabling joint teams to solve the problems that they have identified.

- It will take time to change perceptions, behaviours and ultimately the culture, so be prepared to invest time, resources, energy and enthusiasm.
- Keep the dialogue going even when it gets difficult and nip problems in the bud by talking them through.
- Without commitment from senior parties, it will fail, so make sure you have the continued support of key stakeholders from the outset and keep them involved and engaged during the process.

> **Tip**
>
> Union representatives may be concerned about how their members will react to them working jointly with management, soon after being in conflict. Therefore, it is important to involve unions in shaping and designing any programme of change and develop joint communications to explain the process and benefits to the workforce.

10.9 Conclusion

This chapter has argued that most significant costs of conflict are not rooted in lost production or reputational damage during a strike but in the long-term impacts on relationships within the organisation. What may seem to be a 'victory' for management can undermine engagement, reduce productivity, increase labour turnover and lay the foundations for conflict to re-emerge. However, it does not have to be like this—if an organisation takes the opportunity to try to understand why a dispute occurred and address its root causes, it can create a more positive environment, making conflict less likely in the future.

However, this is not straightforward and takes commitment and expertise to rebuild relationships and restore trust. This is where processes to uncover the root causes of conflict, structured joint facilitated sessions to better understand perspectives, and problem-solving to rebuild trust can be invaluable. The most important aspect of all of these approaches is that they are joint endeavours—they are not solutions imposed by the organisation. Fundamentally they are processes of collective voice which can build trust and create lasting change.

> **Questions**
> 1. Using an example of a dispute with which you are familiar, explain how you would develop a strategy to restore positive employment relations and minimise negative impacts.
> 2. Discuss the main challenges in making team mediation work. Can these be overcome and if so, how?

References

Blake, R. R., Shepard, H. A., & Mouton, J. S. (1964). *Managing Intergroup Conflict in Industry*. Gulf Publishing Co.

Cummings, T.C., & Worley, C.G. (2008). *Organization Development and Change* (9th ed.). South-Western Cengage Learning.

French, W. L., & Bell, C. H. (1984). *Organization Development: Behavioral Science Interventions for Organization Improvement* (3rd ed.). Prentice-Hall International Editions.

Schein, E. H. (1988). *Organizational Psychology* (3rd ed.). Prentice-Hall International Editions.

11

Measurement, Evaluation and Reporting

Abstract There are many reasons why it is important for organisational leaders to measure, evaluate and report on the effectiveness of their collective employment relations strategy such as the cost of conflict, damage inflicted on brands and the management of risk. There is also increased external scrutiny on organisations to demonstrate positive employment practices, seen by how organisations treat their people. However, collective employment relations is not regularly assessed in organisations, despite the benefits of doing so. Gathering robust data on the effectiveness of the employment relations strategy and activity can inform a continuous improvement approach, thereby reducing the likelihood of conflict as well as providing assurance on workplace culture to investors, potential investors, and current and potential employees. This chapter discusses why organisations should measure and evaluate, provides examples of a range of practical tools, discusses problems with measurement and reporting while also providing examples of good practice.

Keywords Measure · Reporting · Risk · Governance · Continuous improvement · Audit · Evaluation · Behaviours

11.1 Introduction

In this chapter we focus on why organisations should measure and report on the effectiveness of their employment relations strategy and consider various methods for doing this. Measurement and audit are a key part of the methodology which we have set out in this book. If organisations take a strategic view of employment relations, invest in capability and skills, and ensure constructive dialogue amongst employees and their representatives, the final stage of the process is to assess the benefits of this approach and make changes to improve performance—instilling a continuous improvement approach to employment relations. There are also other reasons for measuring and reporting, such as increased external scrutiny, the cost of poor employment relations and the risks to the organisation. We propose that organisations undertake a regular assessment of the effectiveness of their ER strategy rather than waiting until there is a dispute or breakdown in relationships.

11.2 Why Evaluate Your Collective Employment Relations Strategy?

There are multiple reasons why organisational leaders should invest in undertaking a regular audit or assessment of their collective employment relations climate. But, in our experience, it is rare to find organisations that do this. This is despite the risk and cost of poor employment relations and the benefits of good employment relations. Many organisations adopt the approach described by a Human Resources (HR) leader in exercise 11.1, in that they only know it's not working when something goes wrong.

> **Exercise 11.1: We know it's not working when it goes wrong...**
>
> **The following is a quote from a senior HR leader, who we interviewed for this book, explaining their approach to employment relations evaluation.**
>
> > We don't measure the effectiveness of employment relations, like we do our diversity, equality and inclusion strategy (DEI), for example. With DEI we have a clear strategy, we roll it out with a lot of stakeholder engagement, there are targets and we evaluate if it's working. We only know if our employment relations approach is not working when it goes wrong. With employment relations, it is hard to define the deliverables, not everyone is touched by it, so who do you share it with, and the other party – the union – has a different set of objectives.
>
> Thinking about this explanation consider the following questions:
>
> 1. Is it possible to define the deliverables of an organisational employment relations strategy?
> 2. How would you go about defining joint objectives with a union or are joint objectives impossible between organisations and unions?
> 3. Does the employment relations strategy only affect or impact union representatives and managers or the whole organisation?

The lack of evaluation is arguably surprising when you consider that a breakdown in collective employment relations is often at the top of a corporate risk register in highly unionised organisations, with substantial costs associated with disputes, negative impacts on customer service, consumer confidence and share prices. There is also increased scrutiny of an organisation's Environmental, Social and Governance (ESG) performance from investors who are looking for a business to demonstrate actions leading to a positive employment relations climate. To analyse this further, investors will look at the risks and statements made in annual accounts. There is no doubt that workforce issues have risen up the corporate agenda and this includes collective employment relations (CIPD, 2023a, 2023b).

Therefore, we now explore four major arguments that employment relations practitioners can use to make the case for measuring, evaluating and reporting on the organisation's collective employment relations climate on a regular basis. These are:

1. To establish if your strategy is working.
2. Increased external scrutiny.
3. The cost of collective conflict.
4. The management of workforce risk.

11.3 Establishing if Your Strategy is Working

As we have mentioned in earlier chapters, employment relations can be costly to individuals and organisations when it goes wrong, so is often high on the risk register. It's therefore likely that board and executive members will require data to enable them to talk with confidence about it. In large organisations and those spanning various countries, the employment relations landscape can be complicated, decentralised to operational teams with lots of moving parts and different players involved. Regularly assessing if this is working is critical. Deloitte reports that corporate directors are requesting more data about "engagement and sentiment and exploring enriching ways to get feedback from the workforce in a much bigger way than they had before" (Deloitte Insights, 2023).

It makes business sense to evaluate the impact of any strategy that the organisation has set out and committed to. If the organisation has defined a strategic direction for collective employment relations, has set achievable goals and has a clear idea of where it is trying to get to, a review of how it is working should be part of the plan. If there has been organisational investment in employment relations, capability building initiatives and time spent managing effective structures, the organisation should ask if this investment is worthwhile, assess the benefits and report on this.

11.4 Increased Scrutiny from Investors and Shareholders

The second reason to measure, evaluate and report on the employment relations strategy is the growing interest amongst shareholders and investors in ESG issues, including workforce issues such as employee voice. While not as prominent as environmental issues like climate change, measurement and reporting on people issues (the "S" in ESG) continues to grow in importance as investors and regulators expect external disclosure of reliable data to make informed decisions about an organisation's responsible and sustainable business practices. The growing focus is global and has been driven by the impact of the Covid-19 pandemic, the rise in inflation and a renewed labour movement with spikes in strikes in key industries.

In the US, the Securities and Exchange Commission introduced human capital disclosure requirements for publicly traded companies and the European Union (EU) has also introduced reporting requirements. The Corporate Sustainability Reporting Directive requires large employers operating in the EU to publish more information in their annual reports on how they manage and develop their workforce. This will include workers and those in the organisational supply chain and will cover diversity, employee voice, employee relations, work-life balance, investment in training and health and safety. It will also include non-EU companies which have subsidiaries operating within the EU or are listed on EU regulated markets. This directive, along with another on pay transparency, requires organisations to involve their employee's representatives in the process.

In further evidence of increased scrutiny, chief people officers in the UK are beginning to report greater numbers of conversations with investors about workforce issues (CIPD, 2023a). In the US, Bloomberg reported that company executives and analysts discussed trade unions and labour relations issues on earnings calls more in 2023 than at any time in the last two decades (Constantz, 2023).

One asset management company specialising in sustainable and socially responsible investment by integrating ESG factors and shareholder advocacy is Trillium. It has targeted companies that don't uphold human rights conventions and has exposed gaps between the public commitments of the companies and what their actions display. In the US, this has meant Trillium has put companies like Starbucks and Apple under pressure for their attitudes and actions towards employee efforts to unionise. One investor coalition letter to the Starbucks CEO, led by Trillium, called on the company to "adopt a global stance of neutrality to worker organising efforts, cease all anti-union communications, negotiate with all elected unions in good faith and initiate dialogue with trade unions in how Starbucks might implement its stated labour rights commitments" (Trillium Asset Management, 2022). Both Starbucks and Apple agreed to independent audits of their employment relations practices although, at the time of writing, there is concern from the investor group about the quality of these external audits (Mundy, 2024).

Exercise 11.2, sets out the arguments that Trillium makes for investors to support unionisation and outlines why it believes this stance is aligned to sustainable, long-term investment.

> **Exercise 11.2: The business case for unionisation**
>
> Trillium argues that there are six reasons why investors should support unionisation and other worker empowerment efforts to ensure sustainable long-term returns.
>
> - Greater worker productivity in firms with collective agreements
> - Improved worker health and safety
> - Increased worker satisfaction and decreased worker turnover
> - Avoiding reputational risk from anti-union activity
> - Holding companies accountable to their commitments and legal norms
> - Upholding commitments to racial and gender equity
>
> *"The Investor Case for Supporting Worker Organizing Rights"* Trillium Asset Management (2022).
>
> 1. Looking at your own organisation or one you know of that recognises unions, have you seen the benefits that Trillium describes? How do you measure these benefits?
> 2. What reasons does Trillium use to explain why it believes that organisations with empowered workers are more aligned with sustainable investments?

As further evidence of the investor interest in collective employment relations, the Labour Rights Investor Network has been established and describes itself as "a global investor network for exploring the risks and benefits associated with workers' rights to freedom of association and collective bargaining.

The Network assists investors by acting as an education and exchange platform and a place to connect on issues related to freedom of association and collective bargaining. The Network is composed of investors who commit to integrating labour rights into their stewardship practices". (Committee on Workers Capital, 2023).

> **Tip**
> While investors may take different perspectives on employment relations, increased investor interest is something which our employment relations professionals should be aware of. They can use this as a valid reason for influencing the organisation to build positive employment relations and subsequently evaluate, measure and report on impact and progress.

11.5 The Cost of Collective Conflict

As we discussed in previous chapters on conflict and rebuilding after conflict, an industrial dispute is costly to organisations and its employees. If conflict has culminated in a dispute, it is likely that the relationship has been in decline for some time. There will have been signals of a deterioration in relationships. There may have been missed opportunities to resolve. We know that once damaged, the relationships between representatives and employers can take many years to rebuild.

The cost of conflict is far-reaching and goes beyond one organisation, according to the Centre for Economic and Business Research in the UK (CEBR, 2023) which states that, "the small direct impact of strikes must be considered in the context of wider economic, social and environment costs that disruption to services like rail, education and health causes". It explains that, in the longer term, employers may find it harder to recruit to their sector, thereby incurring costs of recruitment and problems of retention. In the health service, costs of disputes will be felt by the wider population over a long term as the costs of delayed treatment and diagnosis, and this will continue to pile pressure on the health system for years to come.

The wider financial and economic impact of strikes has also been analysed by economists in France at the National Institute of Statistics and Economic Studies (INSEE). Strikes in the transportation sector negatively impact all tourism-related activities. Strikes in refineries cause industrial production to fall in the impacted companies and every economic sector contracts in parallel.

> **Tip**
> Understanding the full cost of conflict and disputes, including potential reductions in dividends and falls in share price, would assist organisations to get a more complete picture and may provide an incentive to put in place measures to reduce the likelihood of disputes. If one understands the true cost of conflict and dispute, it is also easier to make the case for investing time, resources and effort in good employment relations.

11.6 The Management of Workforce Risk

The next argument in favour of evaluating and measuring employment relations is the management of risk. Considering the costs of dispute, it is understandable that a breakdown in employment relations is often high on the risk register of unionised companies. We are aware of a global airline where a breakdown in employment relations was the second most significant risk on the risk register after a global pandemic. A strike had the potential to dramatically impact flight schedules, damage customer service and reputation as well as impact operational and financial performance. Often, employment relations risks can be so significant that they are classed as "principal risks". In the UK these are defined by the Financial Reporting Council (FRC, 2022) as *"a risk or combination of risks that can seriously affect the performance, future prospects or reputation of the entity. These should include those risks that would threaten its business model, future performance, solvency or liquidity"*.

However, a dispute is normally the tip of the iceberg and in many organisations, it is a very rare event. Just because there is no dispute, doesn't mean there are no employment relations risks. These risks are more likely to come from a slower deterioration in the relationship between the employer and the unions or its employees, due to multiple reasons over a long period of time. It may not be obviously discernible. Managers may notice that meetings are not as constructive, or agreements are harder to conclude. In industries that rely on voluntary overtime or goodwill to complete tasks, they may start to see a reduction in completed tasks and a reluctance to work overtime. This can have a big impact on customer service and operational delivery. In our experience, organisations with robust mechanisms for worker voice have more opportunity to hear directly from employees about the issues which could become risks, and this enables managers to support resolution of these issues or escalate them.

Risks could also increase due to a lack of action over a bullying or discriminatory culture which leads to a fall in productivity or higher turnover. Risks can also manifest in a resistance to change which can then hinder the organisation in its modernisation plans and negatively impact employee commitment and engagement. Risks in the employment relations field can also include issues around discrimination, sexual harassment, working practices or bullying as well as mental health, equality, diversity and inclusion—all aspects of the non-financial reporting on the social aspects of the global ESG agenda.

> **Tip**
>
> Managers, employment relations specialists and HR colleagues need to be fully aware of the employment relations climate in their organisation, industry and externally. It is often the job of the employment relations leader to report on the employment relations risks at the audit or risk committee, along with their mitigating actions to reduce the likelihood and impact. Insight and data are required to enable the risk management process to work effectively.

Understanding your workforce risks is therefore the key first step. According to management consultancy Deloitte, this involves developing a definition that takes into account the "full array of potential and underlying internal and external sources of workforce risk". The next step is to measure and monitor using metrics and tools which enable the organisation to identify future risk and "more transparently reporting and disclosing workforce-related information". Mitigation strategies should then be developed and owned "both vertically (from line managers to the board) and horizontally (across functions outside HR)" (Deloitte Insights, 2023).

> **Exercise 11.4: Workforce risk management**
>
> So far in the chapter, we have discussed the importance of understanding workforce risks. In light of this consider the following questions.
>
> 1. Why is it important to clearly define organisational workforce risks?
> 2. What data and metrics do you use in your organisation to identify risks?
> 3. Where do workforce risks sit in your organisation—with HR, with the line manager, at board level, somewhere else? Why is it important where the risks sit in the organisation?

11.7 Methods of Evaluating and Auditing Collective Employment Relations

In this section, we will discuss different methods of evaluating and auditing employment relations. We look at how to adopt a simple continuous improvement approach into day-to-day working, an annual behavioural audit, a more formal employment relations audit and also discuss a range of qualitative and quantitative data. An audit needs to be thorough but not overly complicated. Whatever data is collected, it should give the organisation a clear indication of gaps and risks, and, if repeated, it should provide an idea of where employment relations has improved and areas where less improvement has been made. It can involve a range of stakeholders such as senior leaders, key managers and union representatives, and organisations will differ in what they need.

11.7.1 Adopting a Continuous Improvement Approach

A simple and effective approach to evaluating collective employment relations is one based on the principles of continuous improvement. This does not require a specific formal audit, but it does require a specific mindset and support from both parties. It is widely recognised that collective employment relations requires ongoing maintenance and regular efforts to understand how the other party is seeing or perceiving an issue (Muench, 1960). It is also our experience that when the employment relations leader, operational managers, leaders and the lead union representatives have a trusting relationship, they are more likely to be able to have honest and open discussions on what is working, how people are feeling and what can jointly be done to make improvements. They are, in essence, able to give each other timely feedback. We don't think that evaluation needs to be all about complicated surveys and audits. A continuous improvement approach enables organisations to regularly learn what is or is not working, allowing the parties involved to resolve issues that arise in a timely way. The opposite is a culture that allows issues to fester and remain unresolved. These become serious irritants which leak into the whole system until it collapses, damage is done and much investment is needed to repair and rebuild.

> **Tip**
> Take a proactive approach to collective employment relations—ask 'is this working' regularly rather than waiting for relationships to deteriorate or conflict to erupt

Continuous improvement usually relates to production processes and a lean methodology where small changes are made, identified by those doing the job, to streamline process, to improve production and lower costs (see below). Applying this to employment relations enables ideas for improvement to employment relations to come from those in the system—leaders, managers, union representatives and employees. This, in turn enables better engagement and any changes are more likely to be effective, easier to implement with more buy-in.

> **Important**
> Continuous improvement is a "culture of sustained improvement targeting the elimination of waste in all systems and processes of an organization. It involves everyone working together to make improvements without necessarily making huge capital investments. Continuous improvement can occur through evolutionary improvement, in which case improvements are incremental, or through radical changes that take place as a result of an innovative idea or new technology. Often, major improvements take place overtime as a result of numerous incremental improvements" (Bhuiyan & Baghel, 2005: 761).

In our experience, a continuous improvement process can be used quite simply to assess the interactions between union representatives and managers to, for example, improve meetings at all levels of the organisation. This type of 'after action review' simply asks everyone to rate the meeting in terms of a set of agreed principles (e.g. we solve problems jointly; we listen and respect each other's contributions) and ask what needs to happen to make the meetings more effective. It is simply giving each other feedback at the time, rather than disparaging each other outside of meetings or keeping your thoughts about the ineffective meeting to yourself without offering ideas on how it could be better. It can also be used in other circumstances. For example, we have used an 'after action review' with a joint group of union representatives and managers after difficult pay negotiations. With a facilitator, both parties gave their views of what was constructive about the negotiation process and what could be improved for next time. In this example, the review looked at all aspects of the negotiations, such as arrangements for setting up the meetings, the timings, who was involved, the behaviours in the negotiations and the communication during and after. The review identified the areas that worked well and would continue and those areas that didn't work well, with ideas on what should happen differently next time. All this data was captured to ensure that these improvements were put in place for the following annual pay negotiations.

11.7.2 Annual Survey Based on Behaviours in Employment Relations

As we saw earlier in the book, the behaviours of leaders, managers, HR teams and union representatives play a critical role in employment relations. In case study 11.1, we provide an example of an organisation in the UK that chose to design an annual employment relations audit based on behaviours or ways of working. These behaviours had been jointly agreed as the fundamental behaviours that would lead to positive employment relations. If these behaviours were being adhered to, the outcome would be constructive dialogue and problem-solving between the unions, managers and leaders. If they were not being adhered to, the manifestation would be a fractious relationship and an inability to listen and respond constructively to each other, leaving issues unresolved and conflict escalating.

The annual audit gave both parties an opportunity to rate the adherence to the behaviours from their perspective and identify which parts of the business needed support to improve. It also enabled the parties to build an annual improvement plan and embed the notion of continuous improvement into employment relations. This allowed the organisation and its unions to identify what 'good' looked like and how this could be replicated elsewhere.

> **Case study 11.1: Measuring changes in behaviours**
>
> **Annual survey designed around joint behaviours**
>
> Both parties—leaders and union representatives—agreed a set of behaviours to guide how they would work with each other in formal and informal meetings. Every year a survey was sent to the key union representatives and managers across the company to ask if these behaviours were being adhered to and were regularly observed. The results were analysed across the company and by business area. This enabled the parties to see improvements, discuss what had led to these improvements and identify areas of good practice. It also enabled a discussion about the lowest performing areas and what was needed to support these areas to improve their employee relations climate.

The purpose of the survey

The purpose of the survey was to:

- Assess the views of key managers and representatives on the state of the employment relations climate.
- Provide the basis for the development of local, business unit and company-wide employment relations action plans in the spirit of continuous improvement.

The joint behaviours

The annual survey was designed around a number of joint behaviours seen as important in delivering positive employment relations. The consequent questions are outlined in Table 1 Case Study 11.1. Participants were asked to say if these behaviours were being used effectively across the organisation.

Table 1 Case Study 11.1 Annual Survey

	Poor	Needs improvement	Good	Very good
We share information to enable genuine and timely consultation to take place				
We value and listen to each other's contribution				
We are clear about our roles and responsibilities in delivering effective employee relations				
We have the right skills and capabilities to deliver highly effective employee relations				
We recognise how both informal and formal discussions contribute to good employee relations				
We have a shared responsibility for resolving issues in a timely way, and local problem-solving is the norm				
We communicate jointly where appropriate				
We assess the partnership and relationships regularly at local level and learn from our experiences				
We acknowledge that there will be times when we disagree, however our behaviours keep the relationship intact				
We welcome interventions to help move issues forward without apportioning blame				

Participants were given a description of "poor" to "very good" and an additional question asked respondents to sum up the employment relations climate in the year.

Thinking about the last 12 months, which of the following sentences best describes the overall employment relations relationship between management and representatives in your business area? Please choose the statement that best fits the majority of the time over the last year, rather than focusing on any one-off incidents.

- The working relationship is poor, negative and ineffective. Problems are not solved jointly and issues are left unresolved.
- The working relationship needs improvement and can be negative at times. Problems are occasionally resolved, sometimes by working together.
- The working relationship is usually positive and we work together to keep it on track, although there is room for improvement.
- The working relationship is positive. We solve problems jointly and don't allow issues to remain unresolved.

Output

Each year, the survey results were discussed at the executive and trade union meeting and then at each business unit joint meeting. At the end of the joint discussions, an employment relations action plan was produced with priority areas for the following 12 months.

Key questions

1. Would a survey of this type be appropriate for use in your organisation?
2. How could this approach be adapted to fit the organisation that you work in?
3. What would you need to do to make sure that a survey of this type is effective?

Tip

If you undertake an employment relations survey, share the results with your union representatives and key managers, and ask them to devise the action plans. Actions can be jointly owned by managers and union representatives to encourage a climate of working together on improvement. This may be a capability building programme or a plan to improve meeting behaviours, for example.

11.7.3 Formal Employment Relations Audits

Those organisations that have a high risk of industrial action should periodically undertake an audit of their employment relations processes. In our experience, some organisations also typically undertake an audit when the external environment has changed and this may have impacted the risk (e.g. increased conflict or strike activity in their sector or in the economy as a whole), or the business may have changed (e.g. merger or acquisition) and this also may have impacted the risk.

The audit may be undertaken by an external consultant and could be requested by the audit committee as part of a more thorough analysis of a specific high-profile risk. If using an external consultant, in our experience they will typically look at the following areas:

- Is there a clear, high-level strategy for the approach to be taken with the recognised unions and is it clear to senior leaders how this fits the business strategy?
- Is there a clear understanding of the employment relations strategy and the organisation's appetite for risk amongst senior leaders?
- How is the collective employment relations environment taken into consideration in the decision-making process (e.g. acquisition or merger, closure of a site, expansion into a new country)?
- What internal governance is in place to provide a timely and accurate flow of management information for appropriate oversight? Is the organisation able to analyse trends, causes of conflict and is there appropriate escalation?
- Are the roles and responsibilities of managers clear for engagement with unions to ensure a co-ordinated process and to avoid duplication or confusion?
- What training is provided on collective employment relations for managers and is there an ongoing upskilling programme?
- Is there appropriate capability and capacity in collective employment relations in operational areas and in HR?
- Is there an assessment of suitability for working in unionised environments when a manager is recruited to key positions in the business?
- If accountability for collective employment relations is devolved to local managers, are there defined escalation processes? Do local agreements reflect this and are they consistent with strategy?
- What is the process for managing collective agreements?

The consultants will request data and interview key people identified by the organisation, compiling a report for the audit committee, for example. This data is used to give assurance that risks are being managed and also to identify any gaps which will then need focused attention by the operational or employment relations team. The information gained in this report could also provide some data which can be used for reporting purposes in the company accounts.

11.8 Collecting Qualitative and Quantitative Data on Collective Employment Relations

In addition to periodic audits and a continuous improvement approach, some organisations, via their HR departments, also regularly collect qualitative and quantitative data and we have presented examples of the type of commonly collected data in the boxes below. The level of data will depend on whether you are undertaking an international or country-specific audit. Whatever the scope, HR teams should be wary of overloading managers in this type of activity and should always be clear on the value to the organisation of collecting regular data. In Tables 11.1, 11.2 and 11.3, there are questions related to the employment relations strategy (Table 11.1), line manager capability (Table 11.2) and the effectiveness of collective forums (Table 11.3) which can be used to gauge the opinions of different groups. The survey could be followed up by group discussions to identify areas for improvement.

Table 11.1 Measures—employment relations strategy

	Agree	Disagree
The employment relations strategy is well defined and reflects the business strategy		
The employment relations strategy is well understood by the senior management team		
The employment relations strategy assists the business to manage change		
The employment relations strategy is regularly reviewed to ensure it continues to support the organisation		

Table 11.2 Measures—line manager capability

	Agree	Disagree
Line managers have clear objectives derived from the employment relations strategy		
Line managers have training plans to develop key employment relations competencies		
Line managers understand their role in delivering the employment relations strategy		
Line managers know how to use the 'employee voice' forums and when to resolve issues themselves		
Line managers manage local employment relations issues effectively		

Table 11.3 Measures—effectiveness of collective forums

	Agree	Disagree
Collective issues are resolved effectively		
The forum focuses on issues of relevance to employees and the business		
The forum shares relevant business information		
Consultation at the forum is genuine		
Managers and representatives solve problems outside of the forum		
The forum is seen as being beneficial to the business		
Employees understand the forum, how to use it and what it does		
Communication from the forum is timely and informative		
The forum is regularly reviewed and changes made to format, constitution etc		

11.9 Employment Relations Measures

In the example below, we share some common measures that organisations use to assess the quality of employment relations. Some organisations choose to share this quantitative data with their union representatives in a regular meeting, often developing a dashboard of key indicators to form the basis of a discussion on the current employment relations climate and steps to be taken to improve, learn or intervene.

Quantitative employment relations measures

- The length of time taken to resolve collective issues
- The number of collective grievances
- The number of disputes
- Number of grievances
- Length of time taken to resolve grievances
- Number of disciplinaries
- Length of time taken to resolve disciplinaries
- Number of tribunal cases
- Time taken to resolve tribunal cases
- Cost of tribunal cases
- Employee engagement scores for division/team
- Exit interviews
- Confidential reports from whistleblowing service and/or Employee Assistance Programme (EAP) on trends

11.10 Problems With Measurement, Evaluation and Reporting

Recognising the increased scrutiny from investors on workforce issues, the cost of poor employment relations and the risks to the organisation, we turn our attention to a few current problems around measurement, evaluation and reporting of collective employment relations.

The first issue is concerned with what data gets collected and reported. Reports suggest too much is being collected which is irrelevant for the business, while there is also concern about too little being externally disclosed. Collecting the right data should be able to suit both purposes—it can be used internally to improve performance, create effective employee voice and manage risk while also be used externally to assure investors and other stakeholders of the organisation's current picture and future plans.

Research on workforce reporting in the UK found that HR teams are collecting a lot of data without a clear aim or outcome and much of it is not being used for business decision-making (CIPD, 2023a). With regards to the quality of data disclosed externally, "the quality of this reporting remains low in many cases, making it challenging for stakeholders such as investors to assess the working practices and culture of an organisation" (The High Pay Centre, 2022). In 2023, the UK's CIPD argues that while more is written in annual reports on people issues in the UK today, much of it is "unsubstantiated narrative, not concrete data" and is often "uncritical, positive and not an objective assessment".

To investigate this issue around reporting and disclosure from an investor's perspective, Pensions and Investment Research Consultants (PIRC) undertook a review of the workforce-related data disclosed by the UK's FTSE All-Share (excluding investment trusts) (PIRC, 2022). Specifically on the issues of collective employment relations (and more specifically labour disruption), PIRC found at least two companies that had experienced significant labour unrest but had failed to disclose labour disruption as a principal risk within the same period. In its recommendations, PIRC requests that "companies which have potential for Labour Disruption to list this as a principal risk and demonstrate to shareholders the processes in place to monitor this risk and ensure that the issues are managed, and that strikes can be avoided where at all possible". If companies have disclosed labour disruption as a principal risk, they should disclose information on union relations including collective bargaining coverage, union density and any other relevant information to labour disruption. Also, where companies have, or expect difficult industrial relations, PIRC "would expect to see commentary in the annual report and for boards to consider its inclusion as a principal risk".

The final concern is whether those at board level have the expertise in people and collective employment relations issues. In the UK, for example, people issues have risen up the corporate agenda but the majority of UK boards lack directors with people expertise. One very clear recommendation from a 2023 report from the CIPD is that "the board should ensure it has the necessary knowledge of workforce policies, practices, behaviours and data to inform its understanding of people risks, in the same way as it would have sufficient understanding of financial risks" (CIPD, 2023a). It goes on to argue that senior level understanding of people risks is key to organisational success.

We are not encouraging employment relations and HR teams to produce another dashboard for the sake of it. We are encouraging these practitioners to consider what we have seen work in organisations, what we have described in this chapter and ask how this could help to improve their organisation's employment relations culture. This can also provide data and valuable insight for their external reporting on collective employment relations at the same time.

> **Tip**
>
> Consider the value of the information that you are collecting on workforce issues. Can it be used for external reporting as well as providing valuable insight to help your organisation to improve its employment relations climate?

11.11 Conclusion

There are various ways of evaluating an organisation's employment relations strategy, through qualitative surveys, formal audits, quantifiable data and also by taking simple, regular 'continuous improvement' style temperature checks which allow both parties to suggest areas for improvement. Each will enable you to create a better employment relations climate and positive workplace, better manage risk and cost, and determine if your strategy is working effectively. Robust evaluation gives an accurate assessment of risk, enabling control or elimination of that risk and the development of robust mitigation plans. It will enable senior leaders at executive and board level to feel confident of the facts, data and perceptions of those working in the organisation and believe that the investment in good employment relations is worth it.

Evaluation will enable you to spot a decline in mood and relationships before there is damage to the organisational culture and brand and to its employees. It enables the organisation to learn about what works and apply that good practice elsewhere. Taking a proactive rather than reactive approach to employment relations, incremental change is made through regular discussion, annual action plans and a continuous improvement mindset is embedded in employment relations. This data, invaluable to the organisation and its employees, is also valuable to investors, enabling them to see how worker voice is heard, issues are identified and resolved. This gives assurance to investors that the leadership of the organisation is well informed and able to make good decisions based on robust employee voice.

Questions
1. What are the different ways you can evaluate the effectiveness of an organisation's employment relations strategy?
2. What ways do you evaluate in your organisation?
3. What are the benefits to the organisation of this continuous improvement approach?
4. What is the rationale for evaluating and measuring employment relations?

References

Bhuiyan, N., & Baghel, A. (2005). An Overview of Continuous Improvement: From the Past to the Present. *Management Decision., 43*(5), 761–771.

CEBR. (2023). *Industrial action cost the UK economy £243m in Q1 due to lost working days, but indirect costs will drive bigger overall impacts.* [Online]. https://cebr.com/blogs/industrial-action-cost-the-uk-economy-243m-in-q1-due-to-lost-working-days-but-indirect-costs-will-drive-bigger-overall-impacts/. Accessed 15 September 2024.

CIPD. (2023a). *Effective Workforce Reporting: Improving People Data for Business Leaders.* Chartered Institute of Personnel and Development.

CIPD. (2023b). *The value of People Expertise on Corporate Boards.* Chartered Institute of Personnel and Development.

Committee on Workers' Capital. (2023). *Labour Rights Investor Network.* [Online]. Workers Capital. 17/12/2023. https://www.workerscapital.org/labour-rights-investor-network/. [Accessed on 17/12/2023].

Constantz, J. (2023). Wall Street is Talking about Unions More than ever. [Online] *Bloomberg*. 10/11/2023. https://www.bloomberg.com/news/articles/2023-11-10/actors-uaw-strikes-big-pay-raises-capture-wall-street-s-attention?leadSource=uverify%20wall. [Accessed on 14/11/2023].

Deloitte Insights. (2023). *Managing Workforce Risk in an era of Unpredictability and Disruption.* [Online]. 24/2/2023. https://www2.deloitte.com/us/en/insights/topics/talent/workforce-risk-management-solutions.html. [Accessed on 10/12/2023].

FRC. (2022). Guidance on the Strategic Report. [Online]. *Financial Reporting Council*. June 2023. https://media.frc.org.uk/documents/Strategic_Report_Guidance.pdf. [Accessed on 15/9/2023].

High Pay Centre. (October, 2022). *Worker Voice in Corporate Governance: How to Bring Perspectives from the Workforce into the Boardroom.* [Online]. https://highpaycentre.org/wp-content/uploads/2022/11/STA0922916658-001_aFFT-Pay-Ratios-Report_1022_v5.pdf. [Accessed on 7/11/2023].

Muench, G. A. (1960). A Clinical Psychologist's Treatment of Labour-Management Conflict. *Personnel Psychology, 13*(2), 165–172.

Mundy, S. (2024). Apple Stand-Off Tests Investor Concern Over Workers' Rights. [Online] *Financial Times*. 4/3/2024. https://www.ft.com/content/7b161f44-d1ac-4d7a-95e8-bd8ab5459534. [Accessed on 13/3/2024].

PIRC. (2022). *Companies' Reported Workforce-Related Risks not Backed by Data.* PIRC.

Trillium Asset Management. (2022). *The Investor Case for Supporting Worker Organizing Rights.* https://www.trilliuminvest.com/whitepapers/the-investor-case-for-supporting-worker-organizing-rights. [Accessed 19/11/2023].

12

Concluding Remarks—Building a Strategic Approach to Employment Relations

Abstract The world of work is rapidly changing and creating new challenges for employers, workers and their representatives. However, the skills and knowledge which organisations developed to help them to create positive employment relationships, negotiate change and resolve conflict have been fundamentally eroded. This book has aimed to fill this gap. This concluding chapter highlights the key messages we have tried to convey and provides a number of recommendations for practitioners.

Keywords Collective voice · Trade unions · Strategy · Trust · Skills · Capability

12.1 The Aims of the Book

The motivation for writing this book was a growing unease that organisations no longer had the capacity, skills and knowledge to navigate the complex challenges of contemporary employment relations. The decline of trade union membership and the growth of HRM has seen the practice of collective employment relations disappear from mainstream management education. Even those textbooks that explore employment relations often pay little attention to the way in which employment relations is conducted in the workplace. Therefore, this book seeks to complement existing literature and, in particular, provide those working in and studying employment relations with a practical perspective and guide. Moreover, it also attempts to give practitioners a structure and a business case for encouraging a positive approach to collective voice in their organisations. We hope that the concepts, cases and practical examples—many taken from our own experience—will provide key insights into the role that can be played by employment relations professionals and the contribution they can make to organisational effectiveness.

12.2 Influencing Organisational Leaders

Employment relations professionals who understand and respect collective employee voice can help to build better workplaces and better jobs. Of course, those working in this field need supportive leaders who set the culture and tone for them to develop effective collective voice and work constructively with trade unions. In our view, trade unions respond to how they are treated so leaders have a vital role in role-modelling positive behaviours that acknowledge the legitimacy of trade unions and recognise the contribution they can make. As we have discussed in this book, employment relations strategy will be shaped by a range of contextual factors, however in our experience positive employment relations climates are more likely to be found where unions are not seen as a hindrance but as holders of valid, diverse viewpoints.

However, organisational leaders may not automatically have a positive attitude to collective employment relations in general and trade unions in particular. Indeed, we explored the growth of unitarist perspectives earlier in the book. Therefore, practitioners have a key role to play in encouraging leaders to listen to the views of employees, influencing leaders to acknowledge that worker voice often leads to better decisions and coaching them to see the benefits of structured feedback and engagement. This book is explicitly designed to help practitioners to do this—to understand unions beyond the stereotypes, the politics and fear and focus on the positive role they can play in work and the wider economy.

12.3 The Importance of Collective Voice

Research shows us that investing in collective voice is good for productivity, organisational commitment and critical for improving engagement. It makes work more meaningful, purposeful and utilises the talent, experience and creativity of an organisation's workforce. In particular, trade unions can play an important role in battling inequality, improving wages and experiences of work. In this way their impact is not just felt in the workplace but in the economy overall. Effective collective bargaining can improve wages and conditions across industries, boosting incomes and driving economic growth. Sectoral bargaining can provide stability and certainty for organisations, increase incentives for investment and prevent wage costs becoming a source of competitive advantage.

As part of our research, we spoke to many people in the field of employment relations—employers and unions. The common ground they have is that they all aim to build healthy workplace cultures and structures which give workers a strong voice. A union General Secretary in the UK, describes the downside of ignoring worker voice in today's complex world and the dangers of not building the organisational skills to develop collective voice:

> There are some big global issues to deal with in the workplace at the moment. Flexibility is a great example – who can and who cannot work remotely. Issues such as mental health and the impact of AI. All of these issues require a collective workforce perspective, which needs to be listened to if we are to make the best decisions. Unions play an important role in speaking up for workers on issues such as these and without unions, where is the worker voice? The unions play an important part in helping navigate some complex, social issues. In the UK, there are now very few tripartite bodies left. So, the voice of workers is not being heard and this has big consequences for the country. We have lost these skills at a national level and a sector level.

Although the long-term trend in most economies has been declining trade union membership and influence, attitudes to organised labour in countries such as the US and the UK are increasingly positive, levels of industrial action are rising, and new unions and alternative forms of representation are emerging. It can be argued that these phenomena may be a short-lived reaction to unusual economic conditions. Moreover, unless trade unions can convert increased popularity into increased membership, they will struggle to be relevant outside of their traditional strongholds. Nonetheless there is a very plausible case that we are seeing a more fundamental shift in attitudes to work, with a growing demand for a collective voice to address fundamental issues of equality, work-life balance, wages, insecurity and dignity at work. If this is the case, employment relations skills, neglected and ignored, will be needed even more.

12.4 Building Employment Relations Capacity

Constructive relationships with union or employee representatives do not materialise simply because an organisation decides they might be beneficial. They can only be built over time and through the development of employment relations capabilities throughout the organisation. This provides managers, leaders and practitioners with the confidence they need, so that they can accept challenge and manage conflict. They are no longer surprised or offended when their employees and their unions have a different opinion or propose alternative solutions. They see this as positive, as a sign of a healthy and inclusive culture. They learn to listen to it, work with it and encourage it. They do not always agree and sometimes this boils over into conflict. But skilled practitioners can resolve conflict, solve problems and sustain high-trust relationships.

It is possible to find solutions that are good for employees and the organisation, as this quote demonstrates from a union official to a departing senior employment relations manager:

> Whilst we have had to engage in some difficult discussions during your tenure as Head of Employee Relations, the union believes that these have always taken place in the correct spirit. The nature of the relationship between yourself and the union obviously meant that we were unlikely to agree all the time, but we do believe that the way we worked together in these instances has benefitted both our members and the company.

This is why we have focussed on understanding positions, interests and needs, and why we have shared an approach to problem-solving which is often outside the traditional remit of employment relations processes like consultation and negotiation. When you can't reach agreement using your usual approaches, a mature organisation with skilled leaders and union representatives recognises that the problem still needs to be solved and will agree to try something new. This requires a level of trust which is at the heart of employment relationships. Trust is built when you are credible, empathetic and authentic. This can come naturally or be developed as you are empowered in your organisation to solve problems and build relationships and rapport with union representatives.

Investing in problem-solving skills for managers, including HR and union representatives, helps parties to accept conflict as part of working life, seeing it is as good for workplace culture, enabling diverse views to be accepted and valued. This is reflected in the following comment by Dennis Rocheleau, retired Head of Labour Relations at General Electric quoted in an article in

Harvard Business Review (2023) authored by Roy Bahat, Thomas A. Kochan, and Liba Wenig Rubenstein.

> We are not so naïve as to believe that our mutual interest in a peaceful, equitable settlement will automatically produce a consensus on how such an agreement should be defined. If we both see the world in precisely the same relief and hues, one of us is probably unnecessary. We recognise that the world is wide, and there is room enough in it to accommodate an expansive range of opinions and attitudes….listen to others' perspective on an issue, explore many alternatives, eschew a reflexive retreat to the homely confines of your preconceived ideals or traditions. (Bahat et al., 2023)

12.5 Ten Steps to Build a Strategic Approach to Employment Relations

In summary, we urge organisations to take a strategic approach to employment relations, building skills, creating effective channels for collective voice and evaluating and reporting outcomes in a transparent way. In order to achieve this we suggest the following steps, distilled from the insights provided in this book.

1. Set out a clear strategy aligned to business goals. Make sure your employment relations strategy will help you to achieve your goals and if it's not going to, change it.
2. Assess the organisation's attitude to the risk of conflict and effects of poor collective employment relations. Are you comfortable with some conflict or risk to the business or does this need to be avoided or managed better?
3. Foster a leadership culture which encourages diverse opinions and perspectives, truly listens and knows how to adopt a problem-solving mindset. This is one of the foundations of good collective employment relations.
4. Build the competence of your line managers—they have the biggest impact on day-to-day employment relations. Target those in the organisation who have the most critical interfaces with union or employee representatives. Invest in conflict resolution as a core leadership skill.
5. Listen to the views of your employees. Many issues and changes will be better resolved and implemented with an input of employee voice. Leaders don't have all the answers, all the time.

6. Trust your employees and their representatives to know as much, if not more than you, on issues about how work gets done. Tap into their knowledge and enable their contribution. Work jointly with union and employee representatives where possible, as much as possible.
7. Make sure your managers and your HR teams stay connected and don't sit in 'ivory towers'. Understand your employees—find out what motivates and demotivates them and the factors that shape their well-being.
8. Use employment relations competence as a key criterion in talent management, succession planning and leadership development. If good employment relations is a critical skill and capability for leaders, make sure your current and future leaders have the competence to implement the employment relations strategy.
9. Coach the representatives and managers who aren't demonstrating a constructive approach to employment relations.
10. Gather data so that you can measure your employment relations climate on a regular basis. Share this information with unions and other stakeholders. Identify problems and develop joint solutions.

Reference

Bahat, R. E., Kochan, T. A., & Rubenstein, L. W. (2023, July–August). The Labor-Savy Leader. *Harvard Business Review*.

Correction to: Informing and Consulting—Practical Processes and Structures for Employee Voice

Correction to:
Chapter 6 in: D. Sanders et al., *Collective Employment Relations*, Palgrave Executive Essentials,
https://doi.org/10.1007/978-3-031-65471-8_6

This book is authored in its entirety by Debbie Sanders, Joseph Perry, and Richard Saundry. However, in the initial printing, Chapter 6, titled "Informing and Consulting—Practical Processes and Structures for Employee Voice," incorrectly listed Francesco Iannone, Natalia Franco, Carmen Parisi, and Rossana Laera as chapter authors. This was an internal error and has now been corrected to accurately reflect the true authorship.

The original version of Chapter 6 was previously published with incorrect author names, which have now been corrected. The chapter has been updated with the changes.

The updated version of this chapter can be found at
https://doi.org/10.1007/978-3-031-65471-8_6

Index

A

Active listening 89
Alliance of Motion Picture and Television Producers (AMPTP) 136, 139, 140
Amazon 8, 30, 32, 33, 55
Apple 8, 139, 221
Artificial intelligence 4, 36, 69
Asda 51
Attitudes and relationships 49, 88
   attitudinal restructruring 94
   attitudinal structuring 97
   managers and union representatives 59
   relationship patterns 50, 88
Audit 221

B

Bargaining power 138
Beneficial constraints 24

C

Centralised employment relations 70
Centres of excellence 70, 72
Changing attitudes to work 28
Changing behaviour 101
   a framework for collaborative behaviours 101
Codetermination
   definition 109
   pros and cons of Works Councils 119
   Works Councils 114, 120
Collective bargaining 132
   definition 109, 135
   disputes procedure 186
   lack of skills and experience 136
   scope 132
Collective conflict
   costs 222
   impact on relationships 200
Collective representation 20–22
Collective voice 4, 7, 23, 24, 30, 108, 237, 238
   leadership 9
Communication
   definition 109
   information-sharing 111

non-union fora 113
structures 113
Consultation 109
  consultation at a time of crisis 117
  Covid-19 pandemic 116
  definition 109
  international comparisons 115
  legal frameworks 115
  role of leaders and managers 115
  role of representatives 112
  structures 120
Corporate sustainability 220
Covid-19 pandemic 5, 20, 29, 33
Curiosity 89

D

De-industrialisation 25
Disengagement 27
Distributive bargaining
  definition 147

E

Employee engagement 108
  definition 21
  disengagement 27
  survey data 29
Employee involvement 109
  Involvement Groups 111
  role of representatives 112
Employee silence 27
Employee voice 24, 34
  direct voice 21, 22
  multiple voice channels 21
  Staff Councils 111
Employment contract 20
  rules 20
Employment relations
  accountabilities 79
  accountabilities and skills 75
  behaviours 89
  building capacity 240
  marginalisation 26
  perception gap 86, 87
  scope of activity 76
  skills and capability 79
Employment relationship 21, 23
Employment relations strategy 11
Equality, diversity and inclusion 50, 68, 224
Evaluation
  collecting qualitative and quantitative 231
  continuous improvement 225
  measures 232
  measuring changes 227
  methodology 226
  problems and challenges 233
  rationale 214
  survey methods 227

F

Financial Reporting Council 223
Frames of reference 22
Freie Arbeiterinnen- und Arbeiter-Union 37

G

Globalisation 7, 20, 25, 26
GMB 37, 51
Great Resignation 29

H

HR business partnering 31, 73
Human Resource Management
  business partnering 31, 68
  employment relations capability 12
  knowledge of employment relations 31
  strategic HR 31
  unitarism 9

Index

I
IG Metall 37
Inclusivity 89, 93, 94
   meeting behaviours 94
   role of leaders 94
Independent Workers' Union of Great Britain 37
Industrial disputes 199
Inequality 5, 7, 20, 24, 36, 238
Influencing organisational leaders 238
Information
   information-sharing 111
   structures 111
Integrative bargaining 156
   key factors for constructive engagement 148
International Labour Organisation (ILO) 134
Investors and shareholder scrutiny 220

J
John Lewis Partnership 51

L
Labour Rights Investor Network 221
Line management 95
Line manager lifecycle 81

M
Managerial quality 21
Managing change 13, 54, 62, 68, 78
Managing risk 14
Measurement 233
Mediation
   addressing the root causes of conflict 209
   designing collective mediation 203
Meetings
   good practice 126
   increased effectiveness 126
   managing meetings 123
Multinational corporations 25

N
Negotiation 132
   BAFO (best and final offer) 134
   BATNA (best alternative to a negotiated agreement) 134
   common ground 142
   conflict management styles 143
   counter-offers 142
   definition 135
   finalising the agreement 149
   planning 136
   planning template 137
   selecting the team 140
   starting the negotiation 141
   structures 121
   ZOPA (zone of potential agreement) 134
Networking group 55
New technology 27, 35–37

O
OECD 7, 20, 24, 25
Organisational design 71
   design implications 71
   design principles 71
   devolved employment relations 74
   employment relations operating model 72
   mixed employment relations model 74

P
Pay negotiation 136
Personnel management 68, 116, 209
Platform working 4, 20, 35, 37
Pluralism 22, 38, 97

Populism 25
Positions, interests and needs 96, 124, 240
  mutuality 100, 109
Precarious employment 35
Problem-solving 154
  benefits 154
  challenges and obstacles 172
  definition 155
  difference from traditional employment relations processes 156
  employment relations applications 156
  five whys 164
  group size and composition 165
  key steps in the process 166
  organisational culture 159
  practical considerations 164
  pre-conditions for success 158
  recognition and commitment 160
  structure 162
  suitable topics 157
  trust 159

R
Rebuilding employment relationships 201
  challenges and barriers 213
  key principles 201
  leaders and union representatives 210
  motivation for change 202
  sustaining change 211
  understanding the problem 205
Rebuilding relationships
  facilitation 205
Reporting 233, 241
Representation gap 27, 69, 107, 128
Respect and recognition 89
  union legitimacy 90
Riders x Derechos 37
Risk management 224

S
Société Mutuelle pour Artistes (SMart) 37
Starbucks 8, 30, 221
Strategic choice 9, 45, 50, 51
Strategy
  alignment 60
  behaviours and capability 62
  case for strategic employment relations 56
  change 47, 50
  change in strategy 62
  changing strategy 64
  conflict 47, 50
  conflict management 63
  employment relations strategies 47
  employment relations strategy in a European airline 52
  employment relations strategy in practice 55
  evaluation 218
  formal and informal structures 62
  governance and risk 60
  implementation 59
  key factors 53
  rationale 46
  reputation 47
  risk 47
  strategic employment relations in financial services 56
  ten steps to build a strategic approach 241
  voice 47
Strike action 181
  causes 183
  communications strategy 195
  contingency planning 185
  costs 180
  employee perspectives 194
  escalation 188
  impact on relationships 222
  local knowledge 182
  local union representatives 181

organisational perspectives 185
planning and communication 193
process of escalation 183
role of mediation 191
roles and responsibilities 179

Teambuilding
collective engagement 77
overcoming problems 82
relationship building 77
subject expertise 78
Tesco 51
Tesla 8
Trade union organising
grassroots organising 92
Trade unions
approval and support 30
business case 221
deconing union density 25
dualisation 27
facility time 127
growth and influence 25
HR perspectives 19
investment and trade union organisation 5, 7, 11, 14, 15, 220, 226, 235
marginalisation 26
membership 23
organising 6, 34
popularity 5
public support for 27
renewal and revitalisation 26, 27, 201
replacement 26, 27
skills and capability 128
typology of union representation 91
younger workers 26

Training 127
Trust 4, 11, 13, 15, 22, 86, 201
collaborative working 86
key behaviours 89
role of employee voice 21
sustaining positive relationships 86
trust and resolution - a virtuous circle 86

Unbion organising
in the US 33
Understanding and empathy 89
Union organising 33, 34
community groups 37
grassroots unions 37
new trade unions 37
Quasi unions 37
relevance for behaviours 93
Unitarism
Human Resource Management 31
USDAW 51

Varieties of capitalism
coordinated economies 24

Workplace conflict 177
collective conflict 179
individual conflict 180
mediating collective conflict 191
Workplace culture 4, 13, 34
Writers Guild of America (WGA) 136, 139

The manufacturer's authorised representative in the EU is Springer Nature Customer Service Centre GmbH, Europaplatz 3, 69115 Heidelberg, Germany. If you have any concerns regarding our products, please contact ProductSafety@springernature.com

Printed and bound by CPI Group (UK) Ltd, Croydon, CR0 4YY

18/02/2026

02055594-0003